WIN, LOSE, OR DRAW

By WARREN BROWN

WIN, LOSE, OR DRAW

THE CHICAGO CUBS

Win, Lose, or Draw

By WARREN BROWN

G. P. PUTNAM'S SONS; NEW YORK

Contents

1. My Business Is Yours   3
2. California, Here I Go!   10
3. Touching All Bases   17
4. A City of Characters   27
5. Dempsey Meets Kearns   37
6. How Matches Are Made   50
7. A Not So Long Count   61
8. Roped Arena City   70
9. World's Series Memories   78
10. The Wonder Team   87
11. Who Trained for What?   96
12. Rise and Fall of Shelby   103
13. Benton Harbor Besieged   110
14. "When I Played for McGraw . . ."   118
15. Red Grange Runs   126
16. Rambles with Rockne   134
17. "Six Points or Nothing!"   142
18. Landis Walks In   149
19. Good Morning, Judge   157
20. Break for the Player   165

CONTENTS

21. The Portable A.C.   173

22. The Thoroughbred Develops   181

23. Derby Delights   190

24. For Ways That Are Dark   199

25. The Customer's All Right   208

26. Meet My Gang   217

27. Gentlemen of the Press   225

28. Work or Play?   233

29. "Please Use and Oblige . . ."   241

30. It's a Promotion   250

31. Behind the Box Score   258

32. My Team—All Mine   266

WIN, LOSE, OR DRAW

CHAPTER I

My Business Is Yours

*S*PORTS are my business, win, lose, or draw.

When I came in, the stands were still rocking from the last rousing rally of the nineteenth century. The twentieth was just going to bat.

But don't get the notion that this is to be a matter-of-fact report of the findings of a sports writer. Rather is it the story of one in whom has merged the likes and the dislikes of reader and writer, of speaker and listener, of participant, promoter, and patron. I am or have been all of these, by geographical accident as much as reportorial design.

In the field of sports what has gone before is intimately linked with what is happening now and what is to come. No reviewer can in all honesty tell where the past leaves off and the present begins. A sports personality is a live story topic for all time. His deeds inevitably form a basis for comparison for those who come after him. Otherwise there would be no need for record books. Or for records. A sports character newsworthy enough to make print in his own era remains in type forever. The hell box or the limbo of forgotten stories is not for him.

It is my personal collection of unforgettable incidents that I now propose to share with you.

I do not intend to proceed on the "stop me if you've heard this" basis, for I am reasonably certain that many of the facts and most of the fancies are here being set forth for the first time.

3

The sports-minded are of three general groupings.

There are those who make the news, whether it is to be reduced to printer's ink or engraver's zinc or wafted o'er the air lanes.

There are those who gather the news.

There are those who have the news thrust upon them, in story, in picture, or in figures. It may come to them on the printed page, through the loud-speaker, or on the flickering screen of the cinema or the latest and most astounding news-conveying medium of all, television.

I have never been able to determine which of the three groupings of the sports-minded is the most consistently interesting. In this uncertainty I differ from none of my calling who has endured for very long.

Sports as practiced in this land have no game preserve, no limit, no closed season. No person can escape some manifestation of them completely. Nor can any one person keep up with all of them.

Some of us, believe me, have given it a heluva try, just the same, making up our own rules as we go along.

Thus, when I regard James A. Farley as a baseball, boxing, football, or racing fan, and sometimes guardian of the public's interest in the New York prize ring, you will understand how I got that way. I know Farley does. What he has accomplished as postmaster general, or as first passenger as well as driver of the original Franklin D. Roosevelt bandwagon, is something for the journeyman political writer or the page-opposite editorial columnist. It is not for this part-time dabbler in such earth-shaking activities. Sure, I've written about national conventions, but I once had to review a dramatization of one of Gertrude Stein's triple-talk operas, and I didn't like that, either.

When I write of Kenesaw M. Landis, you may be sure that his chaw-tobacco federal justiceship will be left severely alone. That's for the end book. My Landis is the one of the sport page, a "damn the torpedoes, full speed ahead" Landis.

It is not difficult to hew to this sort of line. More often than not your character himself will run interference for you, as Farley did on one memorable occasion in Chicago.

He had left his base of operations in New York ostensibly to attend an Elks convention in the Pacific Northwest. In reality he was to spread the Roosevelt gospel to the delegates. Between trains, while resting (or so I surmised) in Chicago, he called me up and asked me to come to his hotel suite for a visit. I had no previous intimation he was in town, where he was headed, or why as I strolled the few blocks to pay my respects. It did not occur to me to phone from the lobby and announce myself. I went right on up to his suite, opened the door, and walked in.

I was startled to find the place packed with people whom I recognized as the flower of Democracy in Cook County. Present too were political writers from all the Chicago papers, my own included. It seemed no place for me just then, and as I turned to leave hastily Farley spied me.

"I want to see you," he called. With that he led me into an adjoining room and closed the door. I apologized for bad timing, but Farley shrugged it off.

"Let's call up Jimmy Johnston," he said.

Johnston, manager of ring champions and promoter off and on, was then preparing to stage a show in New York. The call went through. We talked for a while with Johnston. All the while the deserving Democrats in the other room fretted and fumed. When we had finished our phone call and chatted a while on other topics, Farley rejoined the party and I went about my business, being frowned upon by one and all, but most of all by the political writers.

Some time afterward the political expert of my paper returned to the office and sought me out.

"All right," he said. "I know you know Farley and that you rated a private interview with him. What's the lowdown? What did he tell you that he didn't want us to know?"

I protested that Farley hadn't mentioned politics, hadn't even inquired if I were a registered voter, and that we had talked mostly about Jimmy Johnston's fight and a bit about the New York Yankees.

The political writer didn't believe me. He probably will not believe me now, if this catches his eye. But that's the way it was. That's the way it has been with other people who make news apart from the sports page when I have caught up with them, or they with me.

My perspective on Jimmy Walker, New York's most famous mayor in my time, is different from the sort that might be taken by anyone else but a sports writer.

I became acquainted with him when he was a legislator active in getting boxing legalized in New York, and having Sunday baseball sanctioned. He was an avowed fight fan, and took a lively interest in most other sports too. When I choose to recount some of his adventures with sports and sports writers, instead of calling the roll on his political or social life, I am certain the evidence will support my case.

That was the side of Walker revealed to me and my fellow craftsmen. I wouldn't know what he did in a night club. I don't care whether he was early or late for a political clam bake. The Walker I knew and the one I shall never forget was always on time for the first pitch, the bell, the kickoff, or the springing of the barrier.

And so it goes. . . .

Now and then a personage from Hollywood might get wildly excited about sports for the sake of whatever promotional publicity value it might hold for him. I once heard of a band leader whose press agent had spotted him as a member of a famous college football team of the twenties. Amusement-page addicts went for that in a big way, but the journeyman sports writer had the means and took the trouble to find out that the horn blower's entire extracurricular activity in college had been restricted to participation in glee-club doings. He not only did not play on the football team, he was not a member of the squad.

In all journalism there is no person better fitted to detect a sham than is the sports writer. He can pin the out-and-out publicity seeker best two out of three falls, right along. He can also forget him, three for three, and generally does.

If he has to take these folks of stage, screen, and radio in stride, he can always remember that there are many of them who are genuine adherents of sport, and were long before the spotlight of national attention was turned upon them. Their active interest in various forms of spectator sport is such that any resultant publicity is never artificially stimulated. Perhaps that is why they get it so freely from the sports writers who know their way around.

Until now, all I have been trying to do is set up my road blocks. From this point on, you travel at your own risk. May your way be as casual as mine whenever I have shuffled off to Buffalo.

There in the not too dim past I was summoned to be the principal speaker at an annual dinner honoring the football team of Canisius College. Until the bid came I had not paid too much attention to Canisius. It had been a half line of agate type in the fall. Sometimes the line told what Canisius had done in the game with St. Bonaventure. Sometimes it told what Niagara had done to it. So I did a bit of research and discovered that Canisius was a Jesuit College.

I happen to be a horrible example of Jesuit education, having graduated from St. Ignatius University in San Francisco in 1915, A.B. *mirabile dictu* rather than *magna cum laude*. After what seemed not too decent an interval, the good fathers of St. Ignatius not only changed the name of the institution to University of San Francisco, but they moved its site and even changed the colors from red and blue to green and gold. I still think they didn't have to go to all that trouble to eradicate my footprints from their halls of learning, but that's what they did, just the same.

It is quite possible that I knew more about Canisius than Canisius did about me when the dinner was held. As the speaking began I was preceded by the president of the college.

He took no chances on the guest speaker's limitations. He went all out on the subject of football. Canisius football. He reviewed the team's season. He discussed its individuals and its coaches. He spoke of and to the alumni. He gave what seemed to me a complete recital of Canisius football from the moment fall practice began until the dinner guests had thrust aside their coffee cups and began to set up their defense for the words and phrases about to be thrown at them. He was eloquent. He was thorough. He was convincing. He left damn little on the subject of football for the guest speaker from Chicago to discuss.

I had to change my offense hurriedly as the toastmaster proceeded to introduce me.

I arose and said that as long as the president of Canisius had covered the subject of football so completely, there was nothing for me to do but talk about education, Jesuit style.

"Repetitio est mater studiorum," I began. Then I saw two tackles and a blocking back fix me with cold eyes.

"It's all right, friends," I continued. "There are times when we Democrats of Cook County find repeaters very useful as the mothers of pluralities."

The tackles and the blocking back relaxed.

And again, summoned to Buffalo on another occasion, I was to preside as toastmaster at a testimonial dinner being given favorite son Joseph V. McCarthy, who had just won another world's championship with the New York Yankees.

At the speakers' table were many famous figures of the sports world. The audience was presumed to be 100 per cent sports-minded, which left the toastmaster with one pressing problem. For among the prospective speakers was Dr. Alan Dafoe, whom the Dionne quintuplets and Walter Winchell had but recently made famous.

A most engaging sort was Dr. Dafoe, and from our first meeting I cherished his acquaintance and friendship. But how to present him to Buffalo's citizenry gathered there to whoop it up for McCarthy, the baseball manager?

I have no idea how Bob Hope or Georgie Jessel would have approached it, but I managed to come up with:

"Gentlemen, may I present the man with the greatest delivery in the history of the national pastime?"

In Buffalo, they still like me. . . .

CHAPTER 2

California, Here I Go!

THE first blessed event that ever concerned me took place in Somersville, California.

Somersville was back in the hills a piece from Antioch. Antioch was just up the road from Rodeo, where Vernon Gomez, of Yankee pitching fame, originated. You take it from there. Or skip the whole thing.

Most of the residents of Somersville at the time I was born were gainfully employed in coal mines, with no John L. Lewis to lift his eyebrows at them for any deed or omission.

My sire ran Somersville's equivalent of the Stork Club. From meager hearsay evidence that has come my way, the joint may have been more of the Turkey Buzzard than the Stork type. My sire wore a beard such as was standard equipment for the minor prophets, but I doubt very much whether he ever suspected what the last of his sons was to get into.

My formal education began at Somersville. At a very tender age I was led across the main gulch by my mother and up the hill to the little red schoolhouse, as spacious as any Southern Pacific Railroad boxcar you have ever seen. There, some time after the bell had rung, I refused to come out of my corner either weaving or bobbing. The teacher told me I was stupid. My intuition told me that if formal education consisted of being told things already in the public domain, the hell with it.

I got up and went home. I never went back to the little

red schoolhouse at Somersville. To this day the relics of the Browns, one of Somersville's first families, go around boasting that the author of *The Chicago Cubs* was so precocious a child that at the age of five he finished an entire term's schooling in less than half a day.

My private sit-down strike against Somersville's educational standards went on and on. It did not become a matter of national or even local importance, for it coincided with the departure of the First California Volunteers to the Spanish-American War, and its slop-over insurrection in the Philippines.

My oldest brother was in Company L, and he had marched away promising me that he would personally cut off Aguinaldo's ears and bring me back the bolo. He did bring back a bolo, come to think of it, but the nearest I ever got to a Filipino's ears was when I interviewed the great little bantamweight Pancho Villa many years afterward.

Through some upheaval of nature, the mines of Somersville flooded and became unworkable soon after the Gay Nineties War. Old residents began to climb the hills and look about for new diggings. The Browns kept moving until they came to Concord, from which you can see Mt. Diablo even if it isn't a clear day.

If Concord means anything at all to the sports-minded, it probably will be because that was the town whence emerged the three Fighting Shades, George, Billy, and the most engaging of all, Dave.

George was a club fighter with no particular appeal and no championship pretensions whatever.

Billy, a product of the four-round game that flourished at one time in San Francisco and Oakland, took a trip to Australia, as many Yankees were wont to do. He left as a welterweight and a fairly capable one. When he returned he had succeeded in winning welterweight, middleweight, light-heavyweight, and heavyweight championships of the Antipodes. Johnny Dundee, Henry Armstrong, and Barney Ross were thus not the first wholesalers in ring championships to come to my attention.

Dave was the most colorful of the Shades, and in many respects one of the real storybook characters of all ring history. He began as a bantamweight. As he grew in stature and poundage, he became recognized as a master craftsman in both middleweight and light-heavyweight classes. He was perfectly at ease in the ring against all kinds of opposition, but he was just as nifty in white tie and tails, hobnobbing with royalty abroad, or with Leo P. Flynn, his manager, at home, as the case might be ... when it was possible to get it by the case.

These Shades came from Concord. Perhaps others besides Nat Fleischer, the boxing record-book man, will remember it. However, I am satisfied that Concord has pretended right along that the Browns never lit in the place at all.

We moved eventually to the wondrous city of San Francisco, not too many miles away. In it were large buildings, cable and trolley cars, paved streets and sidewalks. On one side of it was a bay. On another was an ocean. It had two coasts. From one, great banks of fog rolled in during the late afternoons. On the other, known as Barbary (though this I didn't know until much later), drunks were rolled late at night.

This was San Francisco. The City, to distinguish it from that upstart Los Angeles, a few hundred miles to the south.

San Francisco was to become in reality my home town, since Somersville was now nonexistent, and Concord a passing fancy ... or perhaps just a Shade of the imagination.

It was in this glorious community that I began to encounter the persons and get a working knowledge of the events that were to fashion my career. Even in short-pants days I was cultivating a lively interest in sports. I was an avid reader of words on the current performers and the heroes of the past, and many of them, particularly those in baseball and in the prize ring, were around and about the city by the Golden Gate.

I was well able to hear and marvel at the tales of a pre-historic third baseman, Jerry Denny. He could do things with his bare hands that were comparable, the ancients still insist, with anything Jimmy Collins, Buck Weaver, Pie Tray-nor, or anyone else of baseball's modern era was able to do with full field equipment. I knew all about Bill Lange and what he was doing with "Pop" Anson's Colts. The Cor-betts, Jim and Joe, were most familiar to me. And why not? We lived in the same neighborhood, a section of San Fran-cisco known as Hayes Valley.

Brother Jim Corbett had been the heavyweight champion, the reformed bank clerk who had licked the mighty John L. Sullivan. He might have remained champion much longer save for the incident at Carson City, Nevada, when Ruby Robert Fitzsimmons poked an exploratory handful of fingers into the Corbett region forever after known as the solar plexus.

Brother Joe was a pitcher with the Baltimore Orioles, who brought into the baseball world John McGraw, Hughey Jennings, Willie Keeler, and other potential candidates of baseball's hall of fame.

It was completely understood by all us kids of Hayes Valley that Brother Joe, a gentle, mild-mannered soul by nature, could, if aroused, lick as many and do it as effectively as Brother Jim ever did.

Contrariwise, there was the belief that Brother Jim, if he had not taken up the prize ring, might well have been a major-league ball player. I was never able to verify this. When I sought testimony in later years from McGraw, from Jennings, and from Jack Doyle, of the old Orioles, I was assured that while Joe Corbett wouldn't bother anyone, it wasn't very healthy for anyone to bother him.

In San Francisco were to be found the great fighters of all classes, as residents or visitors. Here also were many of the ring's most famous referees, such as Eddie Graney, Jack Welch, and Jim Griffin. Across the Bay at Oakland was Eddie Smith, another arbiter in the rings, which had not yet become overmanned with two extra officials known as judges.

No fight was official unless its contestants were sent on their way by the announcements of the picturesque Billy Jordan. He was in the pre-public-address-system days, of course, but the fan in the uttermost reaches of the arena could hear his bull-like bellowing. Jordan, a hefty handle-bar-mustached man, was as much an essential California prize-ring property at the turn of the century as were the gloves, ring posts, ropes, water buckets, towels, and sponges.

For a hero-worshiping youngster, San Francisco was a sports paradise.

While the pursuit of sports and sporting figures was delightful, there was also that matter of education to be considered. In Hayes Valley was located St. Ignatius College. It came equipped with a prep school and a few rooms devoted to upper grades of grammar school. I was deposited in this last section, and made such progress that by September 1905 I was launched on a high-school career, struggling to tell a declension from an unknown quantity, or Ovid from Euclid.

This, of course, was by necessity. By choice I'd have preferred attempting to tell the ball players at the Eighth and Harrison Street grounds without a program. Or perhaps scrap Longfellow's verse for something like a parody of the time that went:

> Good-by, Jabez White, good-by.
> You thought you were it,
> Till you met Jimmy Britt.
> Good-by, Jabez White, good-by.

Jabez White was an English lightweight who had dared challenge Britt, the slick 133-pounder from San Francisco's South of the Slot, and failed dismally, as any of us native sons could have told him he would long before he sailed for our shores.

Life at St. Ignatius went on apace until April in 1906. I was awakened rudely shortly after dawn one day when down from the ceiling came the ceiling. As it came down, the bed upon which I lay seemed to be straining to get up there to meet it. I know it is good and wholesome for all San Franciscans, past or present, to say that the episode of April 18, 1906, was a fire and not an earthquake. But I promised myself at the take-off of this job that I would not hold out on you. It was an earthquake. I know. I was in on it. Or it was in on me. The effect was about the same, either way.

Were I so minded, I could give a play-by-play account of those terrifying days and nights of April 1906. However, the earthquake figures in this recital chiefly because it was needed to get me out of the first year of high school.

It turned the city's favorite arena, Mechanics Pavilion, into an emergency hospital, but had few other points in common with sports and the sports pages. One was the yarn that was told of a diminutive Negro fighter, Deacon Jones. He fought now and then. He was broke always. He liked a snifter and had developed a routine calculated to produce one when the price was lacking.

He was a familiar figure in and out of San Francisco's bars. He went into one that early April morning. He approached the bar and went into his act. The bartender eyed him and said nothing, but went on polishing glasses. The Deacon tried his emergency routine. It also failed. Other stratagems availed nothing. The Deacon would now try force. He advanced to the bar and shouted:

"Ifn you don't gimme dat drink, Ah'll reach down, grab de rail, and push de whole bah in yo' lap!"

The bartender kept right on polishing glasses.

"Ah warned you," said the Deacon, and reached over to get a grip on the rail.

Just then arrived the earthquake.

Several minutes later the bartender and the Deacon hauled

themselves out of the rubble of mortar, plaster, and broken bottles and glasses, and began taking stock.

"Boy, Ah suah give yo' service," said the Deacon.

The bartender simply shook his head. He still didn't believe it happened and nobody was going to tell him it did.

So I'm not going to try. . . .

CHAPTER 3

Touching All Bases

*T*HE earthquake of 1906, which I have damned with faint praise, shook the family of Browns out of San Francisco for a year or so and scattered them as far afield as Sacramento and Oakland. By late summer of 1907 they were nesting again, hard by Golden Gate Park, and a few blocks from the new site of St. Ignatius College.

Now I have said that it took an earthquake to get me out of the first year of high school. That was true, but with reservations. When I returned to my studies, it was decided that I start from scratch. The work I had gone through haphazardly first time around now came rather easily. This gave me more time to cultivate sports and the sports pages.

My favorite sport then, as now, was baseball. I went in for it in a large way. When there wasn't enough of it on the St. Ignatius program, I looked to other fields. One of these was a tournament organized by the San Francisco *Examiner* for youngsters who could make 115 pounds. I was the first baseman of the Telegraph Hill Boys' Club. I made the requisite 115 pounds by starving for two days prior to the weigh-in, and by drinking no water for several days before that.

The pitcher of our club was a lanky youngster known as "Swede" Risberg. He was to become famous first and afterward notorious as the shortstop of the Chicago White Sox of 1919's world's series of unhappy memory. But more of that in proper sequence.

I'd like to be able to report that we ran away with the *Examiner*'s trophy. But we did not. It went to the Columbia Park Boys' Club, whose shortstop was Jimmy Caveney. In due time he reached the Cincinnati Reds, and was a member of an infield all positions of which were manned by San Franciscans. The others were Lou Fonseca, Sammy Bohne, and Babe Pinelli. All had their baseball beginnings in Golden Gate Park's "Big Rec," as its green-turfed recreation field was called.

This was the baseball cradle of more famous players than any other spot in the country. It held space enough for several diamonds, but they were so close to each other that action was hazardous in the extreme. A baseman trying to make a play at first base in one game was in danger of being spiked by a base runner oversliding third on the field next door. At this shooting gallery you learned to keep your eye on the ball, if nothing else.

In between classrooms and full-scale baseball operations, I was able to keep up with the established heroes in other fields and was an avid reader of all their exploits. It was about this time that I met up with heavyweight champion Jack Johnson.

He was in San Francisco training for a fight. His camp was at Seal Rock House on the ocean beach. The most direct route there led along the street on which I lived. Johnson used that route right along, covering it in a low-slung racing-model automobile. He was one of the original speed demons in the days when folks were not quite sure whether the auto would ever replace the horse.

I was going home for lunch one day and was just stepping off the curb when the roar of an infernal machine startled me. I let out a frightened yell and jumped back. It was close, Mom, but I made it. When my addled wits had been reassembled I looked down the street. In the distance I saw the auto come to a stop, swing around, and come chugging back toward me. As it approached I recognized Johnson.

"I just come back to give you some advice, young fellow,"

he said. "If you watch where you're going, you'll last longer. And you'll keep out of a hell of a lot of trouble."

With that he turned the car again and roared on his Seal Rock House way.

Many times since, when the chance was afforded me to know more of Johnson and his debit and credit sides, I wondered what might have happened to him if he ever thought of following his own advice. He never did, of course. But then, he would not have been Jack Johnson if he had.

My high-school days moved rapidly along. There was an interlude in a ball game in which Joe Corbett, my first coach, sent me up to the plate with instructions to make a sacrifice bunt and advance two runners who were on base.

I bunted . . . a line drive that was turned into a triple play! As I passed Corbett, fully expecting to draw down the wrath such as only a member of the old Baltimore Orioles could exude, the coach merely shook his head a bit sadly.

"The theory was correct, my boy," he said, "but the execution was a trifle faulty."

Not for nothing had we been neighbors in Hayes Valley years before. . . .

My name was in various San Francisco papers, off and on, generally set down as "Brown 1b" or "Brown cf" in a half-column line of agate type. None of the contemporary journalists seemed to appreciate (as I did) the importance of an event in 1909. Then, while in the third year of high school, I earned my letter playing on the college varsity team. That does not make sense now, but in my days elastic wasn't quite the word for eligibility codes.

However, it was not until 1911, and as a high-school competitor, that I made the sports pages in the grand manner, action picture and story.

Our team was engaged with Sacred Heart High in a game for the city championship. The game was played at the Presidio Athletic Grounds. Two home runs were hit. One, which went over the right field fence, was propelled by Harry Heilmann. He found St. Ignatius pitching as soft a touch for him as American League style was to be for so many years afterward while he was a member of the Detroit Tigers. The home run that cleared the left field fence was mine. All mine.

The next morning's San Francisco *Call* presented pictures of each of us crossing the plate.

Since that memorable event Heilmann and I each have had our own ideas about the proper place of that game in San Francisco's history. Mine is that the *Call* ceased publication as a separate entity not too long after it had printed my picture. Heilmann, who now has the radio broadcaster's imagination, is mindful of the fact that the Presidio Athletic Grounds was soon dismantled to be used as the site for the Panama Pacific International Exposition of 1915. My home run, he says, is the only one ever expanded into a world's fair.

As I crossed the dividing line between prep school and college and had some vague ideas of an A.B. that meant more than the heading of a box score's first column, there was baseball every day, spring, summer, fall, and winter, if one wanted it. This one did.

Besides a full schedule at St. Ignatius, there was action with the semipros on Sundays, with the Olympic Club, and with two oddly assorted winter and early spring groupings known as Ireland's Independents and Louie Lowenberg's All Stars. On these latter two might be found many famous professional players whose homes were in San Francisco, and who were not averse to playing a bit of baseball in the off season.

Because of all these outlets it has never been any wonder to me why San Francisco has developed so many great ball players, from Bill Lange of the Anson era to Joe Di Maggio. Any youngster with talent at all could not help but get both encouragement and development in that environment.

For my purposes, those days were most useful in forming acquaintances and friendships that were to prove most helpful when I became a collector, rather than a producer, of baseball news in later years.

It was in 1913 that I met up with my first major-league club, close enough to see the whites of their eyes.

St. Ignatius was given a spring exhibition game by the Chicago White Sox, who were training on the Coast. They licked us, 3 to 2, but that game brought into prominence our slim left-handed pitcher, "Dutch" Ruether. Going into the ninth inning, he had allowed but three hits and had the Sox beaten 2 to 1. A base on balls and a line shot by Buck Weaver that may be rolling yet turned up in the ninth to give the Sox two runs.

Our side still had a chance. I led off our half of the ninth and hit one over third base, which Harry Lord blocked and threw hurriedly far over the head of Babe Borton, the Sox first baseman. Mine was the tying run, and in the rush to get to second base—to which a ground rule entitled me, bonehead that I was—I tripped over first base and sprawled out. Arising sheepishly, I went on to second, where the ball had already arrived. Second baseman Morris Rath tagged me and umpire Jack McCarthy said I was out, of all things, for failing to tag first base! I raved. I ranted. Nor did it help when Rath, the big leaguer, spoke softly in my ear:

"There are only three of 'em out here, kid. You ought to be able to touch 'em all!"

Some years later, when I was a baseball writer, and Rath was playing in the Coast League, he one day missed a base.

You may be sure that I had ready for publication the soft answer that turned away Rath.

That game against the White Sox earned Ruether his first major-league contract. He was to have many before his pitching course was done, in both National and American Leagues. He had been on various teams with me from his prep-school days on, and when he became a character among the many that Uncle Robbie marshaled at Brooklyn, I was not surprised.

Even in his salad days "Dutch" was a character. Such

as on the occasion when the strong Pall Mall Pool Room team, of which Ruether was pitcher, was scheduled to play at Healdsburg, California, one Sunday afternoon. Ruether, who liked to get around, had made the trip the night before. The other eight members of the team went up Sunday morning, and having duly reached the park, found themselves with no pitcher. No one had seen Dutch since the night before.

Twenty minutes before the game began, a gate opened out in center field and through it appeared a horse-drawn carriage, with the driver whipping the horse in a fine frenzy. Beside him was one of the belles of Healdsburg.

Straight toward second base came the carriage, made the turn to third, rounded it, and drew up in front of the bench assigned to the Pall Mall Pool Room nine.

Out stepped Dutch Ruether. He gallantly assisted the Healdsburg belle to alight and found a seat for her in the stand.

Then he proceeded to warm up for the game, and as a matter of course, win it. Frank Merriwell himself could not have done it nicer.

The game Ruether pitched against the White Sox had the effect of getting all our names in the Chicago papers for the first time. That mine happened to be among them goes to show what queer bounces a baseball takes. Not much more than ten years later I was contributing regularly my share of Chicago's sports page literary output.

The year 1913 was memorable in other respects than our brush with the White Sox, which took place in early spring.

During the summer for a time I was occupied in playing Sunday baseball at Sebastopol. Our hated rival was the team from near-by Petaluma. Our pitcher was Ray Kremer, not long out of high school in Oakland, and associated with us at St. Ignatius before professional baseball beckoned to him and he went on to curve out a great career with the Pittsburgh Pirates.

In one of our games with Petaluma we were confronted

with a spitball pitcher, "Mickey" Shader. In the first inning, with two men on bases, Mickey threw one where I was swinging and it went over the right center field fence for three runs, or all Sebastopol was to get. Kremer was in excellent form and Petaluma did not have a chance until the ninth inning. Then two men got on and the next batsman, with none out, tripled. Two runs were in, none was out, and the tying run was on third.

Kremer dug in and pitched his way out of that jam, retiring the next three hitters and anchoring that tying run at third. The home-town fans who had wagered greatly on the ball game went into hysterics. They showered Kremer with gold pieces as he came off the field.

The center fielder who had knocked in the three runs that made the victory possible had been badly off in his timing. He opened the show, and the star act came on last.

True, the story of the game in the next issue of Sebastopol's weekly newspaper did say that the folks up that way would remember Brown long after they had quit moaning about the condition of the country roads. But at the time I'd have preferred to stop a few of those five- and ten-dollar gold pieces.

It was this small-boy resentment of the cruel public that led me to switch my Sunday baseball farther north and join the Eureka team. It was located in the heart of the lumber country, and Eureka, on Saturday nights when those loggers came in out of the woods, was really something to write home about.

One of our games was against the Ferndale team, whose pitcher was Joe Oeschger, a St. Mary's College right-hander of considerable skill and endurance. There were no less than three Browns on the Eureka team. One of them scored the game's lone run, which beat Oeschger 1 to 0. The game went nineteen innings.

It was therefore no surprise to me when Oeschger, pitching for the Boston Braves in 1920, engaged Leon Cadore of

Brooklyn in a twenty-six-inning game, longest on major-league record. I had been present when he rehearsed it.

It was while acquiring a baseball as well as a college education that I came to the lasting conclusion that Hal Chase was the greatest fielding first baseman who ever lived. As a small boy I had seen him play many times when he was working for the outlaw California State League team at Stockton, California. Now I was to have a chance to study him close up.

I had gone to Santa Cruz for a Sunday game, and Chase was filling in with the home team. There came a time in the game when our side put a man on first base. Chase was holding him on. The batter sent a sharp bounder well to the left of the second baseman on a hit-and-run play. Chase, a left-hander, tore down the line from first, fielded the ball, and in a play that happened so rapidly it seemed one movement, got it to second, forcing the base runner. How Chase stopped, reversed himself, and got back to first base to take the return throw, completing a double play, I will never know. But that's what happened, and the way Chase executed it, the play seemed rather simple.

Having seen that, I was ready (and still am) to believe any of the stories about Chase, such as one that Jim Morley, a Los Angeles magnate of the early days, once related.

There was a man on third base (Morley said) and the squeeze play was tried. The batter pushed the ball along the ground toward first as the runner dashed for home. Fast as he traveled, Chase moved faster. He raced in, scooped up the ball, and without missing a stride kept on, tagging out the runner just as he slid for the plate.

All of this adventuring in baseball quite naturally caused me to give some thought to the game as a means of livelihood.

Offers of sorts came my way and had been coming since my last year in high school. A Pacific Coast agent for Connie Mack told me what a fine education I might get at Holy Cross at Mr. Mack's expense if I would give his Athletics first search on my baseball talent, if any. I passed that one up, as I was later to pass up one from Kansas City, where Cliff Blankenship was manager pro tem.

Blankenship, a former member of the Washington club, had once traveled out to Idaho and placed the stamp of approval on the youthful Walter Johnson, who was to become one of baseball's immortals. Blankenship was denied the chance to get me for Kansas City. That may have been a mistake on my part. Had I taken root in Missouri in 1913, who knows but what I might have been a member of the Cabinet in 1947?

Among all the baseball offers that came my way, the one that seemed most logical came from a friend, Harry Wolverton, who managed the Sacramento club. He knew that badly as I wanted to play baseball, I wanted my college degree more. He proposed that I join his club during my summer vacation of 1914. If I made the grade, permission would be given me to return to college and graduate before taking up the game for good.

I took him up on that. Somebody's old score book will show that I broke into professional baseball in a game against Vernon, getting a pinch hit off Doc White, who had outlived his major-league usefulness with the Chicago White Sox.

Somebody else's old scrapbook will show that later in the series I batted again, this time against another former major-league left-hander, Roy Hitt. I singled, which pleased Wolverton so much he sent me into the outfield to finish out the game. I was stationed in a sun field, without glasses. A "busher" in those days was not offered any help by teammates. Presently one of the Vernon batsmen sent a fly out my way, which I promptly lost in the sun. My floundering around prompted a Los Angeles baseball writer to say that I had all the grace of an underfed elephant on a waxed ballroom floor. (I knew, fifteen years later, just how Hack Wilson felt in that tragic world's series moment of sunlight in Shibe Park when he lost the fly that precipitated a ten-run inning against the Chicago Cubs.)

There isn't much more that records will show of my professional baseball career. At the end of my vacation I went back to college and was content to bat the books around until a degree flew out of them. By that time the urge to play professional baseball had left me.

I have never regretted one instant of my baseball. It threw me in contact with hundreds of players who had made, were making, or would one day make the history that I would eventually help to chronicle . . . though I had no definite thought on this at the time.

Somewhere in my inner consciousness, I suppose, was the suggestion that it might be easier to tell how others have or should have played a game than to play the game myself.

It was not very long after my college career was ended that I was to attempt the practical application of this theory.

CHAPTER 4

A City of Characters

*E*MERGING from college in 1915, I became greatly interested in the candidacy of Eugene E. Schmitz. He was attempting to regain the office of mayor from which he had retired under a cloud during a graft prosecution several years before. My man ran second in a race in which place and show were *out*. Thus ended any further ambitions I might have had to become a practicing politician.

At the time I was heartbroken, but I did learn that in politics, as in sport, there is an axiom—they never come back. Five years before Jim Jeffries had tried it, and came to a cropper at Reno, Nevada, when he essayed proving it could be done at Jack Johnson's expense. This notable milestone along pugilism's route had served to make me aware of George L. ("Tex") Rickard, with whom I was to become much more closely associated in the years to come.

Tex was making his first big bid as an international figure among fight promoters, though he had dabbled in it previously, also in Nevada arenas. At first Tex proposed to hold the Jeffries-Johnson fight in California. So much stir did the $100,000 purse and the game's first major exposition of the ballyhoo create, the governor of California invited Rickard to take his show elsewhere. That was where Reno came in. That was where came in also the famous sports writers, cartoonists, and picture makers. All the storied figures of the prize ring moved in. The ballyhoo pace was not to be equaled again until Rickard, at the instance of Jack Kearns, descended upon Toledo with the Jess Willard–Jack Dempsey fight in 1919.

For all the mass of expert opinion most favorable to Jeff, the old fellow couldn't quite make it. He was knocked out, and into the lingo of the times went the expression: "They never come back."

Nor did Eugene E. Schmitz, whose bid for a return to San Francisco's City Hall I helped sponsor.

For lack of something better to do after I had crawled out from beneath the voting landslide, I joined my brother, who was heading for the desert on a job of work for the state in southeastern California. While I was there a message from a close friend reached me.

"Mannix is quitting the *Bulletin* to practice law," he advised. "Why don't you come back and try for that job?" Mannix was a baseball writer with whom I was well acquainted.

Well, why not? I felt that I had a working knowledge of baseball. I had the normal amount of confidence in my writing ability. It had been exercised in various college publications and in preparing publicity releases for the newspapers. I rushed back to San Francisco and sought out Mannix—Francis J. was the rest of it. He confirmed the report that he was giving up baseball writing. But he didn't know when. Maybe three months, maybe six months, maybe a year. That was a great help.

"Why don't you go up and have a talk with Baggerly?" he suggested. "Maybe he'll have some ideas."

Hy Baggerly was the sports editor of the *Bulletin,* and a kindly man who had a reputation for encouraging newcomers in the field of journalism. It was he who had discovered Charley Van Loan. He had given Tad his start. He had believed in Ripley before anyone else did. He had something to do with the start of Rube Goldberg and many others who had gone on from the *Bulletin* to larger fields.

It would be nice to say that Baggerly welcomed me as just the man he had been looking for all these years. It would be nice; but it wouldn't be true.

He had his feet propped up on a desk and was reading a book when I first called on him. He did not even turn around to greet me. There was no job, he said. There wasn't going to be any job. He told me that on my next two visits, by which time he had finished the first book and was part way through another. The fourth time he showed signs of weakening. He admitted that he had been looking for someone to write semiprofessional baseball notes twice a week, but that Al Erle, manager of Spalding's, a headquarters for baseball's coming wonders, was going to look after that for him.

Like hell he was! Spalding's wasn't very far away. Not even as far as I had once hit a home run off Doc Moskiman while Erle was catching him at Santa Rosa, Ripley's home town. I put my case squarely before Erle. He was very gracious. He had not intended to do any writing. All he had ever promised Baggerly was that he'd keep track of items about the comings and goings of the "bushers," as the semipros were called.

Next thing Baggerly knew, he found on his desk a batch of bright and breezy banter, boots and bingles of the bushers. He must have liked them. The *Bulletin* printed them. For that I was given $5 a week, which was considerably lower than an outfielder's pay, but it was a start in this curious business. I was asked to make contributions twice a week and did so for a while. One morning I encountered Mannix on the street. Corner of Stockton and Market, if anyone wants to put up a plaque on the spot.

Mannix said he was resigning that afternoon and that I had better get a story ready for next day, since I was the new baseball writer. Just like that.

The Salt Lake club was in San Francisco at the time. It was managed by Cliff Blankenship, the same who had attempted to get me to sign a contract with the Kansas City club that time he was guiding its destinies.

I wangled a story out of Blankenship. I took it to the *Bulletin* and into the sports department, which was deserted. I left it on Baggerly's desk, where I had been accustomed to deposit my semipro material. I could hardly wait for the next day's papers to roll off the press.

The story was printed with my name at the top. I was in. I have had a story or more printed in some newspaper or other from San Francisco to New York every day since, save for a stretch in 1917–18. Then I was occupied as a member of U.S. Army Intelligence and fought like hell through several western states and Alaska to keep the dread Hun and his loathsome agents at bay.

But the first story is the one that counted, in my life. The boss did not tell me to start. However, he did not tell me to stop, either. At the end of my first week I took my $25 as proudly as if Fremont Older, the famous editor of the *Bulletin,* had personally sent for me, saying that the paper would suspend publication if I did not go in to bat for Mannix.

As a separate entity it did suspend later on, but I refuse to take the rap for that.

During my leave of absence while I was catching spies up and down the Coast, Older and most of his key men surrendered to William Randolph Hearst and went over to the *Call-Post*. This was also an afternoon paper. Just to show you how complicated this newspaper life can be, the *Call* had been a morning paper originally, before combining with the *Post*. As I remember it, there had been a reasonable doubt as to just what the *Post* was while it operated on its own.

After World War I subsided, I returned to the *Bulletin* and by easy stages soon made my way down Market Street, turned right, and landed with the *Call-Post*. Presently the *Bulletin* gave a death rattle, but *rigor mortis* never did set in. A plant surgeon was called in and what had been the *Call-*

Post suddenly became the *Call-Bulletin*. The patient has done well ever since.

Life on a San Francisco newspaper in those days was not very restful. There were four-round fights to be covered two or three times a week in San Francisco and Oakland. Wrestling was packing 'em in. In season there were baseball games five afternoons a week with double-headers on Sunday, the morning game in Oakland, the afternoon game in San Francisco.

You might also qualify, as I did, as a dramatic critic specializing in vaudeville and musical comedy. You might be drafted on occasions to help out on local assignments. You slept and you had your meals when you could get either, on or off the cuff. But you thrived on it.

I had become a fight writer on very short notice while in the employ of the *Bulletin*. The established boxing expert, Marion Salazar, a hot-tempered soul, had one of his periodical flare-ups and quit, taking over a job with another paper. I was impressed into service at a time when my previous experience had been solely that of a fight fan.

Salazar, from three thousand miles off, had always delighted in writing catty things about New York boxing writers. His chief object of attention was Bat Masterson, who was accustomed to reply in kind in his own column in the New York *Telegraph*.

He must have hated Salazar greatly, for in about the length of time it took a copy of the *Bulletin* with my first fight story to get to New York, and for a copy of the *Telegraph* to get to San Francisco, I found out that Masterson had hailed me as a worth-while boxing expert, such as San Francisco generally, and the *Bulletin* in particular, had sorely needed for years.

Just for that, Salazar, in his column down the street, really let Masterson have it.

Sal and I got along well, whether we were associates or rivals. Or did on all but one occasion, which happened to be the night I found out all I ever needed to know about professional wrestlers, and Sal found out more than he had ever suspected.

Our town's leading exponent of the mat game at the time was Ad Santel, whose name had been Adolph Ernst before he moved in. He was not as bulky as most of the heavyweight wrestlers, but he was large enough for all practical purposes. He specialized in the arm scissors. He was matched one night with one of the more important of the Middle Western heavyweights, whom we shall call Mr. X.

Mr. X had called upon Salazar one morning while I was in the office. I was charmed with his culture, his refinement, his dress, his cane, and his cauliflower ear. But I was not fascinated enough to go see the match. Mr. X was resident at the St. Francis Hotel, and about eleven o'clock on the night of the match I happened to pass by there on my way to the *Bulletin* to do an overnight story. Mr. X was just walking up the block to enter the hotel. He looked every inch the conqueror and swung his cane very jauntily as he strode along.

When I arrived at the *Bulletin* I found Salazar at his desk. He seemed very perturbed. He was calling hospitals, first the Central Emergency and then all the others in town, as rapidly as he could thumb the phone book and get their numbers. He was cursing as he went along.

I finally asked what was up.

"I'm trying to locate Mr. X," he said. "He fell out of the ring. I want to find out if his back was broken or not."

"It wasn't when I saw him about five minutes ago on Powell Street," I said.

Salazar simply stared at me, and I repeated that I had just seen Mr. X about to enter the St. Francis Hotel.

Then Salazar really opened up. Not more than an hour ago, he said, with his own eyes he had seen Mr. X thrown from the ring at the Auditorium. When all efforts to revive him had failed, he had been removed hastily to a hospital, it was announced.

"His back must have been broken," insisted Salazar, "and I don't think you saw him at all."

Well, what was a baseball writer to do but preserve the peace? I had seen Mr. X, of course. I have seen him many times since, in Chicago, and while his back may have been bent a trifle with the years, it definitely has not been broken.

That incident, more than anything else, endeared the professional wrestlers to me. There may have been better actors than they since Shakespeare's time, but I have never run across them.

During practically all of my newspaper career in San Francisco I had certain advantages that do not come to the average young man who gets caught up in this curious business. There stemmed out of the city by the Golden Gate characters in all walks of public life who either were or were destined to be an endless source of interest. Wherever I have been since, or whatever has been occupying my attention at the time, more often than not my approach to it has been easier because of this background.

Then, too, I was under the early guidance of Edgar T. (Scoop) Gleeson, who was one of Fremont Older's men. Gleeson was an all-around newspaperman, if ever there has been such a thing. There was no phase of its activity, reporting, writing, art, photography, or make-up, with which he was not at home. He had unbounded enthusiasm for the job, any job. At his urging I was willing to try anything. Since Older stood squarely behind his men, there was no pussy-footing around dangerous topics. Nothing was too hot for us to handle. We had only one house rule. We didn't like phonies. I still like that rule.

We were continually plunging into action, swinging away with both typewriter fingers. One of our adventures was the pursuit of a theory that all things were not what they seemed in the Pacific Coast League. Gleeson and I both manufactured the ammunition for that campaign, but I did the firing. When we had finished developing the theory the league had a new president and several clubs had new owners.

One of these was Charles H. ("Doc") Strub. He took over the San Francisco club in association with Charles Graham and George Putnam.

If baseball ever produced a rugged individualist Doc Strub was it. It was not long before he was asking for and was getting such sums as $100,000 for Willie Kamm, a third baseman the Chicago White Sox craved. Perhaps it was the memory of those baseball $100,000 tags that moved him, in a later existence, to make racing history by offering $100,000 purses annually for the Santa Anita Handicap and Santa Anita Derby at the successful racecourse that he promoted, built, and has so ably directed.

Yet it wasn't Doc Strub's financial wizardry in baseball or racing presentation that endeared him to me. It was an episode in his reorganization of the San Francisco club's affairs that stamped him as a dominant figure.

He had suspected that two of his pitchers, both stars, one a former major-leaguer and the other an up-and-coming youngster, were in league with gamblers. Strub carried on a quiet investigation until he had his proof. He had established that the pitchers actually had a signal code whereby they tipped off to their gambling associates what they intended to do with a pitch, so that important "bet he gets to first base" money could be put down. If necessary, a hit by pitched ball or a walk would accomplish that.

Once convinced of his pitchers' guilt, Strub did not hesitate. He summarily dismissed the two and published all the details of the unsavory mess. More than that, he barred from his park all their known gambling associates. As long as Strub remained an active force in baseball those gamblers remained barred.

One of the many satisfactions I have had out of sports writing has been that I was the unwitting cause of bringing into professional sports promotion a sound character such as Doc Strub.

It has been my personal observation that the prize ring has produced just three notable promoters. James Wood Coffroth was the first, Tex Rickard was the middle man, and the cycle has ended with Mike Jacobs of New York.

Uncle Mike has lacked the imagination of Coffroth and the gambling instinct of Rickard. Perhaps that was because of the three he was the one who had no early San Francisco experience. Rickard had just enough to do him. Coffroth had more than his share. When he exhausted the possibilities of the prize ring he turned to racing and popularized the sport at Tijuana, a not too lovely spot across the border from San Diego.

There in due time he was moved to inaugurate the first $100,000 added attraction in racing history, the Coffroth Handicap. This annual feature continued for the duration of the Tijuana track and endured on the same lavish scale for a while after Agua Caliente had displaced it as racing's port of call in that corner of the world.

Nowadays there are almost as many $100,000 stakes as there are major race tracks, but the first to recognize the crowd appeal of the record purse were Coffroth and Strub.

If there has been an inescapable linking of past and present in this presentation, and if as I go along the urge takes me to flit from one sport to another, it must be accepted that from the beginning I have been in a continuous variety show. I have never known for sure just what was coming off next. Nor have I cared, since all of what I now deem worthy of recalling was most interesting.

It will become necessary, however, to make the report objective now and then. To try out this formula I shall take up first the life and times of two of the most interesting characters who have ever found their way on to the printed page, the two Jacks, Dempsey and Kearns. I, who have known and liked both in most of the years of their respective lives, have never been able to tell which is the more remarkable. Perhaps you will when all the evidence is in, and I shall have returned to a consideration of others who were contemporary with them, and who performed nobly in the center ring of the sporting circus in what time the two Jacks were off stage.

CHAPTER 5

Dempsey Meets Kearns

*J*ACK DEMPSEY's story, in so far as his fights are concerned, has been presented early and often since I first wrote it for a San Francisco newspaper following his speedy knockout of Fred Fulton. So I have no particular intention of following the record book to its logical conclusion.

Since it was given to me to be associated with Dempsey from his very early days, I prefer to view his career through many incidents that were not all on the record. Many of those made a more lasting impression on me than did any series of left hooks to the body and jaw that this most formidable of all the heavyweights ever threw at an opponent.

Kearns, his manager, close friend and pal through Dempsey's rise and his days of glory, has a story, too. As far as I know, it has never been told in its entirety. As far as I am concerned, it never will, on the same general theory that moved Wilson Mizner to resist appeal after appeal that he write his autobiography. "No," said Mizner. "I can't. I'm no cop."

Well, neither am I.

Kearns was the foremost exponent of the ballyhoo. In the fight game, as well as in all sports that depend on box office, continued successful existence depends on just that.

Long before Kearns knew there was a Dempsey, he had been using his persuasive eloquence to sell the wares of himself or his fighters. He had ranged the country. He had been in Alaska during the gold rush. And it was in far-off Australia, I believe, that he first set forth his success platform.

He had gone there with a troupe of fighters, good, bad, and indifferent. He had seen all of them, and others from the States who were much better, beaten into helplessness by the brawny native Les Darcy. He visualized the gold and glory that might be forthcoming from an American tour of Darcy under the Kearns management. He sold the idea to Darcy.

In Australia at the time was a fiery flinger of words and phrases known as the Boxing Major. He was quite annoyed at this turn of events and sat himself down and wrote a piece:

Jack Kearns, or Karns, or Kearney, the Yankee manager of Murray, Bonds and Watson, who sends out dollops of dope, has bombarded the Sydney press with the announcement that he has become the manager of the middleweight champion of the world, Les Darcy.

His announcement was typewritten on blue paper suggestive of a summons for non-registration of a dog, and bearing a flaming printed heading in black and red, and two portraits of Darcy. It read:

"Just a line to inform you I have taken over the management of Les Darcy. We leave in the middle of December for America where Darcy opens at the Pantages Theater in San Francisco for a 32 weeks vaudeville tour. I am also in receipt of several cables from New York fight promoters for Darcy to box there. His first American appearance will be in Philadelphia against Leo Houck. Darcy is guaranteed twelve thousand pounds. We expect to box Mike Gibbons for James W. Coffroth at Teewona, on the Mexican border near Los Angeles. Such a contest should draw in the neighborhood of twenty thousand pounds."

The Boxing Major was so indignant he forgot to take note of Kearns' weakness in spelling and geography, since Tijuana and not "Teewona" was much nearer San Diego than Los Angeles. But if the Boxing Major forgot to touch all the bases, Kearns did not. He sought out the Australian author and let out a squawk that could be heard around the world.

"Can it be that you don't approve anything but a kindly press?" asked the Boxing Major.

"No, it ain't that," said Kearns.

"Don't you believe you are liable to censure for luring away from his country a fine young man like Darcy, to subject him to temptations and inevitable disaster in a strange and unfriendly land?"

"No," said Kearns. "It ain't that, neither."

"Then would you mind telling me, my dear fellow, what in hell is all the row?" pursued the Boxing Major.

"My name," said our hero, "is Kearns, K-E-A-R-N-S. It ain't Karns. It ain't Kearney. It's Kearns. See that you remember that."

Most sports writers have.

Kearns had been dubbing around as a manager of fighters from his Alaska days onward. He had control of a lightweight, Maurice Thompson, and was in San Francisco at the time of the earthquake in 1906. He was shaken loose of all his worldly possessions save the contract with Thompson. As did so many other visitors, Kearns got away from the stricken area as quickly as possible. He reached Spokane, where he became interested in the publication of a sporting weekly, and through it caught up with Dick Hyland, a San Francisco lightweight of promise.

An offer came for a fight between Thompson and Hyland at Cripple Creek. Kearns accepted. Irregular for one manager to have both fighters? Don't be silly. It was highly regular by contrast with what actually did happen at Cripple Creek.

The Colorado altitude affected Hyland so that he was unable to go through with the engagement. Even that did not trouble Kearns too much. He put on fighting trunks and took the bout himself. It is probably the only time on record in which a manager went into the ring to fight one of his own men because his other man had pulled up lame.

A contemporary author had this to say of the bout:

"Last night at the Victor Opera House, Maurice Thompson of Butte won from Jack Kearns of Spokane in the middle of the fourth round of what was to have been a twenty round go.

"Kearns' seconds jumped into the ring and took their man to the corner after he had fallen to the floor and seemed unable to continue. His wind failed him and his seconds rather than see their man take unnecessary punishment, threw in the sponge."

This is the only evidence on record that Kearns ever ran out of breath.

Kearns revisited San Francisco in 1913. On its Barbary Coast, which still flourished, he borrowed enough money to get himself well plastered. When he recovered he discovered that he was part owner of a dive called the "Breakers." In sober consideration, its only value to Kearns was that it was close to Spider Kelly's. As long as there was a Spider Kelly and he ran a joint, that would be a base of operations for Kearns, as it was for all others of San Francisco's sporting world.

Kelly was one of the sizable colony of ex-fighters who had helped make ring history in and around San Francisco. His own career at an end, Kelly, slatlike and with beetling brows, was a perfect subject for many a caricature by Tad, who recognized in him one of the most cunning handlers of fighters who had ever crawled through the ropes.

It was in Kelly's joint that Kearns discovered Billy Murray, the young Portuguese middleweight, who was one of the trio taken to Australia to tangle with Darcy.

Australia had taken but mild interest in Kearns' ballyhoo antics until he came up with the announcement that he was the manager of the native Darcy. Then all hell broke loose.

Foremost in the attackers was the Boxing Major, of whom mention has been made already. He foresaw nothing but evil ahead for Darcy, and the greatest pitfall of all was the vaudeville engagement Kearns had promised. Of this the Boxing Major had to say:

Then the alleged vaudeville engagement. Thirty two weeks on the Panturges Circuit. Thirty two weeks of mad unrest; of night traveling by rushing, roaring trains; of one night stands; of temptation to take stimulants and temptation at the fair hands of the lovely but deadly sirens of the American vaudeville stage. And to top off, three shows every week day and four on Sundays. It's not an engagement; it's slavery and degradation. Can you fancy merry, young Darcy, accustomed to warmth and friendly devotion and truth and honor, suddenly cast in that hideous maelstrom, and in the depths of an American winter, at that. And to crown all, he'd not only be a friendless stranger in a strange land, without any personal freedom, but even debarred from visiting the newspaper offices or fraternizing with the writers or others likely to be of use or help to him.

Verily the Boxing Major viewed America and the Pantages Circuit with considerable alarm!

Kearns went right on perfecting his plans, but he had not reckoned with the European war. The conscription act prevented any able-bodied man from eighteen to forty-five from leaving Australia. Darcy was certainly able-bodied. He had not enlisted. He had tried to, earlier, and had been ruled off as underage. Kearns tried for a six-month leave of absence for the lad, and when it was denied, chose to abandon the whole project until after the war. He sailed for San Francisco, Darcy having promised to follow when circumstances permitted.

Kearns had hardly reached the States before the news broke that Darcy had slipped out of Australia and was bound for America, thereby bringing down on his head the hue and cry of "slacker." While Darcy had cabled Kearns he was on his way, there was much mystery surrounding his place and date of arrival.

Then, too, Kearns learned that others were in the running for Darcy's services, among them Tex Rickard, who then was an acquaintance made in Alaska, and someone glimpsed at Goldfield, Nevada, while Joe Gans and Battling Nelson were settling the lightweight championship of the world. Tim O'Sullivan, who, it seems, had engineered the break from Australia, accompanied Darcy. By the time they had reached

New York, the Darcy incident was international in its scope, a *cause célèbre*. Australian papers had magnified the incident to such an extent that it seemed as if Darcy, singlehanded, might have won the war had he remained and declared for military duty. He was accused of dodging "his plain duty to a country that fed and pampered him." They demanded that America do something about it. The heat was on.

Darcy turned to his sponsor, Rickard, for help, but Tex wasn't having any. There wasn't much that Kearns, from afar, could do. He tried, but Rickard and his minions had blocked him at every turn.

Darcy, worried, friendless, knowing not which way to turn, left New York, and in Memphis, Tennessee, on May 24, 1917, he died. The doctor's certificate said pneumonia. Doctors' certificates rarely record deaths from a broken heart.

If Kearns were unable to do anything for the living Darcy, he did not desert him in death. He accompanied the remains to San Francisco, where a final tribute was made to the lad who was probably the greatest fighter next to Bob Fitzsimmons Australia ever sent to these shores, but who was a martyr to the greed of prize-fight managers, promoters, and flag wavers generally.

The Darcy chapter's ending was the bleakest in Kearns' career, and he accepted it as such. This had been his first long shot with a chance at the big money. For a time thereafter Kearns was back on his heels.

There was always Spider Kelly's, and one night Kearns hied himself there. At a corner table were seated one of the Bay section's four-round fighting luminaries, Al Norton, with his manager, George Sharkey, and a third person, a dark-haired, black-browed, sullen youngster, obviously underfed and down on his luck. Norton was drinking. Sharkey was drinking. The stranger was drinking. Kearns sat down to do some drinking too.

After a time Norton remembered the proprieties. With a patronizing wave of the hand he indicated the stranger.

"Meet young Dempsey," he said. "He's the boy I licked

over in Oakland a while ago. Strong kid. Don't know nothing, though. But he's game."

Young Dempsey said nothing, but his dark features twisted into a scowl.

"So this guy licked you, did he?" asked Kearns.

And then came the first words ever spoken by Jack Dempsey to Jack Kearns: "He got the decision, but he didn't lick me!"

Norton didn't like that. He was for proving it all over again, right there. Dempsey was willing, but Sharkey acted as peacemaker. He took his fighter away, leaving Dempsey and Kearns together. They were to be together a long time thereafter. Before the night was over Kearns' persuasive eloquence had aroused a spark in the young warrior, which was in time to be fanned into a conflagration that lit up the entire prizefight world.

Kearns had under his control at the time a middleweight, Marty Farrell, a clever boxer who lacked a finishing punch. He had a peculiar weaving style and fought from a crouch. It was Farrell's style that Kearns adopted for the long hours of ring schooling Dempsey needed, and in the meantime Marty was the meal ticket for the combination.

He had a match at Dreamland Rink in San Francisco with Mick King, Australian middleweight, also a clever boxer.

Now, the fight fans of the four-round game were not too partial to boxers. They craved action from bell to bell, and the sooner someone was knocked for a loop, the better were those fans pleased. They didn't care for the exhibition between Farrell and King one bit. And they said so, their clamor becoming louder with the passing minutes.

Referee Toby Irwin went right along with the crowd. When the din was louder than his sensitive ears could stand, he tossed Farrell and King out of the ring and called it "no contest."

Every paper in town but mine put the blast on the fight. Some even hinted that Kearns, adjudged the cause of it all, should get out of town and stay out. I had rather enjoyed the boxing match as a variation from the usual knockdown-and-drag-'em-out stuff, and had so written. I didn't care for Irwin's letting the crowd make his decision for him, and said so.

About an hour after our paper was on the street, Kearns and Farrell dropped in, accompanied by one whom I was unable to place just then. We discussed the fight and what Kearns proposed to do about it, and just as my visitors prepared to go, Kearns thought of something else.

"I'd like you to meet the next heavyweight champion," he said, and called over the third member of the delegation.

Jack Dempsey said he was pleased to meet me. I said I was pleased to meet him.

"What makes you think you're the next heavyweight champion?" I asked.

"Kearns," said Dempsey, as if that settled the whole thing.

As indeed it did, come to think of it.

And that is how my follow-up story on the Marty Farrell–Mick King fiasco had to do instead with my meeting with the next heavyweight champion of the world. Before Dempsey's course had run through a strange assortment of fighters on his way up to Jess Willard, many others of my craft scrambled on the bandwagon. But it was I who put the horses between the shafts, before the bandwagon had even begun to roll.

Dempsey went through several fights when Kearns felt he was ready, and the results were uniformly satisfactory.

However, in private conversations with me, Kearns indicated that there was one question that had yet to be answered: Could Dempsey take it?

"I know he's got guts," said Kearns, "to get as far as he has after what he's been through. But there's two kinds of gameness. One is to take a terrific beating without quitting. Lots of guys have that and wind up cutting up paper dolls. The other kind is to be able to take punishment and come back strong from it and go on to finish your man. That's what I want to find out about Dempsey."

And that, in Dempsey's record, is where Gunboat Smith came in.

The Gunner had seen his best days in the ring, but he could still swing a right hand. Kearns knew that when he made the match. So did Spider Kelly, attached to the company as chief second. Many were the words of caution and advice given Dempsey about Smith's right hand, but midway in the fight one landed flush on the chin. Dempsey's knees sagged, but he did not go to the floor. Instead, he went into a clinch, not to hang on, but to beat a tattoo about the Gunner's body with both hands.

High above the roar of the crowd at the landing of the Gunner's punch and its immediate aftermath arose the shrill voice of Spider Kelly:

"He can take it! Kearns, he can take it!"

In that instant Kearns knew that all his fond hopes were not in vain. He was sure then he was gazing upon the next champion of the world.

It has been told, often enough, that Dempsey had been "out" all through the remainder of the fight, but battled on by instinct, not coming to until he was in the dressing room afterward, with the decision over Smith securely his. It made a good story.

This fight was all Kearns needed for his ballyhoo purposes. He had friends in the newspaper profession all over the country and he bombarded them with lurid claims for his man. The newspaper gentry hopped to the new sensation, and for a while, though Dempsey wasn't making money nearly as fast as Kearns was spending it, not even the champion, Jess Willard, was getting so much attention. Not that Willard wasn't getting attention from Kearns. He was. Indeed, Jess counted that day lost in which he did not get some new proposition whereby he might be induced to enter a ring with Dempsey.

In between attempts at lining up a title bout, Kearns kept Dempsey busy with fighting and following a tour with a burlesque company. They didn't make much money, but they had a lot of fun.

One evening in New York, broke as usual, and in company with his newspaper cronies, broke as usual, the party decided to descend upon "Cap" Huston, a favorite touch of New York sports writers affected with the shorts. Huston was the partner of Jake Ruppert in the operation of the New York Yankees.

Huston had been sighted at the Biltmore bar, and the party headed there. Upon arriving Kearns was hailed by John McGraw of the Giants, who suggested a drink.

"But first you ought to meet this fellow here," he said. "You should know him. He's Tex Rickard, just in from South America. He's a big promoter."

"He's a big bum," said Kearns. "I don't want to meet him. You can have him."

McGraw would not take no for an answer. He shoved Kearns forward and attempted to introduce him to Rickard.

"Kearns?" said Rickard. "Oh, you're the fellow who has that western fighter Dempsey."

"Yes," said Kearns, "the next champ."

"He's too small," said Rickard.

"That's what you said about Les Darcy," replied Kearns.

Rickard thought that over. "What do you know about Darcy?" he asked finally.

"Plenty," said Kearns. "I talked him into coming over here and you tried to steal him from me."

At this Rickard surveyed Kearns more carefully. "Haven't I seen you before?" he asked.

"I guess you have," said Kearns. "When I was a kid I worked at your joint, the Northern, in Alaska."

It required at least an hour to develop the "what a small world it is" theme, and by that time Kearns was willing to take McGraw's tip that maybe Rickard could do him some good.

"Why don't you put on a Dempsey-Willard fight?" Kearns asked. Rickard still argued Dempsey was too small, and the public would prefer a match between the huge Willard and someone approximating his size—Fred Fulton, for instance.

"Fulton lasted eighteen seconds with my man," said Kearns, who went into a lengthy sales talk on Dempsey's terrific punching power, his youth, his speed, and so on. He even had an explanation for the memorable four-round decision Dempsey had lost to Willie Meehan in a war benefit show promoted in San Francisco by James W. Coffroth, following the Fulton fight.

"Eddie Graney [the referee] was all in at the end of the bout," he said. "He reached for something to steady himself and it happened to be Meehan's arm. That's all there was to that. Let's send Willard a wire asking him to fight Dempsey."

Rickard protested that it would take a lot of money, and he wasn't holding too much just then.

"What's money?" said Kearns. "We can always raise that. What I want is somebody to get Willard to agree to fight. Maybe he'll do it for you. He must know you're the greatest promoter in the world." Rickard admitted with due modesty that he guessed he was.

With that Kearns rounded up a telegraph blank, filled out a message to Willard, and signed Rickard's name to it. There was a reply in the morning. Willard was interested and proposed a meeting to discuss details. After a conference with Kearns, Rickard agreed to meet Willard in Texas.

Three weeks later he was back in New York, with word that Willard wanted $100,000 for the fight. That had stopped Rickard, but not Kearns.

"Swell," said Kearns. "We'll get it for him."

"But how?" asked Rickard. "Where? How do I know the fight will draw that much?"

"It'll draw enough to pay Willard," promised Kearns. "We don't want any money. All we want is a crack at the title."

Several weeks passed before Kearns was again called into

executive session. Willard was to get his $100,000 guarantee, and Rickard spread out the contract for Kearns to sign.

"Certainly," said Kearns, "but I want training expenses."

"How much will that be?" asked Rickard.

"I figure this match will draw three or four hundred thousand," explained Kearns. "Dempsey ought to get half as much as Willard."

"You're crazy," said Rickard.

"Maybe so," said Kearns, "but you'll have to admit I've made sense so far. I'll take twenty-five per cent for Dempsey; or after Willard is paid and the promotion expense is taken out, I'll take half of what's left."

Rickard couldn't see either of those propositions, so Kearns kept advancing new ones. At last it was decided to put the matter to a vote by the gentlemen of the press who were present, whether Kearns should get $30,000 or $27,500. The vote saved Rickard $2,500.

Rickard now had his heavyweight championship fight, lacking only a place to put it.

Kearns had the answer to that, too, producing Ad Thatcher of Toledo, and after an inspection of the site at the Ohio city, Rickard agreed. A citizen of Memphis came through on schedule with the $150,000 to prove that the fight business as well as show business has its angels.

The din aroused by this fight was terrific. It was excelled in Dempsey's championship career only by his adventures with Georges Carpentier at Jersey City, with Tommy Gibbons at Shelby, and with Gene Tunney, first at Philadelphia and then at Chicago. Oddly enough, for sheer fighting fury none of these bouts furnished the sustained thrill of Dempsey's memorable engagement with Luis Angel Firpo, by long odds the most savage combat between heavyweights the ring has ever known.

The prefight and postfight stages of the others will be remembered longer by anyone whose business it was to try to keep up with them, but Dempsey's furious two rounds with Firpo was *the* fight of all ring time.

To two of his best friends in the newspaper profession, Dempsey's sensational gaining of the title at Toledo was a mild letdown.

Damon Runyon had wagered his money that Dempsey would knock Willard out in the first round. In a San Francisco paper I had predicted the same thing, and was threatened with dismissal for daring to make such a rash statement. Actually we were both right, for Willard was down seven times in the first round, and out for all practical purposes, though a mix-up over the bell forced Dempsey to return to the ring after he had left it, and keep on pounding the helpless hulk before him for another two rounds.

Runyon lost his money, but I kept my job.

The fight drew $452,000 . . . and nothing like that had ever been recorded in the prize ring before.

CHAPTER 6

How Matches Are Made

THUS far in the story of Kearns and Dempsey not too much stress has been placed upon the champion's actual performance in the ring. There is reason for that. Dempsey, schooled by Kearns, was so far ahead of his field that the element of reasonable doubt did not enter the calculations of anyone interested in the outcome of a given fight involving the man who had slaughtered Willard.

And yet the first million-dollar gate of the prize ring— Dempsey was to participate in four others before he retired— was attracted to a fight in which none of the 80,000 present gave the champion's opponent a semblance of a chance, but that did not stop them from expending $1,729,238 in order to see it.

Ballyhoo, and nothing else, did that. Which is one of the reasons I have stood squarely on my platform that what goes on apart from the actual field of competition in sport is often much more amazing than the contest itself.

Let us look, therefore, into the circumstances of the "Battle of the Century," held July 2, 1921, at Boyle's Thirty Acres in New Jersey.

Georges Carpentier, the Orchid Man of France, was the opponent. He was the ring idol of his country, if not of all Europe. He had a gallant war record, while Dempsey's was negligible. He had gained much of his ring prestige by laying a right hand on the jaws of British heavyweights. He was a bit of a glamour boy, but he had absolutely no business in the ring with Dempsey, unless it were to pose for a picture with him.

He had come to this country to fight Battling Levinsky and had won this engagement handily enough. He was preparing to return to France when Kearns began to have thoughts about him.

Kearns had considered the war angle, the international angle, and all the other angles. He was sure that, properly exploited, they would bring a huge gate, if he could but interest a promoter in putting on the fight.

He turned to Rickard, but Tex was wary. He foresaw too many complications.

"I'll put you into it," promised Kearns. "It may draw a million dollars."

"I never seed anybody like you," said Rickard. "You're crazy as a loon."

Kearns next took up the subject of fight promotion with William A. Brady, famous figure in the theatrical world. Brady had dabbled in the fight game before, and was not averse to another whirl. He allowed that he might be induced to promote a fight with Dempsey in it.

"Who'll we get to fight him?" he asked.

"Carpentier," said Kearns.

From long experience, Brady knew his fighters, so his reaction to this was natural.

"I see why you've picked me to promote that fight for Dempsey," he said. "If anything happens to the champ, I can go in myself, old as I am, and lick Carpentier."

"But it will draw a lot of money," Kearns argued. "Carpentier can be built into something great."

"Maybe we can't get him, anyhow," said Brady. "I understand he's under contract to Cochran, that English fellow who's over here putting on a show with me."

"That's fine," said Kearns. "We'll declare him in, too. We can put the fight on in Europe or in Cuba or in Tijuana. I'd just like to see an old-timer like you back in the game."

(Brady had been a famous figure in the Corbett-Jeffries-Johnson era.)

It was arranged for Kearns to meet Brady and Cochran the next day. Meanwhile Kearns looked up one of his intimates, Dan McKetrick, who had a working knowledge of French.

"You know Carpentier," said Kearns. "Speak to him about fighting Dempsey, will you?"

"Dempsey will kill him," said McKetrick, "but I'll ask him. Maybe he's lived long enough, anyhow."

McKetrick reported back that Carpentier had an agreement with Cochran, and that neither he nor his manager, François Deschamps, cared to go beyond that.

At a party celebrating the opening of the Brady-Cochran show, Kearns moved in on the English promoter.

"I've heard a lot about you," he said, "and what a sportsman you are. I understand you have a contract with Carpentier. You wouldn't want to stand in the way of his making two hundred thousand dollars, would you?"

Cochran was staggered at this. No champion and certainly no challenger who had ever lived commanded that sort of price for his services. It was twice as much as Willard had drawn for his trouncing at Toledo.

A wild jabbering broke out among Carpentier, Deschamps, and their satellites who were present at the party. That Kearns was utterly mad. Rickard was now not the only one who "never seed" such a man.

"The fight will draw a million and a half," said Kearns. "Ain't that right, Bill?" he asked, turning to Brady.

While making a mental note that the fight was already drawing a half million more than when Kearns had first discussed it with him, Brady nodded agreement. He was beginning to enjoy this sort of drama very much. "A cinch," he said.

Cochran remained hesitant. He knew of no one who would guarantee such a sum for a prize fight.

"Let me put it this way," Kearns offered. "If I can get

Georges two hundred thousand to fight Dempsey, will you stand in his way?"

"Certainly not," said Cochran, still certain that such an event would never come to pass.

"That all I want to know," said Kearns. "You gentlemen have the fight. I am more or less honor-bound to go along with Tex Rickard, however, and he will have to be in on the promotion."

By that time, the bewildered Cochran would have been willing to declare the King of England in on the promotion, so dizzy was he from Kearns's high financial flights.

Announcement was duly made that Carpentier had agreed to accept $200,000 as his end for the fight with Dempsey. There was no reason to keep that a secret, and Kearns was never much of a hand for palming a secret, anyhow. But the problem of promotional who's who and where the money was to be found was unsolved, and stayed that way for a time.

Bob Edgren, famous sports writer and cartoonist, was brought in as an arbitrator at Kearns's suggestion, and the argument went on and on.

Kearns was desperate by this time, but as resourceful as ever. In a restaurant in downtown New York he rounded up two Cuban waiters, outfitted them, and rehearsed them carefully in their parts. From some place known only to himself he produced what looked like a certified check for a great sum of money. Armed with this, and flanked by the waiters, he moved in on Rickard, who was now the only one of the original trio who wasn't ready to forget the whole thing. The "million-dollar fight" had gone completely out of Cochran's range of vision, and Brady's interest from the start was no more than a gag. Rickard, however, had his reputation as the world's greatest promoter to worry him.

"What's this?" he demanded, when Kearns appeared with his Cubans and his check.

"You fellows have been stalling so long," said Kearns, "I am preparing to accept an offer from the syndicate of rich Cubans these gentlemen represent."

The Cubans, letter perfect in their part, broke into the proper lines. Rickard was visibly impressed.

"Besides this," said Kearns, "I have a five-hundred-thousand-dollar offer from Jim Coffroth. He'll put it on at Tijuana. He was promoting fights before anybody ever heard of you, Tex. When Coffroth goes after something, he gets it. If he comes back as a fight promoter, you might as well go back to the Yukon."

That was too much for Rickard. He agreed to promote the fight on his own.

Kearns was so elated at Rickard's capitulation that he agreed to let Dempsey go on for $300,000, neglecting to secure a percentage option. That was a costly error. A normal champion's percentage privilege would have returned more than twice that amount from the gate eventually drawn. This error in calculations has been advanced as one of the reasons Kearns and Dempsey finally came to a parting of the ways. Actually it had nothing to do with it, for in those days Kearns and Dempsey were operating strictly on the "you can't take it with you" basis.

It was argued by Kearns with Rickard that the only way to keep interest at a fever heat for the fight was to have Carpentier remain as much of a mystery as possible. For his own place of operations, Kearns chose Atlantic City, as quiet a spot as Times Square on New Year's Eve.

Carpentier's training was very much in secret, and apart from the information that his manager, Deschamps, had a hypnotic eye, very little was known about the Orchid Man's camp. Indeed, the only pair of newspapermen who penetrated Carpentier's hide-out on Long Island were Tad and Bill Farnsworth. They had been sunning themselves on a porch at Bayside one Sunday afternoon when the idea of visiting Carpentier struck them. That there were no visitors allowed and that there were wire entanglements around the camp meant nothing. Tad and Farnsworth drove through the wire and right on up to the cottage where Carpentier was rocking at the moment, perhaps wondering what was going on in the great world outside.

He was glad to see his strange visitors, and while Deschamps didn't like it and tried to fix Farnsworth with the hypnotic eye, Bill didn't scare worth a darn. Carpentier was genuinely sorry when they drove away, and they were even sorrier when they thought about this nice young man in there while Dempsey was pitching punches. But their respective stories of the incident were printed the country over.

In due time, after almost as many words had been written about it as coverage of World War I required, Dempsey and Carpentier entered the ring at Jersey City. Dempsey was very nice about it all, and drew enough deep breaths to make the motion pictures of the fight of value, before crumpling the Orchid Man with a punch in the fourth round.

The momentum of the first million-dollar-plus fight kept Kearns and Dempsey going for more than two years before they took up defense of the title once more. That was at Shelby, Montana, where the misguided citizenry collapsed under the pressure of providing Dempsey's $300,000 guarantee in three $100,000 installments, as arranged between Kearns and Loy Molumby, the promoter. Tommy Gibbons was the opponent, and he went fifteen rounds to gain the distinction of being the only man fought by Dempsey in a seven-year span who was not knocked out. Literally, Gibbons fought for nothing.

In a subsequent chapter or two, when the antics of the gentlemen of the press in sports are dealt with more adequately, there will be more about Shelby, as there will be more of the round-the-clock doings at Dempsey's Atlantic City camp when he trained for Carpentier.

But for the moment, pride of coauthorship moves me to reprint the "Battle Hymn of Shelby" as it was played by Bill Cunningham of Boston, and sung by a badly mixed chorus of newspapermen as Shelby's bankers, butchers, bakers, and candlestick makers were vainly struggling to raise one of the $100,000 payments Kearns demanded.

The hymn, which was mine, for the most part, lacked a punch line until my old friend Scoop Gleeson of San Francisco came to the rescue. Here was the lyric:

> O Molumby, the gent with the notion
> On whom Dapper Jack put the bee,
> The cause of the whole damn commotion,
> * The world offers *fromage de Brie.*
> Thy contracts make bankers dissemble
> In the town where the mud sticks like glue;
> All the oil men of Shelby will tremble
> When the last hundred thousand falls due!
> *Refrain*
> Three cheers for the prize fight that blew,
> Three cheers for the prize fight that blew!
> All the oil men of Shelby will tremble
> When the last hundred thousand falls due!

* Gleeson batted for Brown.

Dempsey and Gibbons huffed and puffed and blew the financial house down at Shelby, the champion retaining his title by decision at the end of fifteen rounds. At no time was he in imminent danger of losing the fight, and at the finish he had enough left for a quick sprint out of Shelby, which didn't like him any too well just then.

Jack Kearns was left behind to wrestle for any odd dollars the combine had not extracted already from the scene.

Two months later Dempsey was caught up in as ruthless a battle between big men as ring history records. This was the two rounds it required for the champion to show that he was master of Luis Angel Firpo of the Argentine, whom Damon Runyon had termed the Wild Bull of the Pampas.

Firpo had reached the championship round by shrewd manipulation on the part of promoter Tex Rickard, the springboard from which Dempsey was reached being an eight-round knockout of the former champion Jess Willard. This took place in July 1923, at Boyle's Thirty Acres in Jersey City, scene of Dempsey's victory over Georges Carpentier in 1921.

Old Jess was presumed to be fighting for another chance at Dempsey on this occasion, and while he had seldom reached heroic stature as a champion, there is no doubt but that the crowd's sentiment was with Willard. Particularly was this true in the seventh round, when Jess rocked Firpo with right upper cuts. The roar of "Come on, Jess!" was one of the most thrilling episodes of this fight. But Jess was not destined to come on much further.

In the next round Firpo belted him solidly enough to warrant Willard's taking a trip to the floor. He rested on one knee while the count of ten was being reached, and then leaped to his feet, apparently delighted that it was all over.

Firpo was a ponderous swinger, with little or no knowledge of ring science, and possessed of a better than average amount of animal courage. He had many advisers, and some of them convinced him that his best chance—perhaps his only chance—with Dempsey lay in letting go a right hand as soon as he came out of his corner . . . or even sooner.

Dempsey's previous fights, from Gunboat Smith through Willard and Bill Brennan, proved that he could be hit by a right hand. Even the fragile Carpentier had managed to caress his chin with a right that looked well in the motion pictures.

So the Wild Bull was ready for that charge. He surely let the right hand go, and it met Dempsey's chin squarely as the fight began. There is no doubt but that it stunned the champion. He did not go down, but he went into a clinch. Then began the wildest three minutes of swinging, pushing, and hauling. It is improbable that either of the fighters had a clear picture of what was going on. They were banging away with no regard for boxing skill. Each was moved by one thought: to get rid of that fearsome object before him as soon as possible. Firpo was knocked down. Dempsey waited scarcely until the Wild Bull was struggling to his feet to continue with the assault. Dempsey was down, or partially down. And still the brutal battle raged.

Once in this furious mix-up, Dempsey literally stood

astride his fallen foe and swung upon him at the first indication that Firpo was to get up again. Perhaps this was the crowning blow that truly turned Firpo into a maddened creature, for it was shortly after this that his bull-like rush and his hefty right-hand swing carried Dempsey against the ropes and right on through them.

The champion's feet were in the air as he landed in the press row. He was not without aid in getting back in there, and for the balance of the round the fighting fury of both abated not a whit.

Never in ring history had there been so much confusion in the ring and around it. It was days afterward before there was any agreement on the number of knockdowns that had taken place in that first round. My count showed seven, Dempsey scoring five and Firpo two.

When the bell ended the round, the commotion did not lessen. Dempsey's handlers, led by Kearns, worked feverishly over their man, and did so while in a hysterical state. It was during this one-minute rest period that Kearns was alleged to have yelled for the bottle of smelling salts, only to be reminded that it was in his own hip pocket. After he took a whiff he felt much better.

So did Dempsey, for the minute's rest, but the minute didn't mean much to Firpo. He had fired his whole month of Sunday punches and they were not quite enough.

When they came out for the second round, Dempsey was warier than he had been at the start of the fight. Firpo's surprise wallop could not happen again, and the Wild Bull was weakened greatly by the amount of punishment he had taken in the wild first round.

Dempsey merely bided his time until the opening presented itself, and when he landed on Firpo's chin this time, the man from the Argentine went down . . . and stayed there.

Following the Firpo fight, and in the interval before the first engagement with Gene Tunney came along, Dempsey and Kearns agreed to disagree. Many of the original Dempsey followers remained steadfast. Others, in looking toward his fighting without the benefit of Kearns's manipulations, were inclined to give Tunney a splendid chance.

Three years went by between the time Dempsey stood over the fallen Firpo and the day he was asked to make a defense of his title against Tunney. Three years in which there had been no tough fights to keep him battle-sharp and battle-wise. Three years of living in which he drifted far away from fighting condition. However, the memory of the Dempsey that had been was so strong with the fight public that though it was known the champion was not in the best of shape and did not figure to be too well advised, he entered the ring at Philadelphia an eleven-to-five favorite.

The day before the fight I had encountered a group discussing the outcome. I found myself the only one to give Tunney a chance. In the group were Jim Coffroth, whose friendship for Billy Gibson, Tunney's manager, had been most helpful in getting the match made; Jimmy Hussey, of vaudeville fame; and Gleeson of San Francisco, one of the original Dempsey men.

Hussey listened to my attempt to present a case for Tunney. Then he asked if he could ask one question.

"If a guy had you down in an alley and was beating hell out of you, who would you yell for, Dempsey or Tunney?"

However, as it turned out, Dempsey was up against a man in that rain at Philadelphia who was his master at every turn, and went on to gain the championship by decision. Dempsey was a pathetic figure to those who had watched him from his rise in the four-round game of San Francisco and Oakland and who had ground out hundreds of thousands of words about his exploits up and down the land.

But in all that discomfort of falling rain, the irritation of breaking telegraph wires, of bogged-down portable typewriters, in all the excitement of a championship changing hands, there was one figure who had as much to do with it all as if he had been inside the ropes. He sat instead in the press section, close by Dempsey's corner.

He was Jack Kearns.

There was so much sameness in each round as Tunney relentlessly cut and slashed the slow-moving Dempsey that many in the press section were able to steal an occasional glance at Kearns. He was a decidedly interested spectator when Dempsey entered the ring, defending his title for the first time without Kearns in the corner, come what may.

Kearns watched perhaps half the first round. He saw no more of the fight. His head rested on his hands and he did not once look up, nor did he squirm, though everyone else was moving uncomfortably in the pelting rain. At the end of the fight, such as it was, Kearns was still sitting there, head in hands.

A newspaperman reached over and tapped him on the shoulder. "Thinking of the Dempsey of Toledo, Doc?" he asked.

"Hell, no," said Kearns. "I was just wondering where I'll find the guy to lick that Tunney."

CHAPTER 7

A Not So Long Count

AT the time the first Dempsey-Tunney fight was in the making I was a resident in Chicago. Boxing had become legalized but recently, after fans had been satisfied for many years with odd jobs performed at near-by Aurora and East Chicago, most of them by fighters, distinguished or otherwise, who had been matched by Jim Mullen.

Soldier Field in Chicago is one of the country's largest arenas and its seating possibilities appealed to Tex Rickard.

Chairman of the first commission appointed in Illinois to look after boxing was O. W. Huncke, a most honorable man and a fight fan. He was of the opinion that a fight of the magnitude of Dempsey and Tunney was too much of a proposition for Chicago and the state of Illinois to handle under a law that had not been operative long enough for even the lawmakers to be familiar with all the whereases and be it resolveds.

As is too often the case with a major boxing operation, there were political angles, and Huncke was in a bit of a dither over the situation. He discussed the matter with me, and I held to the same opinions he did, but it looked as if Chicago was going to wind up with the fight, regardless. In fact, Tex Rickard was due any day to discuss final arrangements.

The law said that the promoter had to be a resident of Illinois, which would seem to eliminate Rickard. But the

practice of getting the license in the name of some resident
stuffed shirt was an easy out.

"The Commission can regulate the price scale of tickets,
can't it?" I asked Huncke, and he said that was correct.

"I see what you mean," he smiled, and presently went
about his business.

A day or two later Rickard arrived, and I met him shortly
afterward but before he had visited the Commission.

He was most enthusiastic about Soldier Field and Chicago.
I heard him out. He told of all the "big people" he had with
him. Tex was a great collector of "big people." Everything
was set, he said.

I told him I didn't think it was.

He offered to bet me a hat that the fight would take place
in Chicago. I took the bet.

"Have you read the papers?" I asked.

He said he had not. I told him I thought he might find
them interesting, and he said he knew that he would, because
the newspaper boys were always very nice to him.

He excused himself then, saying he had to go and talk with
the Commission. When he did, he found out what the papers
might have told him, and what might thus have saved him
cab fare.

The Commission had passed a rule limiting the price of
tickets to a very nominal sum. Dempsey and Tunney were
not going to fight for any nominally priced ticket scale, so
back to New York went Rickard, and to Philadelphia went
the fight.

I guess Rickard forgot about the hat. Nor did I ever remind him of it.

Word went around, as word has a habit of doing, that it
was I who had caused Rickard to abandon Chicago as a site
for the heavyweight championship fight.

I did not give much thought to it; no more, indeed, than
I had when San Francisco had been abandoned by Tex in
1910 when the governor of California decreed that the
Jeffries-Johnson fight was too hot to handle. But when I

arrived in Philadelphia a few days before the fight and dropped into Rickard's headquarters, many of my sports-writer friends seemed surprised. One went so far as to say that I had better not let Rickard see me, or he'd beat me over the head with his cane.

Having known Rickard longer than most of those present, I said I doubted that. It was established by then that the gate receipts might reach the incredible $2,000,000 figure, and without being as familiar with Philadelphia as I was with Chicago, I thought it was reasonable to suppose that Tex could not possibly have any more "partners" in a Pennsylvania project than he would have had declaring themselves in in Illinois.

"I think Tex will be glad to see me," I said, "and I'll be surprised if he isn't happy about the whole thing."

He was, too. When he entered headquarters while I was there, he hailed me with a flourish and invited me in to his private office.

"It's all for the best," he said. "I guess you're sorry now you didn't get this one for Chicago."

I said I did not regret it one bit. There hadn't been a single one of the paper's advertisers bothering me to get him ring-side tickets at the last minute, and even Rickard couldn't be happier than I was that Philadelphia was getting the big show.

"I'll tell you something," promised Rickard, "if you'll not print it until after this is over. The return match will be held in Chicago next year."

I didn't print it until after Tunney had gained the championship ... but even that delay gave me a long start on everyone else, most of whom were still busy marveling at the toll Dempsey's years out of action had taken, at the 120,757 who had paid $1,895,733 to be present, or perhaps were still trying to dry themselves out after that soaking rain which had fallen throughout the fight.

A few months later when it suited his convenience Dempsey put Jack Sharkey away with a punch on the jaw while his man was arguing with the referee over the legality of a previous Dempsey punch. So now Rickard, Dempsey, Tunney, the Illinois Commission, from which Huncke had resigned, and the world generally were ready for the return match between Jack and Gene at Soldier Field, leading up to the notorious "long count" episode.

In the years that have intervened, Tunney, Dempsey, referee Dave Barry, and practically everybody else has told his version of this incident. I have a bit to add, some of which has seemed my own business until now.

Chicago in those days was getting many a notice, none very favorable, concerning the activities of the "boys." They were reported to be interested in politics, in racing, and in various angles of the fight game.

One story that reached me was that Jack Kearns was not going to attend the second running of the Dempsey-Tunney stakes, the "boys" having hinted that they didn't want him around causing unrest for Dempsey. I don't know whether he paid any attention to them or not. On the night of the fight I did not have time to look for him in that sea of $40-top faces, which seemed to extend from Hyde Park to Evanston, and which was in reality the longest "ringside" the business of prize-fight promotion has ever known.

I was about to have an early dinner at the Bismarck Hotel when one of the Rover Boys of Randolph Street met me. He had a tale to tell, which was interesting, if true.

It went on to say that a well-known New York character who had Chicago connections had bet a chunk on Tunney before coming out to the fight. Upon arrival he had been advised by the "boys" to get smart, that the judges for the fight had been "seen" and that it was in for Dempsey. The New York man, the story went, got word to Tunney, who was sequestered in the Hotel Sherman, and it was said that somebody, Tunney or Billy Gibson, his manager, thought I should see what I could do about it.

"The way it is now," said the Rover Boy, "Tunney ain't going to come out of that bungalow a-tall."

I was able to reach Gibson, whom I had known much longer than Tunney. He guardedly verified some of the Rover Boy's tale. I told him I thought it was just one of those silly rumors that abound at all fights of any importance, but that if it would give Tunney any peace of mind I'd go to the Commission and place the whole matter before Chairman John Righeimer.

When I reached the Commission it was in session. In one of the outer offices were several of the licensed Illinois referees, including the ranking trio, Dave Miller, Dave Barry, and Phil Collins.

Several days before, Leo P. Flynn, who was handling Dempsey's affairs, had appeared before the Commission to discuss referees and the conduct of the fight. He indicated rather strongly that Miller was not one of his choices, so Righeimer told me.

At the time it was pointed out and agreed to by Flynn that the fighter scoring a knockdown must retire at once to the corner farthest removed from the spot. Dempsey in all his fights, and particularly in those with Willard and Firpo, had not been too particular about this. At times he stood right over his fallen opponent and belted him again at the first sign of rising.

I cite these items since both have been discussed widely in the never ending aftermath of the "long count."

Chairman Righeimer, a friend of long standing, agreed to see me without too much delay, and I quickly placed before him the reasons for my visit.

"But I haven't named any judges," he protested.

"Have you any in mind?" I asked.

Righeimer said that naturally he had considered, as had his fellow commissioners, the judges who were regularly appointed for other fights in Chicago.

"What would you think," he asked, "if I were to appoint two judges out of a group of such outstanding citizens as Sheldon Clarke, Major Frederic McLaughlin, George Lytton, and so on?"

All the men named by Righeimer were familiar with the boxing code, if not with the characters who got into it.

"Well," I said, "if they did make a mistake, no one would be able to say they had been taken care of in advance. That might be the solution to the whole matter."

Righeimer indicated that this was the way it would be. I asked if it would be all right for me to try to get word to Tunney that his rights would be protected. Righeimer saw no harm in that, particularly since he knew Tunney was stubborn enough not to appear for the fight if he had any convictions of a possible "fix."

I took a cab back to the Bismarck Hotel and phoned Gibson, asking if he could drop over. He said he was tied up but that Jimmy Bronson would meet me on Randolph Street in a few moments, which he did, bow tie and all.

"I don't know what Gene has on his mind," I told Bronson, "but if he's worried about not getting a fair shake from the judges, he can forget it. I'll guarantee the judges will be all right. If he wants more than that, I can't help him."

Presumably that was what Tunney wanted to know, for he showed up for the fight. I did, too, but not without further complications.

After leaving Bronson, I was accosted by Jim Mullen, the Chicago promoter, who was a Tunney man and a Kearns man. In those days when the breach was wide between Dempsey and Kearns, most of those interested in the fight game were on one side or the other. Occasionally a true diplomat, such as James W. Coffroth, remained friendly to both.

Mullen wanted to know who was going to referee the fight. I told him I didn't know, but assumed it would be either Barry or Collins, since Flynn had put the finger on Miller. I preferred Miller, all things being equal, since he was well equipped to handle big men in the ring.

"I hope it's Barry," said Mullen.

Barry was in Mullen's employ at a gymnasium he operated, at which most of the fighters trained while in Chicago. Another employee of Mullen's was Paul Beeler, who served as a timekeeper at fight shows.

All the gadding about in the interest of something that was properly none of my business had used up so much time that I had to depart for Soldier Field without having had a chance to sample the Bismarck cooking toward which I had been aiming several hours before. Thus, while the first Dempsey-Tunney fight was to cost me a hat, the second one deprived me of my dinner.

But it did involve me in one of the strangest incidents in ring history.

My recollections of the fight are slightly at variance with some of the popular beliefs. Some of those I have expressed already.

My working press seat was directly opposite the point at which Tunney sank under the barrage of Dempsey's punches, in the seventh round. As he fell, Dempsey stood close by, and referee Barry, having started his count, paused to wave Dempsey to the farthest corner. Dempsey did not move at once, and there was a bit of argument between him and Barry. Meanwhile, Beeler, who was the timekeeper, had paused in his count.

These things I was able to see clearly. I also saw that Tunney, while seated on the canvas, slowly turned his head in the direction of his corner, where Bronson was signaling to him to take full advantage of the count. It is my opinion that Tunney could have risen before ten seconds elapsed, and would have done so. Perhaps he would have fallen a quick victim to the renewal of Dempsey's attack had he done so. Perhaps not.

He was not required to be on his feet before the count reached ten. It made no difference to him if it took an hour and twenty minutes for Barry and Beeler to count that far. Tunney kept his seat . . . and his championship.

When the count was stopped, it had reached four, and a few more seconds were doubtless used up in getting Dempsey to leave the vicinity. The count was *not* resumed then. It was started all over from one.

That was the second mistake of the round. Dempsey had made the first one in not hieing himself to a neutral corner as soon as Tunney went to the floor.

That's all there was to the "long count."

When Tunney rose, he was able to keep out of Dempsey's way for the balance of the round, disdaining the baffled ex-champion's gestures to come on and fight. Dempsey, long accustomed to toe-to-toe slugging, simply couldn't understand a champion in retreat. But then, Dempsey never has understood Tunney completely.

There remains now but one more bit of discussion of the "long count."

That, properly, came from Jack Kearns.

"Judges, referees, timekeepers had nothing to do with the result of that fight," Kearns said. "Dempsey lost it himself when he didn't get to the far corner at once.

"The knockdown took place right beside Dempsey's own corner. Suppose he was excited? Why didn't his handlers shoo him away? They were close enough to him. They could have made him stop arguing with Barry and get the hell out of there.

"I think Tunney would have got up. But he wouldn't have been able to think clearly if he'd been down just nine seconds after the wallop he took.

"Every time I went to the post with Dempsey I had a timekeeper of my own in there, commission or no commission. Sometimes it was Joe Bannon. Sometimes it was Senator Bill Lyons.

"If I'd been in Dempsey's corner that night, and Tunney was on the floor ten seconds, I'd have been in the ring, just like I was at Toledo. I'd have taken Dempsey out of there, and this time I'd not have brought him back.

"I don't think anybody in that crowd would have given me much of an argument, either. A man on the floor ten seconds is knocked out, ain't he? It wouldn't take much to prove that. The very worst I'd have got out of it would be another fight, and maybe just as much dough, or more.

"Suppose Dempsey had marched out of that ring? Darned few people were close enough to tell what it was all about, anyhow, and it would have taken them a long time to be convinced Dempsey hadn't knocked Tunney out."

Some of them, I hasten to add, have not been convinced as yet, but I do hope, after all these years, that some of the foggier patches of that night on Chicago's lake front have now been cleared up. It has been most mystifying how at variance with the facts, easily established from the contemporary reports and from the motion pictures, has been the legend of this second Dempsey-Tunney fight. I have often wondered how many have remembered, or have ever known, that after he did rise, and before the fight ended, Tunney not only succeeded eventually in regaining control of the fight, but actually knocked Dempsey down. But everyone remembers the "long count," even if few ever have understood it.

The fight, incidentally, drew $2,658,660, and I have it on reliable information that when the two principals were paid and all of Rickard's "partners" had been satisfied, Tex still owned his cane when he stepped aboard the Twentieth Century to New York.

There is absolutely no truth in the report that he had to fight in the La Salle Street Station to keep them from taking his cane, too.

CHAPTER 8

Roped Arena City

*I*F I have seemed to thrust aside all comers in my endeavor to keep up with the two Jacks, Dempsey and Kearns,
the actual procedure was not thus at all. The Dempsey-
Kearns story was pieced together at intervals. Prior to its
beginning, and in between its various episodes, there was a
continuous show of sports of all kinds that held my attention.

The San Francisco Bay area, in which the Dempsey–Kearns
juggernaut began rolling, was an ideal proving ground for
any fighter. San Franciscans, from actual experience, knew
a champion when they saw one. Certainly they had practice
enough, for the late nineties and the early years of the twentieth century, before professional boxing was legislatively
frowned upon, found practically all the greats of the prize
ring, in all classes, plying their wares in San Francisco, Oakland, Colma, Daly City, and Point Richmond.

Jim Corbett, first world's heavyweight champion under
the Marquis of Queensberry code, was a San Franciscan. He
had his start at the famous Olympic Club. Toward the end
of his career it was in San Francisco, under James W. Coffroth's promotion, that Corbett's 1903 losing fight with Jim
Jeffries drew $63,340, a sum that stood as a record for many
years.

Corbett was San Francisco's lone heavyweight champion,
but subsequent holders of the title, Bob Fitzsimmons, Jeffries,
Marvin Hart, Tommy Burns, Jack Johnson, and Jess Wil-

lard, all fought at least once in Bay section rings, while the fans were marking time for the advent of Dempsey.

It was in San Francisco that Fitzsimmons, in 1903, made a successful bid for the light-heavyweight championship, beating George Gardner. There two years later Fitz was stopped by "Philadelphia" Jack O'Brien.

In 1904 a welterweight championship fight went to Dixie Kid over Joe Wolcott and precipitated a bit of an uproar, as fights are wont to do, even to this day.

Stanley Ketchel, one of the greatest of all the middleweights, was a frequent performer in this area. It was in a San Francisco ring that he succeeded (though some thought it an optical illusion) in knocking down the great Johnson, a little while before Johnson decreed that the show had gone far enough, and put Ketchel down for keeps.

Ketchel was a colorful character. He would have been an ideal running mate for the free and easy Jack Kearns, who actually did have one chance at managing him and let it get away. However, Ketchel from time to time had managerial direction from the fabulous Wilson Mizner, and his affairs for a considerable time were handled by Willus Britt, brother of the San Francisco lightweight.

Britt, in some respects, was of the Kearns type. He had imagination, a flair for costume, and a gift of gab.

Ketchel himself was no shrinking violet. One of his favorite pranks in San Francisco was to drive down Market Street scattering coins, for which the newsboys (and maybe some of the solid citizens) would scramble madly.

Billy Papke, who knocked out Ketchel and in a return match was knocked out himself, fought many times in the Bay section.

In my personalized report, Papke, Ketchel, and Tommy Burns each figure in one-punch fights that took place at Colma, a suburb of San Francisco. The same story has been told of all, each time with a different cast of characters.

I first heard it in connection with Burns's victory over Boshter Bill Squires, the Australian champion, in 1907. I have been given the same routine in connection with Ketchel's 1908 victory over Mike Twin Sullivan. Not so very long ago Otis Shepard, distinguished artist and a member of the board of directors of the Chicago Cubs, related the story in all its detail, but he fixed the date as 1909 and the fight as Papke's victory over Hugo Kelly.

In those days fights were scheduled for twenty, twenty-five, and forty-five rounds. Some were even billed to a finish.

Since Colma was a bit of a drive in those horse-and-buggy days, the ringsiders used to plan for a big day, taking out to the arena hampers of solid and liquid refreshment.

It was customary to get things all squared away during the preliminaries. On this occasion—say the Burns-Squires well-exploited event—there was so much traffic congestion on the roads that many ringside parties did not reach the scene until the main eventers were in the ring getting their instructions.

The heroes of the story secured their seats and busied themselves unfastening hampers. Many of them were thus engaged when they were startled by a roar from the crowd. They looked up quickly. Squires was on the floor, having been felled by the first punch Burns let go at him. The fight was over.

That's the way I first heard it, and that's my story, but I'm tolerant enough to agree that it could have happened when Ketchel stopped Mike Twin with the first punch, or Papke did likewise to Kelly.

We are all agreed, however, that the three fights took place at Colma. And before I put that brisk little community aside for keeps, I must relate another adventure that took place there as late as 1916, when the area was on the four-round plan for all its fights.

Johnny Coulon, of Chicago, one of the most efficient of all the little men of the prize ring, had come out to box Eddie Campi, a San Franciscan who was approaching the end of a brilliant boxing career. It was stipulated that there would be no decision given at the end of the four scheduled rounds.

The referee was Tom Laird, who was sports editor of the San Francisco *News*.

There was the usual amount of betting upon the fight, with the wagerers agreeing to take the verdicts as reported by the various boxing writers present. Similar methods were used in New York and Philadelphia in no-decision boxing times.

The fight between Coulon and Campi was brisk enough, though neither was damaged to any great extent. At the end of the fight, to the consternation of all and the utter dismay of Coulon, Laird reached out and lifted Campi's hand above his head.

This was the universal token of victory. So here, perhaps for the only time in ring history, was a no-decision fight *with* a decision.

Laird, a blunt-spoken man, brushed it off by saying that he was going to give Campi the decision in his newspaper report, so why wait? But Coulon, the mighty little man from Chicago, was still brooding about it thirty years afterward.

Things like this happened in the fight game in California, and it was because of them that the expression "native-son decision" arose.

Many managers of outstanding fighters worried about such matters. One of them was Jimmy Johnston, the Boy Bandit, who came west with his welterweight champion, Ted Kid Lewis, during 1917, to fill a four-round engagement at Oakland with Battling Ortega, one of the home boys.

Neither Ortega nor Lewis could have scaled above the championship limit without carrying saddle weights, so the title was at stake in this four-rounder. Johnston knew that. While he had utmost confidence in his man, he was fearful of the native-son decision, if both men were on their feet at the finish.

Johnston was a good operator. He found out, long before he left New York, in whom to place his trust in California, but those in whom he placed his trust were not above letting the Boy Bandit dangle on the line for a while.

Ortega, a Mexican, was a rough-and-tumble fighter who might have had a great future in the prize ring if he had ever found time for it. He was in great form for Lewis, and the presence of Jim Griffin in the ring as referee did not soothe Johnston's troubled mind. The best his California friends would tell him was that they "guessed Griffin would be all right."

Lewis was in the ring with Johnston when Ortega arrived. The Battler's first move was to walk across the ring and with suitable profanity tell the champion he was going to be chased right out of the ring. With that he spat in the face of Lewis.

When the fight began, Ortega did not exactly chase Lewis over the ropes. But that was all he left undone. It was a very sorry showing the champion of the world made, and Johnston was in a veritable panic as the fourth and last round ended.

Griffin hesitated not at all with his decision. He lifted the arms of both Lewis and Ortega to indicate that the fight had ended in a draw. Then he and all others in the vicinity began to duck the shower of bottles from an enraged and very partisan crowd.

Johnston, at that decision, was more nearly at the collapse stage than Lewis, and it did not brighten him up too much when a friendly sports writer called up:

"See what is meant by a native-son decision, Jimmy?"

As for Griffin, veteran referee of the good old days of boxing, his explanation was entirely logical from his viewpoint.

"No championship," he said, "should ever change hands on a decision in a four-round fight."

This may serve to explain, after all these years, why the Bay district didn't have a welterweight champion along with its collection in other classes, for Ortega surely won that fight.

It came up with two champions in the lightweight class, Jimmy Britt, a synthetic sort, and Willie Ritchie, who won the title on a foul from Ad Wolgast. Referee Jim Griffin called that one, too.

Wolgast, as well as Battling Nelson and Joe Gans, who preceded him as leaders in the division, was a familiar figure in the ring around San Francisco.

It was at Point Richmond, across the Bay, that Wolgast won from Nelson after forty rounds of the most brutal light-weight fighting. That was in 1910, two years before Wolgast met up with Joe Rivers in a fight at Vernon, California, and helped bring about a situation in which another of San Francisco's storied referees, Jack Welsh, had to make a remarkable decision.

In the thirteenth round both Wolgast and Rivers landed at the same instant. Both went to the floor. Both were completely out. How to unscramble that one? Welsh did not hesitate very long. He simply bent over, lifted the champion, Wolgast, from the heap, and help up his hand. The winner, and still champion—they told Wolgast when he came to.

It was probably as correct a solution as any.

Right on down the weight scale, San Francisco was able to come up with its remarkable fighters. If boxing had a hall of fame, it is possible that Frankie Neil, the bantamweight, would be in it. Pound for pound, he was perhaps as hard a hitter as the prize ring ever knew.

One of the family groups of fighters was the Attells. Brother Abe, the cagiest of the featherweights and the light-weights, was the most impressive . . . when the notion struck him. His name has figured in sports pages as much for his activities outside of the ring as for those in it, but for sheer fighting skill alone he was worthy to be listed among the all-time greats.

Brother Monte was a formidable bantamweight, but it is of Brother Caesar I would write.

The annals of the prize ring will show that Brother Abe, in his time, knew all the angles for protecting himself and his interests, whatever they happened to be. They will show that when Brother Abe, in his after life, became an associate of Arnold Rothstein and others, he knew his way around. Brother Abe knew how to give 'em the business, or how to get it. But Brother Caesar . . . oi!

Tad, the famous cartoonist, loved to relate the adventures of Caesar Attell, a most careful man with a buck.

There was that time when Caesar was fighting the main event at Vallejo, California, from which the boat to San Francisco departed at eleven o'clock. Drop-ins either caught that boat or had to find themselves a hotel room for the night and pay for same, preferably in advance, Vallejo being like that in those days.

There was a little delay in getting Caesar's fight started, and he began his operations with many a fearful glance at the clock. He didn't want to miss that boat. Caesar swarmed all over his man but he couldn't put him away. Round by round Caesar piled up the points, but every three minutes brought that sailing time nearer. It became obvious that if the fight went the limit, Caesar would never make the boat, but no matter how hard and how often the punches landed, Caesar's man wouldn't go to the mat.

Something desperate had to be done. Caesar took one last look at the clock as he went out for the fourteenth round. This *had* to be the last, and even so, it would take some hustling to get out of ring togs, into street clothes, and down to the dock.

Caesar, like all the Attells, was resourceful. He tore into his opponent, gave him the Sunday punch, and drew back. The guy did not fall. He kept coming on. Caesar charged in again, and the first and only punch landed on him that night thudded not too wickedly against his body.

Over went Caesar and was counted out.

P.S. He caught the boat.

Caesar Attell was not the only character the prize rings of San Francisco produced.

I would give top billing to a curious threesome known as Ah Wing, Tanglefoot McGovern, and Cockey O'Brien. Ah Wing was Chinese, and fought in the days when his race affected pigtails. At the start of an engagement in the ring the pigtail would be coiled around his head. Sooner or later, in the frequent round-robin series with Tanglefoot and Cockey, the pigtail would become unwound, and many was the time one or both principals were in danger of becoming strangled as it wound around their respective necks. But it was all in the spirit of good, clean fun.

Before we leave the San Francisco fight colony and its visitors, a bit more should be set down about Willie Meehan, a sort of Tony Galento of his day.

Meehan began his fighting life as a bantamweight, and progressed by adipose degrees through all the other divisions until he retired as a heavyweight.

His place in boxing history is assured, for he was the one man, until Tunney came along, that Dempsey could not handle. They fought many times, always four rounds, the last in a war benefit show in San Francisco after Dempsey had won his sensational victory over Fred Fulton.

In that bout, which marked Jim Coffroth's final appearance as a fight promoter, Dempsey put Meehan on the floor with a savage belt to the body in the first round, but Willie got up and slapped and cuffed his way to what the referee, Eddie Graney, thought was a victory.

I have heard often in baseball of pitchers who can beat one team and few others. I have heard of great pitchers who are unable to get out an occasional hitter who is a soft touch for everyone else. But the Meehan jinx for Dempsey is the only one of the prize ring with which I have ever come in contact.

CHAPTER 9

World's Series Memories

THE year 1919 was the one in which the rest of the sports world seemed to draw closer to California and the Pacific Coast than it had ever done before.

California had more than its share of the great fights and fighters in the past. But they came along at a time when there were no radio broadcasts, no motion-picture newsreels, and not too much emphasis on their features in the sports pages. Certainly there was no general outpouring of writers and cameramen for sports events such as was to become standard practice from 1919 on. The Jeffries-Johnson fight at Reno in 1910 had been accompanied by at least one special trainload of authors, artists, and photographers, and it seemed a tremendous concentration of attention at the time. But it was the exception rather than the rule.

The rise of Dempsey and his smashing victory over Willard in 1919 directed attention to the section of the country in which Kearns had prepared him for his spectacular career.

The same year, 1919, brought with it the first world's series in which I had a personal interest. This was the ill-fated set of games between the Cincinnati Reds and the Chicago White Sox, which was quickly suspect, and almost a year later proven to have been thrown by a cluster of eight Chicago players.

Pitching for Cincinnati was Dutch Ruether, my old teammate of the collegiate and semipro circuit. He was now grown to one of baseball's best left-handers, pitcher and hitter.

On the Chicago side were Swede Risberg, Claude Williams, and Buck Weaver. Risberg and I had been members of the Telegraph Hill Boys' Club in our 115-pound days. Williams had been a teammate of mine at Sacramento as I drifted in and out of professional baseball. Weaver, the greatest third baseman I have ever seen, was as familiar to me as my next-door neighbor. And still is. It was his home run that had beaten my St. Ignatius team (and Ruether) in 1913. Before joining the White Sox he had been a member of the San Francisco club.

From two thousand miles away, awaiting the play-by-play report on a press wire, I was as wildly excited about that opening game of the series as I had been a few months before when my pal Dempsey was dissecting Willard's body at Toledo.

Much as I fancied the White Sox—and I still believe they were the greatest team that ever played baseball—I couldn't see them beating my man Ruether. Maybe Hod Eller and Jimmy Ring and Slim Sallee, but not Dutch.

So when Dutch tripled with runners on bases, hit safely again with more aboard, and was well on his way to his first world's series victory, 9 to 1, nobody could tell me that Ruether wasn't the greatest of 'em all.

But in the midst of the report on that first game, someone tried. . . .

He was a visitor from San Jose who had dropped in to see how things were going. A wise guy. One who knew all the answers.

"The series is phony," he said. "It's all fixed for the Reds to win."

We told him he was nuts. Nobody could fix a ball game. He was probably sore because the White Sox were getting beaten, and they were getting beaten because Ruether was the greatest pitcher who ever lived. We laughed at him. Dirty laughs.

"I ain't kidding," he insisted. "We got the word. You know who from. . . ,"

None of us knew "who from" . . . and none of us then gave any thought to Hal Chase, who sometimes wintered in San Jose. He wasn't in the series, anyhow. None of us thought about Abe Attell, or old Bill Burns, who had pitched on the Coast before he went up to Washington. None of us had ever heard of Arnold Rothstein. We drove our visitor out finally.

Some time after the Reds had won the game and the story was bedded down nicely in the paper, I thought of calling some of the lads on Telegraph Hill who were cronies of Risberg.

I approached the matter cautiously, simply asking if they had heard anything from the Swede about the White Sox chances. Several of them had. The White Sox were a cinch, Risberg had said. Go the limit on them.

I didn't give the matter another thought until almost a year later. By that time the rumblings of a phony series were being heard on all sides, and such able observers as Hugh Fullerton and Ring Lardner had long since denounced the games in their own peculiar ways.

The Dempsey-Miske fight brought me to the Middle West in the late summer of 1920. After it had reached its logical conclusion I went to Cleveland, where Tris Speaker's Indians were about to engage the White Sox in a series on which the pennant might well depend.

The trip was well worth while. It was a blistering series, with the White Sox taking great abuse from the strongly partisan home crowd. In one game the feeling ran so high the White Sox armed themselves with bats leaving the field, just in case their way to the clubhouse would be as rough physically as it had been audibly.

Cleveland won the series, as it was ultimately to win the pennant and the world's championship. One of its leading factors was Walter Mails, a somewhat eccentric left-hander who had come up from St. Mary's College, of Oakland, California, equipped with a fast ball and a hard head.

The White Sox were scheduled to return to Chicago next day, and I was going on to New York. That evening I went to dinner with Risberg. We walked along the street in silence for a while, and then he suddenly blurted out:

"I'll be damned if I'll tell them anything."

I hadn't the slightest idea what he was talking about, and was polite enough not to say so. I found out next day. Upon the White Sox' return to Chicago, Eddie Cicotte confessed that there had been some foul practice in the games with the Reds the year before. The whole unsavory business of the 1919 world's series was out in the open at last.

It had far-reaching effects on baseball. It caused the entry of Kenesaw M. Landis as its commissioner. It led to the banishment of eight members of the White Sox who had been in the series, and brought down baseball's wrath on several others who were believed to have had guilty knowledge of the fix.

The question naturally arises, after all these years: How could a conspiracy (if it were that) to throw ball games in a world's series pass undetected while it was going on, and remain unchallenged until almost a year afterward?

For one thing, baseball was so thoroughly established as a game that could not be fixed that much of the original hinting that something was wrong was written off as scandal-mongering, the wail of soreheads and suckers.

However, there were many forthright writers who were sure there had been "business" done. During the progress of the series, Hugh Fullerton was outspoken in his condemnation of the play of certain of the White Sox. Ring Lardner hummed a parody of a then popular song—"I'm forever throwing ball games"—but nothing was done until the persistent cross-examination of Eddie Cicotte, pitcher (and loser) of two games, by a set of Chicago newspapermen who were not baseball writers, brought forth the first grudging admissions. After that there were court hearings and hulla-baloo galore.

The series in question was taken by the Reds, five games to three. Two of these White Sox victories were won by Dickie Kerr, a tiny left-hander, and the other was gained by the conscience-stricken (perhaps) Cicotte in the seventh game. But long before that Cicotte had pitched and lost two games, and the left-hander Claude Williams had blown two others. The last game of the series, which went to the Reds, 10 to 5, found Williams again the defeated pitcher.

The series abounded with curious plays in which the ball was thrown to the wrong base, flies were misjudged, and "fat" pitches were served to Cincinnati batsmen when runs were in scoring position.

It never was too well established what the asking price or even the final cost of arranging the fix was, or which of the offending players got most of the money, or any at all. Some of those who were eventually banned even had creditable records in all the box scores. One at least is generally accepted to have sinned against the baseball code chiefly by having guilty knowledge, and not because of any overt act on the field.

A few years after the White Sox scandal, when Landis had completed the process of striking from the rolls the name of Jimmy O'Connell, Giant outfielder and one of Doc Strub's $75,000 beauties sold in the San Francisco market, I drew up a brief on ball players who had gone wrong. In a strictly in-formal way, I took it up with Landis, one of my closest personal friends.

I reviewed the case of the White Sox. I recalled that among those implicated, Risberg, Claude Williams, Chick Gandil, Fred McMullen, and Buck Weaver all had their beginnings in the Pacific Coast League, or had served there while in the reshaping process. So, too, had Bill Burns and Joe Gedeon, who were said to have been on the fringe of the 1919 doings. Abe Attell, whose name had been mentioned freely in con-nection with the series betting, came from San Francisco.

O'Connell had started at Santa Clara University, and proceeded from the San Francisco club to the Giants. The player
to whom he was alleged to have made his "don't bear down"
proposition, and who turned him in, was Heinie Sands of
the Phillies, another San Franciscan. Shufflin' Phil Douglas,
whom baseball had given the gate at an earlier date, prepped
with San Francisco in his minor-league polishing term. Then
there were Tom Seaton and Casey Smith, whom Doc Strub
had given the bum's rush for associating with gamblers in the
San Francisco park.

Elsewhere in the Coast League in my time there had been
another wholesale dismissal in several clubs of players who
were caught in a mess.

All these things I placed before Landis, some of them with
more detail than I care to place here.

"Well, what do you make of it?" I asked him finally.

He poked me in the chest with a bony finger and said,
"That, sir, is something for a Californian to determine. I am
a native of Indiana. But don't it beat hell how all those fellows seemed to come from the same place?"

It certainly did.

The exposing of the White Sox late in 1920 cast a cloud
over baseball, but by the time Cleveland and Brooklyn were
ready for the world's series that fall, fandom generally had
been through the period of readjustment and was ready for
its annual excitement.

It held more than ordinary interest for me, since it was
the first world's series I had ever attended. On that count
alone I shall never forget it.

However, it held other items the like of which no other
world's series has offered, over and above the fact that it was
the first one I had seen. It contained the first home run with
the bases filled ever recorded in any world's series. In the
same game there turned up the only unassisted triple play
in series history.

It couldn't have been sheer coincidence that a Brooklyn
team was involved in it.

The teams went into the fifth game, played at Cleveland, deadlocked with two victories each.

Burleigh Grimes, master of the spitball, was the Brooklyn pitcher. The first two Cleveland hitters got on base. Speaker was next up. It was a cinch that he would attempt to sacrifice. Grimes was in favor of that, since he hoped to make Tris do it his way. So Burleigh walked over toward third base and instructed Jack Sheehan, rookie guardian of that post, to remain close to the base, prepared to take a throw for the proposed force-out Grimes had in mind.

Grimes delivered the pitch perfectly and dashed for the plate. Speaker bunted how and where Grimes wanted him to, and Burleigh made a leap for the ball. As he did so his feet slipped out from under him. There he sat, raving mad, unable to make a play. The bases were filled. The packed stands were howling with glee. Grimes was so furious he wanted to kill all present, tearing them limb from limb with his naked hands.

His fever had not abated when he prepared to pitch to Elmer Smith, and the pitch was promptly smacked high and far away over the right-field fence.

The ensuing four runs should have been punishment enough for the Dodgers, but Cleveland wasn't done.

In the fifth inning Brooklyn rallied. Pete Kilduff reached base and so did Otto Miller. Clarence Mitchell, who had succeeded Grimes as pitcher, was the next hitter. With both runners on the go, Mitchell sent a line drive out toward Bill Wambsganss, who was running to cover second base. Wamby speared the ball and continued on to second, stepping on the base to retire Kilduff. As he turned, the slow-moving Miller, dumfounded at the surprising turn of fortunes, was an easy victim. He stood there wondering whether to give up in disgust or to try to get back to first base, and Wamby tagged him out, completing the triple play.

Nor was that all of great moment in this game. Jim Bagby, the Cleveland pitcher, hit a home run with two on. It was the first time in world's series history a pitcher had ever done anything like that. But then, this was the first time Brooklyn had been in a world's series.

After all that punishment in one game, it was no wonder the Dodgers were never the same thereafter. They lost the next two and the series, this being in the days when it was considered sound practice to play best five out of nine, instead of the now standard four out of seven.

All this served to whet my appetite for world's series baseball. I have not missed one since that 1920 affair, and the annual meeting between National and American League clubs is as much a "must" on my yearly schedule as is the Kentucky Derby.

These two events, of all those that are held yearly, are the most fertile fields for the story gatherer. It does not matter greatly how good the competition may be. The crowds are always there, and each renewal of either affords an opportunity for reminiscing. To me, that phase of sports has always been as desirable as the actual event taking place on field or course.

My first world's series, because of that record-charged game, remains among my favorites when I look back.

If I had to select the series that was superlative on all counts, the baseball played, the people in attendance, and general interest and excitement, it would have to be that one in which Dizzy Dean and the rest of the Gas House Gang of the St. Louis Cardinals outlasted Mickey Cochrane's Detroit Tigers in 1934.

It seemed as if there were something going on every minute of the day and night throughout that series, and the most publicized incident, the banishing of Joe Medwick by Commissioner Kenesaw M. Landis, was in reality just one of many exciting events.

In other series I have marveled at the exploits of Babe Ruth and Lou Gehrig of the Yankees, but I also enjoyed the 1922 event in which John McGraw's pitchers, Art Nehf, Jess Barnes, Jack Scott, Hugh McQuillan, and Rosy Ryan, held the Babe to a .118 average for the five games, in which he made but two hits, and *no* home runs.

Pepper Martin's one-man show against the Athletics in 1930; Grover Alexander's fanning of Tony Lazerri of the Yankees with the 1926 series in the balance; the "four straight" sweeps of Yankees under Miller Huggins and again under Joe McCarthy; the ten-run inning the Athletics enjoyed against the Cubs in 1929—all these and more crop up as I look back through old score books.

Then, too, there is the other side, the bad breaks. Hack Wilson's loss of a fly ball in the sun, which helped bring about that ten-run inning for the Athletics in 1929; umpire George Hildebrand's decision in 1922 that it was too dark to continue play in a Giant-Yankee 3-to-3 tie, while everyone else present, including Judge Landis, thought otherwise; Ted Williams' docility in the 1946 games with the Cardinals —the roll of ill-fated exploits is fully as long as that of the successful deeds in the world's series.

I wouldn't want to say I have estimated one world's series as more to be remembered than another. I prefer to say I have liked 'em all, and always will.

CHAPTER 10

The Wonder Team

ONCE the 1920 world's series was out of the way, I returned to San Francisco, prepared to give some thought to football.

California was about to attract national attention for its gridiron game for the first time. This was by no means a criticism of the previous standards of play, but of the sheer oversight on the part of the East and the Middle West, where the national authorities and molders of public opinion seemed to think the only football of consequence was being played. This has always seemed a bit strange to me, who grew up on the Pacific Coast.

As a small boy, and for many years thereafter, I had full appreciation of Yale and Harvard and Princeton, of Pennsylvania, Michigan, Chicago, the Carlisle Indians, and all the other greats before and after the discovery of the forward pass.

Out in San Francisco we knew all about the great men of the East. (Everything on the other side of the Sierra Nevada was "east" to us.) We knew of the coaches and the players and the teams. But did anybody back there know about us? Or admit it? I doubt it. And yet the memories of many of the game's leaders must have been very short and their bumps of curiosity undeveloped if they did not.

Walter Camp himself had served as Stanford coach for a spell. Lee McClung of Yale had coached California for the big game with Stanford. W. W. Pudge Heffelfinger, all-time

All-American guard, had taken a whirl at steaming up California's early disciples of push-and-pull football. So had Garry Cochrane of Princeton. So California and Stanford football could not have been the deep, dark mystery it appeared to be to all those in the "East" until the second decade of the present century.

Camp will be remembered as long as football is played for having popularized the annual madness for selecting All-American teams. Yet he did not give a player from the state of California a tumble on any of his first, second, or third All-American annual selections until 1920.

This could have been due in part to the fact that Stanford, California, Santa Clara, and St. Mary's played Rugby instead of intercollegiate football from 1906 until 1915. After a marked increase in injuries during the 1905 season there had been agitation nationally against the game. In parts of California collegiate and prep-school authorities banned the intercollegiate style, but were willing to accept Rugby as a sport less hazardous to life and limb.

As Rugby addicts, players on those college teams in California got to be so efficient they were able to defeat the famous All Blacks from New Zealand, and in both 1920 and 1924 an all-star team went on from the Pacific Coast to gain the championship of the world at the Olympic games. If the Coast athletes were able to become proficient so quickly in a game that was not theirs naturally, is it unreasonable to argue that they must have been doing all right at their own style of football?

Maybe the intercollegiate football as demonstrated by the Pacific Coast prior to 1905, and between 1915 and 1920, wasn't so hot, generally, after all. But you couldn't tell us that there were *no* individuals worthy of ranking with the best elsewhere.

We were acutely aware that Bobby Sherman of California, with Orval Overall (later a Cub pitching star) running interference, traveled 102 yards for a touchdown against Stanford in 1902. We had our star backs and many of them, great linesmen and many of them. But I guess we didn't know how to project 'em nationally. Parenthetically, I shall be the last to say that the Pacific Coasters haven't since mastered all the promotional publicity angles for their football, and they have more than made up for the lack of press agentry when the century was very young.

The decline of the Rugby code set in on the Coast in 1915. California and Stanford were unable to agree on the freshman rule. California did not want first-year men on the varsity and Stanford did. Stanford foresaw no evils such as an influx of "tramp athletes," a supposed natural consequence of the athletic employment of first-year (freshmen or transfers) men. California did. The freshman and transfer rule is now generally in vogue in most colleges, though the wartime shortage of collegiate athletic manpower caused it to be suspended for the duration.

When California and Stanford broke relations the California advisory board decided this was as good a time as any to abandon Rugby and go back to the "old" game.

The "old" game had been continuously in vogue in the Pacific Northwest. Teams of Washington, Washington State, Oregon, and Oregon State were happy to welcome California back to the fold.

Washington's coach was Gil Dobie, one of football's original glooms. He gave California two games on his 1915 schedule. In the first, while California was still suffering from a Rugby hangover, Washington won, 72 to 0. A week later Washington just did get home in front, 13 to 7, and didn't win the game until the last few seconds of play.

One season convinced California that a big-time coach was indicated, and to ensure action, two famous football figures were imported. One was Andy Smith, who had been chosen on Walter Camp's All-American while at Pennsylvania. The other was Eddie Mahan, the famous Harvard back.

Smith had considerable coaching experience at Pennsylvania and Purdue before accepting the post at California. He took charge for the 1916 season and a great improvement, especially in fundamentals, was noticed in the squad. The Penn and Harvard ideas did not harmonize, however, and Mahan presently went his way.

The outbreak of World War I interfered with smooth progress in football or anything else that was of interest to the collegians of the time, so Smith did not have a fair chance to make a showing until 1919. By this time Stanford had given up Rugby and was experimenting with the American game, as were Santa Clara and St. Mary's.

It was noised about that the California squad of 1920 was really going to be something. It was, indeed.

I have written already that the world's series game between Cleveland and Brooklyn was of great moment, and it truly was. But it deprived me of the chance to see the California team until the week after it had played its third game of the season. It will be one of my everlasting regrets that I missed that third game, for in it California beat St. Mary's, 127 to 0. That is a trifle better than two points a minute. I don't know yet how it was done, but done it was.

That California team went through its season undefeated, scoring 482 points against its opponents' 14, Oregon State and Nevada being the teams to score of the eight California played. Brick Morse, an inspired writer for one of the San Francisco papers, took to calling this the "Wonder Team."

By whatever standards we had on the Pacific Coast, it was all of that. When it went to Pasadena for the Tournament of Roses game, January 1, 1921, scarcely a Pacific Coast football addict gave its opponent, the Western Conference champion Ohio State, any chance at all.

Since these New Year's Day games had been resumed in 1916, Pacific Coast teams had fared quite well. Washington State in 1916 had defeated Brown, 14 to 0, smothering the famed Fritz Pollard throughout the rainy afternoon. A year later, by the same score, Oregon defeated Pennsylvania. Service teams took over the game for the two years that followed, the magnificent Great Lakes team with its Paddy Driscoll, George Halas, and Jimmy Conzelman of later coaching fame being one of these. In the New Year's Day game of 1920 a great Harvard aggregation downed Oregon, 7 to 6.

Now the Western Conference was to give it a try, and what happened to the Buckeyes happened so early and so often it was exactly twenty-six years afterward before permission was given for another of their teams to celebrate New Year's in Pasadena.

California won the game, 28 to 0. In the closing moments of the game it missed at least six more points by inches as "Pesky" Sprott was forced out of bounds in the very corner of the field.

This was the game in which "Brick" Muller, California end, gained national prominence and qualified for a place on many all-time All-American teams.

In the second period Muller pulled back from his position at end and ran around to the right, some fifteen yards behind the line of scrimmage. There he took a pass from Sprott, wound up, and let go one of the most discussed forward passes of all time. It was caught by the other California end, Brodie Stephens, just as he crossed the goal line, fifty-three yards away.

For many years that pass was in record books as a seventy-yard toss. Muller could have thrown one that far. There is no doubt about it. But he didn't happen to, on that occasion.

The pass gained more attention for Muller than his all-around end play ever did, which was an injustice to him. For he was as great as ends ever get to be, on offense and on defense.

He was the first Pacific Coast player ever named by Walter Camp as All-American. Just to prove what a silly business All-American selecting is, Muller was not given a tumble by Camp in the 1920 season. Brick made it at the end of the 1921 season.

With true California fervor, I suppose I criticized Camp for his 1920 omission as severely as anyone, but great as I know Muller was in all the games he ever played, I am inclined to challenge his selection for what he did in 1921, though I appreciate Camp's urge to undo the wrong of the previous year.

However, in 1921 Muller's leg was injured early in the season and he was used sparingly, being brought in now and then to throw a pass. An All-American, in my book, is one who is in there all the time, doing his stuff against all opponents under all sorts of conditions.

In nine games California scored 312 points against its opponents' 33 in the 1921 season. While everybody else on the Coast was hailing it as the "Wonder Team," I was inclined to credit the St. Mary's aggregation as being almost too wonderful to be true in that selfsame year.

St. Mary's had acquired a new coach after its 127-to-0 licking of the year previous, and he was to be a going concern in the Bay section for many years. His personal popularity and his promotional sense gained him a place in the public's regard with Andy Smith, Glenn Warner, and Howard Jones, the three greatest coaches ever to light on the Pacific Coast.

This estimate is certainly not meant as any reflection on the coaching skill or the worth to intercollegiate football of Amos Alonzo Stagg, who reached the Pacific Coast and College of Pacific toward the end of his career. Stagg's fame was established at the University of Chicago, and while he made his presence felt at College of Pacific, his influence on Pacific Coast football was not to be measured with that of Smith, Warner, and Jones.

St. Mary's new man was Edward (Slip) Madigan, who had learned his football at Notre Dame.

Beyond hearing that St. Mary's had assembled some interesting material for the 1921 season, I had not paid much attention to the team, being too occupied in observing the wonders Smith was working at California Field.

One afternoon as the players were assembling for practice, I was chatting with Smith when a very large young man approached and wanted to know if this was Coach Smith.

Andy said it was, and asked what he could do.

The young man gave his name and said he wanted to play football for California.

Smith thanked him, but pointed out that there were such things as one-year, freshman, and transfer rules to be considered.

The young man seemed very crestfallen, and said he had come a long way.

Smith was very sympathetic. "Tell you what you do," he said. "You go out through that gate and across the campus and take a streetcar going downtown. After a while you'll come to a lot of brick buildings. That's St. Mary's College. You go in there and ask for the coach and tell him Andy Smith sent you. Maybe he'll be able to do something for you. The coach's name is Madigan."

The young man started. "Is he out here, too?" he asked, and away he went.

A few weeks later the young man was in the St. Mary's line-up when it met California, and a mighty man indeed was he. Not as well known, perhaps, as Pete Bahan, who had played his normal three-year course at Notre Dame, but who appeared on that 1921 St. Mary's team as captain and quarterback. But quite a man, just the same, and very helpful in cutting exactly 106 points off the California total of the previous year.

The 21-to-0 California victory, once a chance was afforded to study the past performances of many of those who were amplifying their educations at St. Mary's the year Madigan took charge, was in its way as notable as anything the "Wonder Team" ever accomplished.

California's team closed the season with a 398-to-34 record. It returned to Pasadena for the 1922 New Year's Day game to meet Washington and Jefferson, of which the Coast knew little and cared less.

It began to rain the evening before the game, and all of Pasadena's visitors remained indoors. In a suite at the Hotel Green was assembled a group of rain dodgers.

Present was Walter Eckersall, former gridiron great at the

University of Chicago, but then doubling as football writer for the Chicago *Tribune* and as the referee of the New Year's Day game. With him was Tom Thorp, a Columbia hero of the old days who had come west to do a story for the New York *Journal* as well as umpire the game. Johnny Stroud, California graduate manager, and some San Francisco newspapermen rounded out the party at first, and presently it was joined by Andy Smith, who had walked over in the rain from the Hotel Maryland, where his team was quartered.

In no time at all, Eckersall, Thorp, and Smith, who had been collegiate contemporaries, were away on many a run, many a block and tackle of the good old days.

Thorp, a man of tremendous size, recalled "Tiny" Maxwell, the unstoppable Swarthmore battering ram.

"Columbia stopped him," said Thorp. "I'll tell you how."

Maxwell, Thorp related, was one of the most powerful driving backs of his time, and when he played, a man was not stopped until he said so. Maxwell, incidentally, was afflicted with the habit of stuttering when he was aroused.

"Swarthmore started a drive in our territory," said Thorp. "Tiny carried the ball on every play, crashing straight ahead, yard after yard. We were driven back until we had to make a goal-line stand. There was nothing nifty about Tiny. He followed that straight line. When he went for the touchdown, he was aimed right at one of the goal posts. I got in back of it, swung up, and while as many of our side as could grabbed his legs and hung on, I planted my feet squarely on his face. He couldn't move. He couldn't speak. He couldn't do anything. I sometimes wonder why we aren't there yet. Thank God, the goal post held under the pressure."

While Thorp was telling his tale, Smith would open a window and stick his head out. When he withdrew it, soaking wet, he would shake his head and mutter: "We'll kick. The score will be nothing to nothing."

Throughout the long hours Smith kept repeating his act, and in the early morning I went out and filed a story to my paper in San Francisco, quoting Smith as saying the score

would be o to o. Which was exactly what it was. Archie
Nisbet, California fullback on that New Year's Day, in the
mud and rain gave one of the greatest exhibitions of kicking
a wet ball I have ever witnessed, but the break on which
Smith gambled never came.

One of the noteworthy features of that game was the
appearance of Swede Erickson, the W. and J. halfback. As
far as I know he is the only player who ever participated in a
New Year's Day game at Pasadena on two different occasions
with two different teams. His first appearance had been with
the Great Lakes team against the Mare Island Marines, three
years previously.

This game, incidentally, was the last to be played at what
was then known as Tournament Park. When the 1923 game
came around, the Rose Bowl, as it is now known, was in
existence. Andy Smith's Californias were again Coast cham-
pians, but the Bowl bid went to Southern California, 12-to-o
victims of Smith's team.

Regardless of its failure to keep three successive dates at
Pasadena, that 1920-21-22 California squad had made its football history. I place it among the greatest teams of the present
century, well able to stand beside those formidable arrays of
Notre Dame, Pittsburgh, Army, and Southern California. I
place Smith in the company of Knute Rockne, Amos Alonzo
Stagg, Fielding Yost, Glenn Warner, Bob Zuppke, Howard
Jones, Jock Sutherland, and Frank Leahy, as the coaches
who have done most to make collegiate football what it is
today.

CHAPTER 11

Who Trained for What?

*T*HROUGHOUT 1920 and the early part of 1921 I had been keeping up with the progress of my ranking heroes, Dempsey and Kearns.

When all the sleight of hand leading up to the presentation of Boyle's Thirty Acres in Jersey City as a site for the Dempsey-Carpentier fight had been completed, Kearns selected Atlantic City as the champion's training camp. He asked me if I would like to take charge of the press relations. I asked my boss if that would be ethical. He said he didn't know whether it was ethical but that I had damn well better accept the invitation before Kearns changed his mind. So off I went to Atlantic City to participate in an adventure the like of which I had never experienced before, and for which I had more hearsay than practical experience.

I have been to many training camps of fighters in my time, but there are just three that are worthy of remembering. Doubtless Toledo, where Dempsey took charge of Willard, will resent this, but the only incident I care to recall about that was the time Battling Nelson took a bath in a barrel of newly prepared lemonade that was being readied for the parched throats of the visiting firemen.

My training camps, in their proper recollection order, were Atlantic City, Shelby, Montana, and Benton Harbor. All the others had their diverting moments, but these three had nothing else but.

When I arrived at Atlantic City there was but one newspaperman on the job. He was Jack Veiock, who worked for International News Service.

Dempsey, with trainer Teddy Hayes, camp guardian Mike Trant of Chicago, and retinue, was encamped in two cottages at the Airport. Kearns lived in a boardwalk hotel, where headquarters were established.

Since Veiock was the only newspaperman around, Kearns had adopted him. He had also adopted Jack White, a zany comedian who was working o' nights in Joe Moss's Beaux Arts Café, also on the boardwalk.

On my first night in Atlantic City, Kearns, Veiock, and White went on tour after the last show in the Beaux Arts. As they gathered momentum, the visiting newspaperman was caught in between two of the most expert "ribbers" it has ever been my fortune to know.

By degrees White began to resent everything Veiock said. He grew madder and madder. At a critical moment White produced a gun, which was previously loaded with blanks, and menaced Veiock with it. Veiock had the impulse to get out of there, but fast. He did not wait to open the door. He went right through it, White after him, now blazing away with the gun.

First I knew of it was when a sharp knock came at my door. I opened it and there stood Veiock, looking very pale and drawn. He said he was sorry he had awakened me but that he had just received a long-distance call from New York and had to return at once. Would I protect him for a few days until he could get back? I said I would. He left. He never came back. And not until an hour or so later when Kearns and White rolled in did I learn the true facts of the case.

It was not long before there were as many newspapermen in Atlantic City as there were candidates for the Miss America contest, before they began eliminating the outsized numbers and culled the lilies from the tomatoes. To this swarm of writers was added a great collection of nationally known figures from various walks of life. Many of them were actors and actresses, but even those who were not insisted on getting into the act. By way of adding to the confusion, there were times when the convention-infested city found many of the members of Our Set getting mixed up with the delegates, or vice versa.

The championship of the boardwalk, in all weight divisions, was being settled almost every night, though my personal preference for the all-around champion was the night manager of Child's restaurant.

Our playful crowd would wind up in his place about sunup. On one occasion a member of the party thought it would be nice to take a paper pat of butter and plant it on the bald head of an old pal. The old pal countered with a half cantaloupe in the puss. Presently there was heavy firing going on all over the restaurant.

The night manager was a patient man, but when a mess of butter cakes landed on his white jacket he invited any and all to step outside and he'd take good care of them. He did, too. It has always seemed a pity to me that Kearns, on that memorable occasion, was in New York propping up Tex Rickard, the promoter. I still feel that the night manager's punching powers were wasted on those meal tickets Child's used to furnish. I'm sure he, too, could have beaten Georges Carpentier.

After a time it was possible to make some regulations for all my clients.

Dempsey was accustomed to work out in the afternoons. So most of those who had recovered from the night before went out to see him. Those able to see the keys on a typewriter then wrote their own stories, took in the slack for as many of the derelicts as possible, and then stood by.

It was in the standing-by period that a public relations man had to be on his toes.

It became customary for most of the group to gather at the Beaux Arts at night, remain there until the official closing hour, and then remain some more.

White, who had plenty of natural talent, but who had

been in comparative obscurity until then, began to get as much publicity as Dempsey. For the rest of his lifetime, most of which was spent in a basement café on Fifty-second Street in New York, or in the Polo Grounds (White was a rabid Giant fan) , where White was, there were sports writers.

As the training camp grew busier and the date of the fight approached, there was a great influx of foreign writers. They came from England and from France. The English writers I handled without trouble. The Frenchmen were turned over to Dan McKetrick, a sort of ambassador at large.

It was arranged for the visiting delegation to meet Dempsey one morning at his camp. The champion was seated on the steps of his cottage when the party arrived. He rose to greet them and smiled his welcome.

Immediately the Frenchmen began an excited chattering among themselves. Dempsey was puzzled and I wondered what was wrong.

McKetrick stepped aside and explained. "They are amazed that the champion smiles," he said.

"When he sees Carpentier he'll laugh out loud," I said, and drew a reproachful glance from McKetrick, always the perfect host.

Among the visiting English writers was Jeffery Farnol, the novelist, whose works were among my favorites. I could hardly wait until the fight was over and his London paper had a chance to get back to these shores, in order to see the treatment he gave it. I did not know much about English reportorial style in those days, so it took me a long time to recover from the shock. For Farnol's story of the fight had begun: "We arrived at the arena in good time." It went on then for several hundred beautifully put together words, and when you turned over from page 1, you found out at last that Dempsey had knocked out Carpentier. But none of all the hundreds of my clients wrote a more vivid account of the Battle of the Century than did Farnol, for all of his leisurely approach to "who, what, when, and where," American journalese for "get the important facts in the lead."

I believe Dempsey's knockout victory was no surprise to any writer from the British Isles, unless it happened to be George Bernard Shaw, who had declared for Carpentier. But Shaw did not make the trip. To him they all looked good when they were far away.

The American representatives of the press who came from far and near were a merry lot. They all liked Dempsey and none of them liked Carpentier, chiefly because they were barred from his Manhasset, Long Island, camp while the Orchid Man went through all that "secret" training. So they camped at Atlantic City.

They were an imaginative lot, these gentlemen of the press. In their endless search for new angles to what was by now an old story, the writers missed few tricks.

A warrior named Battling Ghee appeared at camp anxious to serve as a sparring partner for Dempsey. He was taken in charge by Charles Wilberforce Dunkley, Associated Press, Chicago. Dunkley gave him a sales talk that this was his big chance. The thing to do, he said, was to cop Dempsey with a sneak punch. In that instant he would be made a national figure. The Battler thought this reasoning was sound.

Thereupon Dunkley sought out Dempsey and confided in him that he had heard the new sparring partner was going to attempt a coup.

Dunkley and all his confreres had a fine time that afternoon writing about the furious burst of fighting Dempsey showed during the time his workout with Battling Ghee lasted, but the poor Battler was never the same again.

In the party at Atlantic City moved many of the notables of the stage. Al Jolson was a steady customer. So was Walter Kelly, the Virginia judge. Eddie Cantor, breaking in a show at a boardwalk theater, was prevailed upon to bring his baseball team, which consisted of both males and females, out to the camp to challenge the newspapermen. Dempsey insisted on getting in the game, and Kearns almost lost his mind, fearing the champion might dislocate a finger handling the baseball.

A compromise was reached and a soft ball was used for the game. Kearns needn't have worried, for his champion, at bat or in the field, didn't come close to a ball while he was in action. Dempsey the ball player was something less than a Ty Cobb.

As the Carpentier fight approached there was still some frowning at Dempsey because of the unfortunate series of events precipitated by his absence from World War I. It was a bum rap from start to finish, but there was nothing Dempsey could do but take it. Fortunately in his lifetime he was to have ample chance by his activity in World War II to make up for any real or fancied dereliction in the days when he was very young.

One paper, particularly ruthless in its riding of Dempsey, sent its highest powered writer to Atlantic City to take the place apart. His arrival was the signal for Kearns to throw the wildest party of all those that were going on night after night. The man with the supply of vitriol in his writing implements was the guest of honor. He loved it. He loved everybody. He not only did not put the blast on Dempsey, but wrote the most fulsome praise of any of the hundreds of observers who had visited the place . . . and he had the words to do it.

Another high-powered columnist from a New York paper came down to do a critical study of Dempsey. He was particularly anxious to know whether Dempsey read much, and what sort of books he fancied.

I hadn't the slightest idea, but I told the columnist that Dempsey, much as the average person, often read himself to sleep at night. He was reading just then, I said, one of Zane Grey's westerns. I even offered to take the columnist secretly to Dempsey's room so that he could see for himself. When he accepted the invitation for later in the week, I had planted a Zane Grey western on Dempsey's bedside table with a page marking the spot where the champion had paused in his last reading. After that, all I had to do was give Dempsey a quick study on what the story was all about, and await the visit of the columnist.

I began to outline the plot of the novel, only to be interrupted by Dempsey, who said in a matter-of-fact way that it wasn't necessary. He knew how that book had come out. All he wanted to know was why in hell I didn't get him one he hadn't read.

Maybe Dempsey of 1921 wasn't up on Shakespeare, but he knew his Zane Grey.

CHAPTER 12

Rise and Fall of Shelby

W<small>HILE</small> my vantage point in the training circus at Atlantic City was in the center ring, the Shelby adventure found me in the role of an observer rather than a participant.

That extremely active session while Dempsey was getting ready to slap down Carpentier had given me the urge to get to New York, where so many other San Franciscans of my calling had traveled and remained.

I returned to San Francisco after the fight with the assurance from several in New York that they would look for a spot for me. Several months elapsed and nothing happened, and one day I presented my case to the higher-ups on the San Francisco *Call Bulletin* and requested more money.

I was told that I was now getting all that the traffic would bear. I served notice then that if a chance to better myself came along, I would feel free to accept it.

Early in 1922 my old Atlantic City six-day bicycle team of Tad, Rube Goldberg, Bill McGeehan, and Billy Gibson informed me that Hugh Fullerton, then sports editor of the *Evening Mail*, was going to Chicago. Was I interested? Was I, indeed! The transaction was completed rapidly enough, I suppose, though it seemed ages of waiting at the time.

I had reached the big league at last. One of the definitely and chronically second-division clubs made the deal for me, to be sure, but it was still in the big league.

Fullerton, an old friend and a very frank sort, wished me well . . . in a left-handed sort of way.

"I know all about you from Tad and Rube," he said. "I wonder who'll give up first, you or the *Mail*."

I still insist that it was a photo finish. Anyhow, it wasn't so very many months before the *Mail* and I came to the parting of the ways, and I was in New York jobless.

I was succeeded as sports editor by a young man who has done all right since as a gossip columnist, even though the *Mail* went out of existence before he had much chance to develop further there. His name is Ed Sullivan. I knew him before he ever heard of Walter Winchell, or vice versa.

When I found him he was a frustrated amateur sports chronicler who liked to talk about Port Chester, Vincent Richards, and sundry New York Celtics basketball players who were his heroes.

I did not remain idle very long after the *Mail* delivery. Tex Rickard had a place for me at Madison Square Garden, which I held until the New York *Journal* summoned me as a boxing expert. It already had Sid Mercer and Tad, so I was needed about as badly as Arthur Brisbane needed ideas. However, it was the *Journal* that dispatched me to Shelby, and I shall always be grateful for that.

Now, it is common practice these days for a great many of my calling to mention that they were among the first to get to the scene at Shelby. But the real pioneer of the party was I . . . nobody else.

When I alighted from the Great Northern train at Shelby and looked around, there was no fight arena. There was no fight headquarters. Tommy Gibbons hadn't arrived. His manager, Eddie Kane, hadn't arrived. Mayor Jim Johnston wasn't in town. Promoter Loy Molumby (of whom I was later to write that song) was supposed to be flitting about the Middle West drumming up trade for the fight.

Buildings were few and far between. There was one that passed for a hotel, but I did not stop to investigate. I had heard it was possible to get to Great Falls by leaving at once. So leave at once I did.

Great Falls was the site of Dempsey's training camp, and

he and Kearns were there already, guarded by the fabulous character Senator Cyclone Wild Bill Lyons.

He was invariably in Dempsey's company after he had adopted him. Before that he was a Benny Leonard–Billy Gibson man, and before that he was a Freddie Welsh man. He had engraved watches from all three to prove it, and carried them with him at all times. The one he got from Dempsey and Kearns had more gadgets to it than any other chronometer in history. All it lacked was a power tube to get Kansas City on a clear night.

I must tell you more about Senator Cyclone Wild Bill Lyons later, but right now I'm trying to establish Shelby and Montana generally.

When I checked into the Rainbow Hotel at Great Falls and was waiting to be assigned to a room, there was a great commotion in the lobby. I asked the clerk what it was all about. "That's So-and-So," he said. "He's one of the big backers of the Shelby fight."

At the moment So-and-So was accompanied by almost as many lovely females as King Solomon was reliably reported to have had under contract when he was going good. I asked who they were, and was told that they were show girls with a musical comedy that was playing Great Falls.

I walked over to So-and-So, introduced myself, and asked if there was any doubt about Shelby's getting up the next $100,000 payment that Kearns was already clamoring for.

"Not a bit," thundered So-and-So, patting his pocket with an expressive gesture. "I've got it right here."

That ended the interview since the giggling gals were anxious to be moving, and the *Journal*'s man certainly did not look like money from home.

I sat down and wrote my first story of the trip, suggesting that there might be a reasonable doubt about the $100,000 materializing on Kearns's next payday.

That story, I believe, was widely disseminated by International News Service. It had the effect of dampening the ardor of many who were supposed to be readying special trains for the trip to Shelby from all parts of the country. Perhaps it was a cruel thing to do, but I have often wished I could call the Kentucky Derby winner that far in advance, that accurately.

The Park Hotel in Great Falls was where Kearns held forth. Dempsey's camp was pitched a bit out of town.

Before long the horde of reporters began moving in on Great Falls. There wasn't much accommodation for anyone at Shelby, though the building program was going on apace. Most of the writers commuted between Great Falls and Shelby. Kearns had promoted an engine and a special car of the early Lincoln period that shuttled back and forth.

Some of the rugged individualists insisted on camping out at Shelby. A few of them, accepting the fact that the fight was in the wild West, arrived with sombreros, bandanna handkerchiefs, boots, and all the cowboy regalia they had been reading about in the better dime novels. And did they look silly!

The Montanans, in Shelby or Great Falls, looked, acted, and dressed no differently than citizens of any other community. Perhaps this was what caused a bit of embarrassment for the dignified and scholarly Lawrence Perry. He was a golf, tennis, and yachting expert, but he dabbled in fight writing now and then. He had heard that there was a rodeo near Shelby and he asked me to walk out with him and look it over. When we got there we found a weather-beaten, mild-mannered man sitting on a corral rail. A typical native of the great West, Perry decided. He engaged him in conversation, using the opening gambit about the nice place you have here before asking about the severity of the winters and the average annual rainfall.

The man on the fence said he didn't know.

"Don't you live here?" persisted Perry.

"Hell, no," said the man on the fence. "I live in Bridgeport. I break horses for Ringling Brothers in the wintertime. I just got out here myself."

It was in Shelby that members of the literati, turned big

outdoor men pro tem, discovered Patricia Salmon in a tent show and so publicized the gal she eventually had a Broadway showing. This has always seemed to me to prove that the press has more power than sense of direction.

In Shelby's hotel there was but one room with bath. That room was occupied for the duration by Solly Harris, a familiar figure about fight camps and race tracks. The bathtub, for the duration, was employed as a container for ice and bottled beer, when either was obtainable.

It was at Shelby the great day the fight rolled around, despite the failure of the guarantees to be produced, that more people crashed into the show without paying than came in with tickets. As soon as the fight started all the gate tenders quit work and went in to see it. The thousands hanging around the outside came right in after them, unchecked.

It was from Shelby that Dempsey and his handlers, save Kearns, made a quick getaway in the special engine and car as soon as the fight was over. But it was at Great Falls, *not* at Shelby, that the fun and games went on.

There hotel rooms were at a premium, and one day there came to town the delegates of a lodge to hold a convention and initiation. They were equipped with a drum and bagpipe corps. They had no place to light, so they formed the entirely reasonable resolve that if they couldn't sleep in the hotels of Great Falls, no one else would. Night after night, for their entire stay, they paraded through the corridors of each floor of every hotel, with drums rum-tumming and bagpipes shrilling. Until you have heard that kind of noise under that kind of condition you haven't heard anything . . . and don't let any American Legion convention follower tell you otherwise.

Great Falls was the scene of most of the discussions over the Dempsey guarantees. Most of the time the newspapermen were either in on it or in the way of it.

In the last analysis, it was Damon Runyon who ensured the staging of the fight. Kearns was holding out stubbornly for the guarantee and was determined to call it all off when the last dismal meeting failed to get anyplace. He had returned to his hotel and was getting ready to make his announcement that it was off when Runyon called him aside and suggested a calmer viewpoint. When Damon had finished making his case, Kearns was ready to go through with the fight, and so announced.

By way of proper celebration, everyone decided to attend a dance that was going on up the street. It was a quiet, homy sort of dance, taking place on the second floor of a building, access to it being by a long and narrow flight of stairs.

When Kearns and his friends arrived, the home folks were enjoying themselves in their own way and minding their own business. Kearns, being in a playful mood, needled Senator Cyclone Wild Bill Lyons, who was now in full dress, western style, lacking only his two guns and chaps.

"Better let these people know you are here," said Kearns.

Lyons let out what he always termed his Comanche war whoop. The Montanans frowned a bit, but let it pass.

"They certainly gave you a tumble," sneered Kearns.

Lyons tried again. He made a speech. He told them he had been born on the banks of the Brazos, and that where he came from (actually he was a traveling salesman for men's ready-made clothing out of New York) men were rough, tough, and ready. He could lick anyone in the house, he said, one at a time, or all together. He finished with another wild yell.

Just then a gentleman detached himself from his dancing partner, came over and picked up Wild Bill, took him to the head of the stairs, and gently but firmly pitched him down the flight of stairs. Then the gentleman resumed his dancing.

Oh, yes, Shelby, Montana, was quite a place, I seem to have read somewhere, but I'll take Great Falls every time.

It was at Great Falls that a young sportsman, John O'Neil, interested in Montana oil, paid in effect what was probably the second largest price ever expended by one man to see a fight.

O'Neil, a Santa Clara man and a member of the U.S. Olympic Rugby champion team of 1920, kept dropping money into the fund they were trying to raise for Kearns until he must have been the largest single investor in the fight. It was O'Neil's theory that as long as they'd gone this far they might as well go the rest of the way—and after all, it was just money.

I have accorded him second place, but he was far behind the man who paid the record price for the privilege of seeing a heavyweight championship fight.

That would be Tex Rickard, who promoted Gene Tunney's farewell to the prize ring, his bout with Tom Heeney, the Hard Rock from Down Under. It was reliably reported that this fight cost Tex Rickard upwards of $200,000.

Whenever anyone starts telling me too much about the terrible "bust" the fight at Shelby was, I am always reminded of this.

CHAPTER 13

Benton Harbor Besieged

J ACK DEMPSEY's fight with Billy Miske at Benton Harbor in 1920 had pugilistic historical importance only because it was his first defense of the championship he had won so sensationally from Jess Willard at Toledo more than a year before.

Miske was definitely on the decline from his former estate as a fairly capable heavyweight, and no one gave him much chance. The lack of the elements of a contest did not prevent the fight bugs from swarming around Benton Harbor.

They came from all distances, and did the best they could under existing congested conditions. Most of the sports writers who served through the Benton Harbor campaign were well adjusted to cope later with the one-for-all and all-for-one housing conditions that endured while spectator sport was struggling to keep going during World War II.

I was one of the early arrivals at Benton Harbor and drew a room in one of the hotels. It was not a very large room. But it was large enough to cause the management to ask me if I would double up with another visitor. I asked who the other visitor was, and found out that it was Tad, the cartoonist, and a sort of godfather of mine in the newspaper business. I hastened to have him checked in. He had with him a traveling companion, Joe Smollen, of New York, who also moved in.

We were hardly settled in what was now about as roomy as a sleeping bag when there came a knock on the door.

Hype Igoe, another former San Franciscan and one of New York's sports literary lights, wanted to know if we could handle his business.

"Sure," said Tad, who was now in charge. I didn't see how we could manage it, but said nothing.

Igoe tossed his bag in the room and departed.

"Put the bag under the bed," Tad ordered Smollen. "That's the last time he'll show up here."

It was, too, for Igoe was one of the busiest little men in Benton Harbor in the time it took Dempsey to get ready for and dispose of Miske.

Directly across the hall from us was a room assigned to Sam Hall and Harry Hochstader, a worthy pair of Chicago writers. Early in the meeting, the room across the hall went on a twenty-four-hour schedule. If it were possible to have kept tab on it, I dare say more people were in and out of that room by day and by night than were present in the arena on the day of the fight.

Hochstader, who had an experimental turn of mind, came up with a great discovery. He learned that if one drank whisky and milk, life would be sustained suitably enough, and all the bothersome detail and time wasted in finding a place to eat, getting served, and eating could be eliminated. It was so ordered, and hour by hour the pile of milk and whisky bottles mounted in the room across the hall.

The presence of the fight so near Chicago caused a great influx of the "boys" from that city. Many and lurid were the tales of the operations of the dips on the common or garden variety of visiting fight fan. It wasn't strictly true that the streets of Benton Harbor were paved with stripped and discarded wallets. It just looked that way.

A few days before the fight there was a story in the Chicago papers of the mysterious disappearance of a freight car from one of the yards. Tiny Maxwell, Philadelphia writer, seized upon that. He said in his report that the pickpockets had finished their training. They were ready to put up the fight of their lives... regardless of how Dempsey and Miske were qualifying for their own test.

Benton Harbor was the home of the picturesque House of David sect, and in 1920 King Ben, the head of the place, was a notable figure. It did not take the writers long to catch up with him. Hochstader and Walter St. Denis, a New York writer, became very fond of King Ben. At one stage of the proceedings they were insisting that they would give up the sordid practice of journalism, grow beards, and join the House of David. Or maybe the proper order was join first and then grow the beard.

Damon Runyon, a bit of a skeptic, charged Hochstader and St. Denis with having designs on the emeralds that King Ben wore as shirt buttons, but the fact remains that before the visiting press had wearied of their exploitation of him, King Ben had done everything save put on the gloves with Dempsey to help give inspiration to a jaded journalist.

My roomie Tad was one of Dempsey's closest personal friends. He had exacted from the champion a promise to be presented after the fight with the belt Dempsey would wear into the ring. That ruffled Igoe's feelings a trifle, and Dempsey effected a compromise by promising Hype his bathrobe.

This was several days before the fight, and I had forgotten all about it by the time Miske was duly knocked out and practically all the literary lights had filed their stories.

A call came in from Western Union that Igoe's story had not cleared. So I set out on a search for Hype. I had last seen him, about a half hour before the fight, crawling under the ring, to escape, he said, the blistering heat of that Michigan afternoon. I was reasonably sure he was not still under the ring, even if he had dozed off, for the crash Miske made on hitting the floor would have awakened a much sounder sleeper than Igoe.

My first point to search was Dempsey's cottage. When I got there the champion was entertaining a few friends. Seated at the table, stripped to the waist, and with Dempsey's belt proudly wrapped around him, was Tad. He announced that his next defense of the title would be against Igoe.

"Where is he?" I wanted to know, and with a gesture Tad said, "In there."

"In there" turned out to be a bathroom. In a well-filled tub of water sat Igoe. Round and round his pudgy frame was wrapped the huge robe Dempsey had worn into the ring.

"I don't like to dry out too fast when I'm training," he explained. I told him the New York *World* was waiting, and he said it would be taken care of in due time. It was, too. For I took care of it myself.

That night in Benton Harbor was wilder by far than any of the not too quiet nights that had preceded it. Most of the visiting writers were going to leave next day and they decided to make the most of the adventure in one last fling.

The Hochstader-Hall room took on the aspects of Grand Central Station. The piles of milk and whisky bottles were now mountainous. The din was terrific.

For all of that, Tad, who was not in the best of physical condition, decided to fold up early. "Hype says he's coming home tonight," he said. "I told him I wanted to sleep and that we'd lock the door and admit no one except on signal. The signal is two quick raps and then a single knock."

Sleep with that bedlam across the hall seemed out of the question, but Tad did not seem to mind.

Long after midnight the noise in the Hochstader-Hall room seemed to grow more violent. One word led to another and presently the sounds of a general battle were heard. Those sounds were principally of crashing bottles and the thud of fists against jaw and body. In the midst of the furor there came two quick knocks and then a single at the door.

"Let me in," pleaded Igoe.

I was about to open the door when Tad ruled otherwise.

"We'll have that fight in here if we do," he said. So Igoe was left on the battlefield, whether eyewitness or combatant I have never known.

"Maybe we should get up," said Tad. "It sounds like a better fight than the one we covered."

Eventually an armistice was reached, and an appalling silence hung over the corridor. Presently from the street below could be heard a resumption of the noise. I went to the window and glanced out.

It seems that a market man was driving in early with a wagonload of produce, principally cantaloupes. The hardy warriors who had gone through the battle of the Hochstader-Hall room had commandeered the wagon and its contents.

With ample supplies of cantaloupes they were lined up on each side of the street, while individual members from each group attempted to run the gantlet of cantaloupe bombardment.

I suppose I should have gone down to find out how the score was kept and who won, but was stayed by Tad.

"Wait till they start throwing watermelons," he advised, "and then we'll both go down."

For a young man accustomed to the peace and quiet of San Francisco's water front, its Barbary Coast, its street railway strikes, and even its earthquake of 1906, Benton Harbor was an unforgettable experience.

In all of the other Dempsey camps, and those of other champions I have visited, there was never so much extra-curricular activity as at Benton Harbor, Atlantic City, and Shelby. Indeed, even Atlantic City lost something when Dempsey, Kearns, and their followers went away.

I returned there when Luis Angel Firpo was training for his memorable fight with Dempsey, but can round up just two unrelated sets of circumstances as worthy of inclusion in this record.

Ford Frick, now the National League's able president, but then a fellow workman of mine under the William Randolph Hearst banner, made the trip with me, and we neglected to make any advance reservations. We knew the manager of the Hotel Traymore and were sure he would take care of us. He told us to check our bags and come back later.

We came back, much later. After midnight, in fact. The manager had kept his word. Our room was ready, we were told. The bellboy took us to the topmost floor, and as we stepped out of the elevator there we beheld the grand ballroom. Far out in its center, almost a full brassie shot from the elevators, we saw two beds. There was a small stand beside them, with towels, basin, pitcher of water, and soap. That was our "room." While some may challenge my statement that I encountered the world's most crowded hotel bedroom at Benton Harbor, there is no doubt at all that Frick and I slept one night in the world's largest bedroom . . . while in pursuit of the elusive training-camp story.

In those early twenties it was customary for the heavyweight champion and his challengers to have by-line stories that sometimes had wide circulation. For obvious reasons ghost writers were assigned to this detail.

This practice was not exclusive to the fight game. Baseball managers and players whose by-lines were of circulation value all had their ghost writers. Ford Frick, for instance, was "by Babe Ruth" for a long stretch. Frank Menke was perhaps the most prolific ghost of 'em all. All sorts of sport figures were under his literary spirit control.

I myself overdid it in a world's series between Yankees and Cubs, when Christy Walsh, who had the world's largest stable of ghosts, prevailed upon me to be both "by Charlie Grimm" and "by Joe McCarthy" in the same series.

Luis Angel Firpo's ghost writer for the Dempsey fight was William Slavens McNutt, a noted magazine writer who insisted upon being in character at all times. While he served for Firpo, Bill McNutt tried his darndest to look and dress like a native of the Argentine.

I have always thought that Firpo's "own" story of the fight with Dempsey was one of the most remarkable ever written. At the finish the Wild Bull of the Pampas was stretched on the floor, utterly unconscious from the fearful beating Dempsey gave him, but at that very instant all over the land there was ticking into newspaper offices the first words of his own exclusive story. Those ghost writers were a resourceful lot, and McNutt was at the very top.

Going toward the fight, I was of the opinion that McNutt, with a little more training and perhaps a slight trim of those gaucho sideburns, might have been able to lick Firpo himself. After I had seen the Wild Bull propel the one and only Dempsey right through the ropes and on to the typewriter of a ringside reporter, I changed my mind. Maybe Bill McNutt would have needed a lot more training.

I have never changed my mind about that three-point landing Dempsey made on the ringside typewriter. After the fifth writer had announced it was *his* machine that was used for a landing field, I was willing to pretend that Dempsey had never left the ring at all. It is much less confusing that way.

The last Dempsey camp I ever visited for long was the one in northern New York at which he prepared for his bout with Jack Sharkey, in between the two engagements with Gene Tunney. That camp produced but one item worthy of remembrance, and that implicated Dempsey but indirectly.

Dave Shade, then grown to great stature in the prize ring, was one of Dempsey's sparring partners. The day I dropped in, Dave and I sat down to lunch. He said that he was not going to work, so he packed in a full-course meal and lit a huge cigar afterward. He was just preparing for a gab fest when he was notified that Dempsey wanted him to spar two rounds.

Shade took his departure and I wandered out to watch the workouts. Presently Shade appeared in ring togs, still puffing away at the cigar. As he prepared to go to the center of the ring, he bent over and placed the cigar carefully on the edge of the platform. Then he proceeded to speed his way around and about Dempsey until the round ended. The cigar was still going, so between rounds Shade puffed it some more. It was burning briskly at the end of his second and last round, and off he went in the direction of the training room, cigar smoke trailing behind him.

I considered that a better story of the day's doings than a routine report on how Dempsey looked or a few hundred words of expert deduction on his chances with Sharkey.

CHAPTER 14

"When I Played for McGraw..."

*I*T was at a training camp of another sort in the spring of 1923 that I had my first opportunity to play ball for John McGraw and Hughey Jennings. They were manager and coach of the New York Giants, and I had gone with them to San Antonio, where the Giants were to train. As was customary, a large delegation of sports writers followed them, for McGraw's men were truly Giants in those days.

One day a San Antonio newspaperman wanted to know if we New York writers had guts enough to get up a team to play the local writers.

We probably didn't, but the defi was issued in the presence of McGraw and Jennings, two throwbacks to baseball's rough and ready days, so we didn't dare say that we didn't care to play baseball, but preferred to write about it, and please go away and let us bask in the Texas sunshine.

McGraw accepted the challenge for us, and said that he and Jennings would manage our team.

That's what he thought....

We lacked a catcher, but the San Antonio scribes graciously consented to let us borrow a Giant rookie whose name was Kernan, a Yale man, no less.

George "Monitor" Daley said he was a pitcher, and there was none to dispute him, not even Bob Boyd, who had lost his left arm in World War I, and who *had* pitched ... and still could. I was the first baseman. Fred Lieb, a veteran writer, was the second baseman, and came equipped with a glove that must have been a holdover from "Pop" Anson's day. Lieb was left-handed. Our shortstop was "Bugs" Baer, also left-handed. Our third baseman was Will Wedge, who wasn't, but should have been, left-handed. Boyd, one-armed, played left. Frank Graham played center. Harry Cross, weaving and bobbing after a bad night, played right.

And McGraw used to think he had troubles with "Bugs" Raymond!

By some hocus-pocus, we, the visitors, went to bat last. McGraw couldn't understand that, and I could see that he was beginning to worry a little. Maybe he should have kept his mouth closed.

The locals, who may have rung in all the semipros in town for all we knew, lit on George "Monitor" Daley. His fast ball would not have made a window curtain sway by landing against it. Five or six runs came in hurriedly.

McGraw was giving us hell from the bench. A local came to bat and hit a pop fly a half mile in the air. It looked to Bugs Baer at shortstop as if it were coming down in his territory. He took no chances. He ran as fast as he could out into center field beyond Graham, threw himself on the ground, and dug in until the emergency was over.

But he couldn't escape the sound of McGraw's voice. None of us could.

The next batter hit a drooping line drive at Lieb. Our gallant second baseman moved boldly toward it and put up his hands. The ball missed them by at least two feet and thudded off his chest.

That was all for McGraw and Jennings. Just then, anyhow. . . .

It was also all for our starting pitcher. Boyd replaced him and retired the side quickly.

It took us two innings to overtake the locals, but we made it finally, owing largely to a homer by Kernan with the bases filled, which put us a run ahead.

As we went out onto the field, no one stopped at his position. All kept on walking until the exit gate was reached.

The taunts of our foes followed us, but we were a determined lot in those days, and most sensible. We knew when we had enough.

But we still had to reckon with McGraw. He was waiting for us at the hotel, and one by one he singled us out. His theme was much the same with all of us. We were the guys, he said, who liked to take typewriter in hand and tell him and his ball players what they were doing wrong. "You should know," he said, "because there wasn't a one of you did anything right out there today. Baseball experts, my eye!"

But when we told him of the outcome of the "game" and how we had snatched victory from the very jaws of defeat, he brightened considerably. He was sorry he had not stayed. We were men after his own heart.

"I never want to see any of you play ball again," he said, "but I'll buy you all dinner and the drinks."

Being McGraw, he did just that.

I have presented this interlude in a sports reporter's life on the off chance that my teammates, much as I, may have found occasion from time to time to say to their children or even their grandchildren in an offhand way, "Now, when I played for McGraw . . ."

These were the years in which the Giants and the Yankees were winning the major-league pennants every season, and the world's series was strictly a subway proposition. For a time, before the Yankee Stadium arose, both clubs played in the Polo Grounds, and it was in that setting I enjoyed baseball writing as a steady diet.

In those days the press coop was directly behind the plate at the ground level. It was thus close enough to the action so that its occupants could not only see but hear much that went on in the dugouts as well as on the field. In later years the press coop was moved back and up, and in some of the major-league parks the writers are so far away from the field even a public address system has trouble in getting to them with essential information.

That nearness to the action made Polo Grounds press-box occupants accurate witnesses to such incidents as the brush between the Giants' catcher Earl Smith and the Yankee outfielder Bobby Meusel in one of the world's series games. They had words while Meusel was at the plate, words that could be heard, but most of which could not be printed.

Meusel got on base and eventually worked his way around to third. He called in to Smith that he was coming in on the next pitch. He did, too, sliding spikes high, wide, and flashing. Only Smith wasn't there. By sheer coincidence he had a passed ball on the pitch.

I enjoyed my stay in the New York press coops as much as any I've ever inhabited, but my stay was not to be too long. In the fall of 1923 I was called into executive session and notified that I was to move to Chicago and join the forces of another of the Hearst properties there.

That was all right with me. It still is.

My arrival took place a few days before the national amateur golf championship was to be decided at Flossmoor.

The publisher of the *Herald Examiner,* George Buckley, was an avowed golfer. He allowed that it might be nice if my first writing efforts for the paper would be on the subject of the golf championship.

That was just dandy. I had known vaguely that there was such a game as golf, had a working knowledge of the famous figures in it, and knew that it was not played on horseback. But that let me out. I explained as much to Buckley.

"I am going to play a round with Grantland Rice Sunday," he said. "Why don't you come out and follow us around? Grant's the best golf writer there is and I'm sure he'll give you enough ideas to get you by."

Which is exactly what Rice did. Off and on, these many years, that grand gentleman of our profession has given many another fellow workman tips that were helpful in his daily chore. I exclude, I hasten to add, Grant's tips on the big horse races, a consideration of which (the races, not the tips) we'll get around to later. In that eternal battle with the pari-mutuels my code has ever been that of every man for himself, bury your own dead, return with your shield or on it, and words to that effect.

At the Chicago Golf Club, out near Wheaton, I saw my first golf match one Sunday afternoon.

While engaged in gallerying, I struck up conversation with one of the caddies. Somehow we got around to a discussion of football. I discussed knowingly the Yales and the Harvards, Bo McMillan, Red Roberts, and Centre College, all the teams I had seen in the East the previous season, and managed to get in a few plugs for Andy Smith, Brick Muller, Pesky Sprott, Crip Toomey, Pop Warner, and all my other heroes of the immediate or distant past.

The caddy was very polite. He heard me out before he did much talking. Then he said, "Wait till you get down to Illinois. They have one of our boys down there this year. His name's Red Grange. Wait till you see him go. I think it was George Dawson who got him to go there. Dawson's a golfer," explained the caddy. "So's his brother Johnny."

"What does this Grange do?" I asked the caddy.

"What does he do?" he repeated. "He *runs!*"

I'll say Red Grange ran, but before I do say it, I must be on about the business of my first golf tournament.

Rice, my custodian, did not let me stray too far from him at Flossmoor. He introduced me to many of the more famous players, and two of them, the golfing immortals Chick Evans of Chicago and Francis Ouimet of Boston, I number among my dearest friends.

It became very evident to me that I was not cut out for a technician in golf writing. My only hope was to try to pry loose some of the human element. Rice thought that might be wise. He was probably influenced by the fact that I couldn't tell a No. 4 iron from a spoon, and didn't show the proper willingness to learn.

Besides, there were too many men in motion, too much to keep up with. There were too many galleryites dashing around and about striving to get to a point of vantage. Golf in its tournament stage is essentially a war of movement, and I'm definitely on the sedentary side.

Perhaps that's how I happened to uncover my first golf story, which my publisher thought was a bit of all right.

I was standing far from the surging mob that was crowding around a green on which one member of a then unidentified twosome was preparing to putt. Between me and the crowd, and perhaps twenty-five yards away, a newspaper cameraman had set up a very high stepladder. He mounted this and prepared to take a telescopic shot of the scene before him.

That was the general idea. But the golfer who was lining up his putt stopped suddenly and consulted with the scorer. There was a general turning of that crowd in our direction, and presently a marshal came loping across the sward and made the cameraman get down off his ladder.

It seemed that he was distracting the man who was lining up the putt.

It took a bit of research on my part to find out who that fussy golfer was, but I made it. He may have been a fussy golfer, but in that tournament, by the end of the week, they paid off on him. It was Max Marston, the 1923 amateur champion, who was allergic to cameramen...and ladders.

By the end of my first tournament, I was an established golf writer. For many years thereafter I had fun in covering major tournaments the country over. Always I adhered to the principle that the golfers who were interesting in their off-course moments were the ones to trail when the championship rounds were in full swing.

Many are the delightful moments I have spent in the company of Bobby Jones, of Evans, of Ouimet, of George Von Elm, and others of the ranking amateurs. I have found many of the British Walker Cup competitors most interesting characters.

I have trailed golfers in all parts of the country, and have seen them in their greatest triumphs and their heartbreaking defeats. In no other sport have I ever met up with any more interesting characters than Walter Hagen, Tommy Armour, Gene Sarazen, Bobby Cruickshank, Macdonald Smith, Billy Burke, Al Watrous, and their contemporaries among the professionals.

I have been told in these later years that the game of golf especially in its professional aspect, has improved tremendously. I have been shown remarkably low scores to prove it. That has been the wrong approach, for me. Scores and course records in my golf writing were never more than incidental. What got me was the personalities, the men who were good for a different story every time you met up with them.

I don't think the current field, whatever its course record-breaking propensities, will assay that high in my critical analysis. Perhaps that is why all I have known about golf in recent years is what I read in the papers.

If that last line is reminiscent of Will Rogers, let me say it was used with due deliberation, for Damon Runyon and I were the medium for getting him to take his first look at a golf competition. It was the occasion of the first Los Angeles Open championship, the leading feature of the winter season.

It wound up in a brilliant battle between Von Elm and Harry Cooper, with Cooper winning. It was understood that Runyon was to present the winner with his trophy, and in the case of the professional, his check. Rogers said he would risk his life to come out on a golf course to hear Runyon's presentation speech.

The final round was well under way before Rogers appeared suddenly beside Runyon and me, who were gallerying. Von Elm was about to putt when Rogers hailed us joyously and quite audibly.

A chorus of "Shhh!" and a barrage of frowns were directed at him.

"What's the matter?" Rogers asked, still in a fairly loud tone.

"Fore!" cried an aroused marshal. "Silence!"

In a whisper, Runyon explained that the code of golf called for cathedral silences while men were playing.

"What kind of ball game is this, that you can't yell at the players?" Rogers wanted to know. Runyon and I led him away from there, lest all three of us be strung to the nearest tree by an irate gallery marshal.

The fame of Rogers as a master of all the entertainment arts, and of Runyon in prose and verse, is well enough established to need no further mention here. But it occurs to me that the side of Runyon the public speaker has never been properly exploited.

I hasten to make amends.

Cooper, the winner, having changed his playing costume for one even snappier, advanced to the clubhouse veranda before the enthusiastic crowd and prepared to accept his trophy.

Runyon, the greatest public speaker of all time, picked up the check from the table, turned to Cooper, and with all the requisite solemnity said, "Congratulations, young man. Here's your dough."

Would that the scores of other public speakers to whom I have had to listen, or whom I have had to present, were able to say it all so forcefully!

CHAPTER 15

Red Grange Runs

ONE of the many reasons that had made me eager to establish a base of operations in Chicago was that this city was in the heart of the Western Conference territory, and not too far away from South Bend, where Knute Rockne's Notre Dame football teams were beginning to make football history.

My observation of Western Conference play until then had been limited to a view of Dr. Jack Wilce's Ohio State team being soundly beaten by California at Pasadena on New Year's Day, 1921, and of Howard Jones's Iowans defeating brother Tad's Yale team at New Haven early in the 1922 season. Now I was to have the chance to see these important teams as often as I desired, schedules permitting.

In order to get the proper background I went on a pre-season tour of the Western Conference, and made a start with Illinois. I was warmly greeted by L. M. "Mike" Tobin, the public relations man. Before going out to the practice field where Bob Zuppke was drilling his charges, Tobin began a recital of facts and figures on the squad.

I remembered the caddy at the Chicago Golf Club and his man, Red Grange.

"What about Grange?" I asked Tobin.

"I thought you just arrived from New York a little while ago," Tobin said. "Don't tell me they've heard about him there already."

I explained the source of my information.

"I think maybe that caddy is right," said Tobin, "but wait till you see Red and talk with Zup."

I saw Red first. I didn't really have to talk to Zup . . . although I did, and have always been happy to do so. He is one of the most interesting conversationalists I have ever known.

I do not pretend to be psychic. I don't believe any sports writer is, otherwise he'd give up work and do nothing but play the horses. But one long look at Red Grange that first day on the practice field at Illinois was enough for me.

Once in a great while you run across an athlete or a personality you see for the first time and know you will never forget. Jack Dempsey was one. Ty Cobb was another. Joe Louis is in that category. So are Babe Ruth, Walter Hagen, Bobby Jones. Cornelius Warmerdam, the pole vaulter, Willie Hoppe, Jesse Owen, the track star, Joe McCarthy, Jim Farley, Jimmy Walker, Colonel Matt J. Winn, Jim Coffroth, Will Rogers, Bing Crosby, Al Jolson, Damon Runyon, and Tad all belong to that select field. So do Knute Rockne and Kenesaw M. Landis.

You sensed at sight that they were champions. You sensed that they would be no less, no matter under what circumstances you might ever glimpse them again. They would never let you down.

I went overboard on Grange and wrote a story about what I thought he would do for the football fortunes of Illinois. After seeing it in print, I suspected that some would think I had exaggerated his prospects. Before his last collegiate course was run and he had trotted off the field into the management of C. C. Pyle and ultimately into the Chicago Bears backfield, what I wrote that day, by contrast with what others wrote later, was downright conservative. But the record will show that I was first past the post with the adjectives decriptive of the young man who has had the most remarkable collegiate football career of anyone I have ever witnessed.

Those who know me have said at times that I have marked leanings toward Notre Dame. It is true that I was one of

didn't know their stuff. But let's see what the guy will do *next* time. Michigan kicked to him again.

Grange was sixty-seven yards from Michigan's goal when he got that one. He was behind Michigan's goal when he put the ball down. Six more points for Grange.

Maybe the guy is good, thought Michigan. But let's see what he'll do when a Michigan man hits him. Let's see if he can take it.

Michigan kicked to Grange once more. Not quite as lengthy a kick as the first two, which is the best reason why this touchdown runback was of but fifty-seven yards. Six more points for Grange.

I'll give Michigan credit for one thing. Its men and its coaches were stubborn. They still wanted to see what Grange would do once he was in the grasp of an opponent. Maybe the Michigan kicker was getting weary by this time of booting the ball with such disastrous results. His effort went out to a point just forty-five yards from the Michigan goal line. That's how it happened that Grange's fourth touchdown needed the shortest sprint of all.

But twelve minutes of playing time had elapsed in the first quarter and Grange had accumulated four touchdowns, or twenty-four points. In his great days at the turn of the century, Yost's Michigan teams were wont to operate on a point-a-minute basis. But here was a young man who was twice that good. He was making two points a minute, and for all Michigan seemed able to do about it, he might have kept it up. But Coach Zuppke was a merciful man. After twelve minutes and twenty-four points, he took Grange from the game, amid the greatest ovation I have ever heard given a football player on any field.

Grange was to return later and score again, this time on a fifteen-yard dash around end, but long before that his place in collegiate football history for all time had been assured. Michigan had not laid a detaining hand upon him as he raced into football immortality.

It was with the plaudits of press and public ringing in his

ears that Grange went to Chicago, where the Illini were to take on Stagg's Maroons.

No one talked much about anything but Grange and his exploits. And no one ever prepared more soundly for his reception than did Amos Alonzo Stagg.

At that stage of his Chicago existence the "Old Man" had some material of his own. For the purpose of cramping the Illini style, Stagg decided on the axiom that the best defense is a whirlwind offense. In that, he followed the philosophy of Knute Rockne, who would tell you, if you asked, that he never saw one football team score when the other side had the ball.

Stagg was willing to concede that Grange was wonderful, as his average of nearly ten yards for every time he carried the ball that season seemed to indicate. But to average ten yards against Chicago, Red must first get that ball.

Chicago took the ball on the kickoff, and with fullback McCarty, on whom I had hung the tag "Five Yards," plunging steadily forward, the Maroons moved downfield until the four-yard line was reached, where the ball was lost on a fumble. Britton kicked Illinois out of that jam, but McCarty, Harry Thomas, and Co. came on and on again, and this time were not to be denied. "Five Yards" McCarty eventually went over for the touchdown, to which Bob Curley added the extra point.

Illinois kicked off to Chicago and once more the Maroons surged forward, not being halted, and presently Thomas scored. For variety's sake Curley passed for the extra point.

Chicago 14, Illinois 0. Grange had not yet carried the ball.

But be patient. Chicago kicked off. The Ghost didn't run it back for a touchdown. But he did everything else. He ran and he passed and the Maroons couldn't do a thing about it, not until the score was Chicago 14, Illinois 7.

Then Chicago did something. It went right out and scored again, made the extra point, and led 21 to 7.

Now, here was the test for which the football world was

waiting. Was Grange one of those front runners? Or was he one who could come from far back, when things looked roughest, and still go on to win? He could. He did. Before the second period ended, on one of Zuppke's dipsy-doo plays, which Stagg described as a "quadruple pass," Grange moved into position to score, and did so on the next play.

Now Illinois was within a touchdown of tying the score. Grange took care of that in due time, galloping something like eighty yards to help get the game tied up. It stayed that way, which was fair enough. The Ghost had come through his severest test like a true champion.

Grange was All-American by acclamation for the second time at the end of his junior year. He was known and had been seen throughout the Middle West. He had been heard of elsewhere, but in the East, where football began, they still didn't believe all they had been hearing. They had to be shown. It was the old vaudeville principle of it not mattering how you might have laid 'em in the aisles on the Orpheum Circuit, or on any other part of Keith's. Until you played the Palace on Broadway, you didn't belong.

So Grange and the Illini went to Pennsylvania, where an admittedly fine football team and a very muddy Franklin Field awaited them.

In the stands were all the great experts of the East, waiting to be shown. Red Grange showed 'em.

Illinois made four touchdowns, mud or no mud. Made them quickly and deftly. Three of them were Grange's. He covered sixty, fifty-five, and fifteen yards on his scoring romps. Wet track or dry, it made no difference to the Galloping Ghost.

After that, what we supposedly overenthusiastic Middle Westerners had been writing about Grange paled into insignificance when those easterners cut loose.

For the balance of his collegiate career, until he ran off the field following his closing effort against Ohio State, Grange on the football field or on the printed page gained more yardage than any of all the famous players who had preceded him.

It was inevitable that his postcollegiate services would be in demand. Somewhere along the line he had joined up with C. C. Pyle, a promotional-minded character who had some of the attributes of Jack Kearns, of Larry MacPhail, and of Tex Rickard, with quite a few that were peculiarly his own.

Pyle led Grange into a tremendous lot of money, and eventually the turn of fortune's wheel led them both out of most of it, but that was simply the luck of the draw. There were not too many regrets on either side.

In his own good time, because he was inherently a champion, Grange struck a balance. He was a most effective professional for many years with the Chicago Bears. He has been more than moderately successful in business and in the radio world. He has never been a disappointment to me, who wrote about him first. Or rather, he has never been a lasting disappointment. He did elude me once, and that was in his final year as a collegian.

I had proposed to him that he take up a job as a football expert for the Hearst papers, and he was offered what seemed an attractive sum to do so. He was urged to accept by George Huff, the athletic director of Illinois, and by many influential members of the alumni, none of whom were elated over the prospect of his tie-up with Pyle.

For a while I thought I had Red in my grasp, but eventually he slipped away. I have taken consolation in the fact that mine was not the only attempted tackle that had missed Red Grange.

I never did find out what Mr. Hearst thought about it.

CHAPTER 16

Rambles with Rockne

*I*N between pursuits of Red Grange and his story content, I was able to cultivate a friendship with Knute Rockne of Notre Dame, whose memory is one of those I shall cherish longest.

In one setting or another I have met practically all the football coaches who have been of any consequence in the last thirty years. I have yet to meet any other one who had the hold on the public's imagination that Rockne did.

He was a most successful operator in football. But he might have been as much a success in the business or in the entertainment world. His influence on football, the people who coached it, who played it, who made rules for it, who wrote and talked about it, was greater than that of any other man before him or after him.

In his playing days, before I knew him, as the receiver of a football thrown by his teammate Gus Dorais, Rockne had been able to make the country conscious of the potency of the forward pass. Now, I am sure that there must have been others who had a way with the pass. It had been in vogue several years before Rockne and Dorais cut loose with it against Army on the plains at West Point. Yet I believe there are a great many people abroad in the land who assume that Rockne discovered the forward pass.

Rockne had not been at his coaching long, succeeding Jesse Harper, when he came up with the first of several outstanding teams. This was the one that featured the immortal George Gipp, considered by many to be the rarest individual performer who ever played at Notre Dame, and possibly anywhere else.

After that Rockne marked time until he assembled the rugged line and the perfectly co-ordinated backs who went undefeated through the 1924 season. These were the Four Horsemen. When their regular season was completed, they accepted a bid to appear in the Rose Bowl against Glenn Warner's Stanford team, a powerful organization built around Ernie Nevers, fullback.

In surveying the football and the football players of his very lengthy stay in the game, "Pop" Warner once characterized Nevers as the greatest player he had ever coached, placing him ahead of Jim Thorpe, the Carlisle Indian. There is no doubt but that Nevers was great while at Stanford, and later on as a professional. He gained great gobs of yardage against Notre Dame in that Rose Bowl game, but somehow the "Seven Mules," as the line was called, or the line backers always managed to stop him when he was touchdown bound.

Nevers was so much the outstanding player on the field that he did some of Notre Dame's work, too. Two of his passes were intercepted by Elmer Layden, and both were carried across for touchdowns as Notre Dame piled up a 27-to-10 victory.

Pop Warner was very petulant after the game. He reviewed all the first downs Stanford had made and all the yards it had gained. Then he looked at the final score. He stormed through interviews in which he insisted that a new scoring system should be adopted whereby a team would get full credit for its first downs and yardage.

By this time Rockne and his team had left the scene and started back home by way of San Francisco. Rockne and his family remained over for a few days there, and so did I.

On the train from Los Angeles to San Francisco halfback Jimmy Crowley was stricken ill, and he was hospitalized for a few days before returning to Notre Dame. Rockne did not want to leave until he was certain that Crowley was coming around in good style. When he did take off for Chicago, Warner had preceded us into the east and the papers were filled with his new plan for keeping track of good deeds in a football game by giving credit for first downs and yardage gained.

If Rockne had heard about this before, he made no mention of it. On the train, however, he read a lengthy account of Warner's plan. When the train reached Ogden, a Press Association writer came aboard to ask if Rockne had anything to say about the Warner plan.

"Sure," said Rockne, "but I'll not say it until they start giving baseball victories to the teams that have the most men left on base."

In the years that have passed since Rockne's time, you may have heard, as I did, that this story originated with Crowley, by long odds the most gifted public speaker of all the Notre Dame football figures after Rockne. But the circumstances that I have related represent the accurate origin of that one.

It was inevitable that while Red Grange was doing his stuff at Illinois and the Four Horsemen were racing to football fame, there would be the urge to have the two meet on the field of play. That they didn't was not for lack of trying on the part of the gentlemen of the press, especially those who were covering a Western Conference schedule meeting in Chicago.

I yield to no one in appreciation of the remarkable qualities Grange and the Four Horsemen had for getting from where they were to where they wanted to be with a minimum of effort. But I also want to give full credit to Bob Zuppke and Rockne for at least one splendid day-long demonstration of artful dodging. They were great, too.

Charley Dunkley of the Associated Press, Walter Eckersall of the Chicago *Tribune,* and I sounded out Rockne on the possibilities of Notre Dame's playing Illinois during the 1924 season.

"Sure, we'll play them," said Rockne.

The interviewers then went in search of Zuppke.

He was willing, he said. In fact, he was delighted that someone had thought of it.

"What dates has Rockne open?" asked Zuppke. The interviewers had forgotten to ask that, but promised to go find out and return.

They were unable to find Rockne, and so reported shamefully to Zuppke. Much later in the day Rockne turned up again, and the committee asked him about dates, saying that Zup was willing, if a suitable Saturday was available.

Rockne listed his dates, and off went the committee to find Zuppke. But he had disappeared. The run-around went on from there, gaining momentum with each passing hour.

We three newspapermen realized that these were very busy men, Rockne and Zuppke, and were inclined to be tolerant about it. But it did seem that the game should be scheduled at once, since both coaches were willing—or said they were, even if not to each other.

To this day, it seems that the game should have been played. Everybody wanted it. Everybody, that is, but Rockne and Zuppke. Getting those two coaches together was as difficult as stopping Grange or the Four Horsemen.

Of all Rockne's teams that passed in review before me, I rate at the top his 1929 and 1930 squads. They were undefeated. They played through harder schedules, for the most part, than any previous Notre Dame team attempted. They had tremendous size and mobility. They were nifty when they had to be, and they could turn on power when that was indicated. They went crashing through two seasons of terrific play, and had the country at large raving about their individuals as well as their team activity. They ranged through the land defeating everything in sight. Their backs, Frank Carideo, Marchmont Schwartz, and Jack Elder, Marty Brill, Joe Savoldi, Larry Mullins, and the most sensational one-game star of them all, Bucky O'Connor, proved their worth

Saturday after Saturday as they went through Rockne's plays, making friends and influencing people.

The O'Connor day in the sun took place at the Coliseum in Los Angeles. It was the closing game of the 1930 season, and against a most potent Southern California team.

It was—though none knew it at the time—to be the last time Rockne would ever send a Notre Dame team on the field, for his untimely death occurred a few months later.

Notre Dame at the start of the season had been well equipped with fullbacks. By degrees, they went out of action. Savoldi left school. Mullins carried on famously until he was hurt. That put the job up to Dan Hanley, a comparatively inexperienced lad. This was the situation as Notre Dame left for Los Angeles to meet one of the strongest of the many great teams Howard Jones ever produced at Southern California.

On the Notre Dame squad Bucky O'Connor had some standing as a right halfback, as much as anyone might be able to get considering that he was outranked by Brill, one of the greatest blocking backs of all time. O'Connor was experienced and very fast. Rockne decided on the noble experiment of making a fullback out of him for that final game.

This was a closely guarded secret. On the train Frank Wallace, magazine writer and Notre Dame alumnus, J. P. McEvoy, ditto, and I were seated in a compartment talking with Rockne when O'Connor, laden with charts and diagrams, stuck his head in the door and asked the coach if he was ready. Rockne excused himself and left us sitting there telling lies to each other for perhaps an hour before he returned and closed the door.

"I have a problem," he said, "and maybe you fellows can give me the answer. What I tell you now is in the strictest confidence. I intend to use O'Connor at fullback Saturday. I am quite sure Southern California doesn't know about it. I am hoping they will not find out until the game starts. But we are to work out in Tucson. Los Angeles newspapermen

are there. They are my friends. They are always welcome.
I never have worked behind barred gates, and I'm not going
to now. How can I keep them from writing about O'Connor,
once they see him?"

All our great intellects went to work on that one.

Wallace and I arrived at a solution finally. We both knew
the Los Angeles newspaper delegation quite well, and how
they would react to direction.

"You like to gamble on plays, don't you, Rock?" asked
Wallace.

Rockne said that he did.

"Well, how about this one? . . ."

Whereupon the Wallace-Brown-Rockne sneaker was dia-
grammed and put into the Tucson practice repertoire.

It was really a very simple play, after all. It consisted in
putting Hanley's jersey on O'Connor and O'Connor's jersey
on Hanley. O'Connor then took his place with the first string
and worked out all over the place at Tucson.

The Los Angeles delegation that awaited Notre Dame's
arrival was taken out to the field. It was furnished with the
names and numbers of all the players. It was permitted to
take as many pictures as it wanted. The gamble consisted in
taking a chance that one of the company might recognize
O'Connor by sight rather than by number. None did, and if
Bucky's picture appeared in Los Angeles papers before the
game under the name of Hanley, in a group with Carideo,
Schwartz, and Brill, no great harm was done.

When his picture appeared *after* the game, it was under
the name O'Connor, and I don't think Southern California
will ever forget him.

Notre Dame took charge of the Trojans from the start of
the game, and things were moving right along and favorably
when one of Carideo's kicks cleared the head of the Southern
California safety man. He raced back after it, turned, and saw
a flock of Fighting Irish closing in on him. Then the Trojan
lad performed a heroic deed. Instead of attempting to run,

he drew back his foot and booted the ball. It went far down the field, rolled on and on, and ultimately came to rest in the Notre Dame end zone.

Thus the ball that had been dangerously close to Southern California's goal line seconds before now went into play on the Notre Dame twenty-yard line. The Trojan adherents made the stands rock with their expression of approval for that sensational recovery.

Carideo, the brilliant and unruffled field general, barked his signal. The ball came back to O'Connor. On his way swept Bucky, through, around, and past all the Trojans, to race unmolested eighty yards for the touchdown that blew Southern California apart. The final score was 27 to 0.

I never got around to ask Rockne what play, of all the spectacular ones his boys had turned in, gave him the biggest thrill. I suspect that he might have named O'Connor's run, all things considered.

Rockne's skill as a coach went beyond the fundamentals of football offense and defense. He had a way with him that caused his charges at times to play even beyond their capabilities. The stories that have been told of his dressing-room exhortations are many and varied.

I do not think that they had as much effect on the players as the legend would have it. Too often have I heard members of his squad, even while they were members, sounding off with imitations of the "Old Man" pep-talking his troops about to go into battle. Too often have I heard Rockne himself scoffing about this form of mass hypnotism to believe that he ever took it very seriously himself, or expected his players to do so.

It was Rockne who popularized the yarn about the coach who delivered a pregame talk to his troops about to go into the Big Game. The talk was given in the dressing room behind closed doors.

"As the coach poured it on, the emotions of his squad were whipped into a fine frenzy," Rockne said.

"The coach finished with a stirring 'Now, men, go out there and *fight!*'

"As one man, the squad tore at the nearest door, broke through it ... and every darn one of them landed in the swimming tank!"

CHAPTER 17

"Six Points or Nothing!"

*I*N establishing his place among the football coaches in
history, Rockne's influence was tremendous on his players,
not only while they were directly in his charge, but after they
had graduated.

A great many of them became coaches and installed the
Notre Dame or Rockne system in college and high-school
teams throughout the country. Many of them, launched on
their own careers, soon took their place with the foremost
of the coaches. But always, in his lifetime, they looked to
Rockne for advice and guidance.

It was he who had a way of locating coaching assignments
for them, and if one job blew up, it would not be long before
Rockne had spotted another. He was a great salesman. In
this manner grew a system that, until the more modern,
streamlined version of the T formation with the man in
motion came along, furnished both collegiate and professional football with its most uniformly pleasing presentation.

Rockne was always experimenting with new plays and
new evolutions, though his system remained basically the
same. When a rival coach was able to prove against Notre
Dame that there was a great deal to be said for the spinner
plays, Rockne did not hesitate at all about adapting spinners
to his own repertoire.

He may not have been the creative genius that Warner
was, or Stagg was, or Yost and Zuppke were. But there was
never a time that he did not know what football stuff was

best suited for the material that came his way. That was his chief concern.

He was a perfectionist. He was not as persistent in attention to the minutest detail as is Frank Leahy, his most successful pupil. He had a system of finding out whether certain types of plays would work before he included them in his own book of offense.

When he met up with a new series of plays, he would have one of his many pupils around the country try them out, either in practice or in actual competition. If they worked, Rockne would adopt them. If they didn't, that was the end of it. He thrived on success. In some respects he followed the reasoning of the first great editor for whom I worked, Fremont Older of San Francisco.

One day in discussing the subject of crusades with Older, who was of the crusading type if the newspaper field has ever known one, he let me in partly on his system.

"Never start a crusade you can't win," he said.

With Rockne that might have been paraphrased into: "Never try anything that will not work."

Many of Rockne's more spectacular accomplishments were made through plays that were basically simple enough, but became a menace to opponents by sheer perfection of execution. Often in company with Walter Eckersall, I listened to that all-time great quarterback expound that "any play, perfectly executed, is a potential touchdown." With Rockne, every play his quarterbacks called had that in mind. With him, it was six points or nothing. It always has been at Notre Dame, since Rockne's time, and field-goal attempts or completions have been few and far between.

When Notre Dame and Army met at the Polo Grounds in 1947, both undefeated, there came a time when the Irish moved within scoring range. Doc Blanchard, Glenn Davis, and Co. of West Point checked what seemed to be a relentless touchdown drive. The second guessers, realizing that Notre Dame had on its bench a goal-kicking specialist in Fred Early, professed to wonder why a field-goal attempt was not made, inasmuch as the game wound up in a scoreless tie. Those that wondered did not know, apparently, that one of the many things Coach Frank Leahy learned from Rockne was that "six points or nothing" plank which is a component part of the Notre Dame platform.

Because of their being relatively uncommon, it may be that a field goal by which Marty Peters was able to win for Notre Dame over Pittsburgh, in the post-Rockne era, comes to mind just now. Or perhaps it is because of a story that goes with it, a story once told me by a president of the University of Notre Dame, Reverend Matthew Walsh, C.S.C.

There is a legend that all over the country when Notre Dame's football teams go into action, people are praying for victory. (It may not be as much legend as fact.)

So, the story goes, when Peters, who had never before made a public attempt at a field goal, prepared for his historic effort against Pittsburgh, the ball was at a bad angle. Peters drew back his foot and booted the ball high in the air, but his sense of direction seemed to be very bad.

The ball, goes the story, was sailing for the goal line, many yards to the right of the posts. It did not seem possible that it would turn the trick. Just then a wave of Hail Marys hit it. The ball, curving gently, arched between the uprights, and Notre Dame had won another.

I think Rockne would have liked that story.

He was one of the best of all the storytellers, in a field in which every football coach has to tell 'em at pep meetings, at gatherings of the alumni, at luncheons and banquets and on the radio.

As his many pupils put into practice all Rockne's plays, so most of them adopted his stories. Some of them even adopted his mannerisms and his tones and technique of delivery.

In Rockne's time there was never much question who had told a football story first. The problem was always who was going to tell it for the last time.

Christy Walsh, the newspaper syndicate man, prevailed

upon Rockne to go literary in the midst of his coaching career. The Notre Dame coach was combined with Glenn Warner of Stanford and Tad Jones of Yale into the All-America Board. With the co-operation of newspaper clients throughout the country, they went in for the annual practice of selecting All-American teams in a big way. They put so much time and effort into their analysis of players' worth that their yearly selections were generally accepted as standard.

In recent years there have been almost as many All-American teams selected as there are players engaged in the game, or writers, coaches, and radio men to jot down the names. Anyone who pays serious attention to All-American selections any more does so at his own risk, for it is a very bad football player indeed who does not find himself named on somebody's first, second, or third team.

My paper in Chicago was the outlet for Rockne's literary production when he first began using the printed page.

His boss, Christy Walsh, decreed that each of his three coaches, Rockne, Jones, and Warner, should furnish a story a week to the clients. Rockne, who had writing facility but no particular knowledge of newspaper technique, turned in his first effort to me. The first page and a half of copy treated interestingly enough of some technical development of football, but midway in the story Rockne had wound up and let go at some of the things that were irking him.

Very properly, I got out a scissors and dissected that opus. When it appeared in print, the technical football was at the end of the story, and the resounding wallop was right up front, where it belonged.

The story had repercussions for several days after it appeared. Thereafter, it was no longer necessary to rearrange the Rockne copy. When he had something to say, he said it, right where everyone could get it at once. When he had nothing to say, he kept quiet. Which wouldn't be a bad idea for all the rest of us.

Rockne brought into football a particular bit of strategy

that has been found useful by many other coaches down through the years, though the unlimited substitution rules of the present era have outmoded this procedure. This was the introduction of what were called "shock troops."

The shock troops were usually the first Notre Dame team to go into battle. They served a dual purpose, or so it was alleged. One, some charged, was the purpose of softening up the enemy, so that the first stringers, upon entering the game, might take charge without delay. The other and more logical reason was that Rockne liked to have his quarterback and his strategy workers beside him until they had a fair chance to size up the other side, and have ideas on what might work quickly.

Sometimes according to the prowess of the opposition Rockne would vary procedure. Instead of sending out eleven shock troops, he would send out a second-string line and a first-string backfield. Sometimes he would use the first team's line and the second backfield. On rare occasions he would send his regulars out to start from scratch.

In a game against Minnesota, while "Doc" Spears was coaching there, an impasse was almost reached. Spears vowed that he would not decide on his starting line-up until he saw what Rockne would send on the field. Rockne had made up his mind to regulate his starters by the line-up with which Spears opened the game. For a while it looked as if neither side would go on the field at all.

It is possible that all this pregame master-minding wore out both Rockne and Spears. The game ended in a tie, and at no time in it did either side appear to have taken undue advantage over the other.

At one stage of Notre Dame's football under Rockne, some of the rival coaches, notably Dick Hanley of Northwestern, were bringing the crowds to their feet by launching quick kicks against Notre Dame. More often than not, these quick kicks went far downfield, and when Notre Dame recovered the ball was dangerously deep in its own territory.

An inquiring alumnus, having been told that Rockne's

teams were suckers for a quick kick, took up the matter with the coach at great length, and finished by saying that he thought something should be done about it.

"Why?" asked Rockne. "If they quick-kick, that means they've given up trying to advance the ball themselves, doesn't it? They want to give us the ball, don't they? You go back and tell those fellows who have been kidding you that Rockne's team will gladly take that ball any time they can get it, anyhow, anywhere on the field. You can't score without it, you know."

Even after he had become a member of the All-America Board and was committed to the selection of All-American players on a big scale, Rockne remained true to his standards. He was of the opinion that no player should be named as All-American until he had reached his senior year. Perhaps that was because he had encountered too many varsity men who followed one well-publicized personal season by trying to get by the rest of their careers on press clippings.

This rigid rating system created a curious turn of events in the 1930 season. Marchmont Schwartz, the highly efficient left halfback who had starred in 1929, was even more brilliant in 1930. He was named on all the All-American teams there were, save one—the team his own coach selected.

It wasn't that Rockne, more than anyone else, was not keenly appreciative of the worth of Schwartz as a player and as a man. Marchy was a junior in 1930, his greatest year.

It was to come about that Rockne was not living at the end of Schwartz's senior year. Thus it is one of those queer turns of life that Marchy's football career found him named All-American by everyone save the man whose endorsement he wanted most—his own coach, Rockne.

I was a Schwartz man myself, and still am. I took the matter up with Rockne, pointing out that it looked very strange to have a man named All-American by everybody else, but passed up by his own coach.

"How can all those other selectors justify their choice, if

a man's own coach passes him up?" I asked. "It makes the whole All-American process look silly."

"Well, isn't it?" was all the satisfaction I ever got from Rockne.

That, and a few others, are the reasons why I have studiously avoided picking All-American teams, no matter what the provocation.

I have heard it alleged that Walter Camp, who picked up the All-American torch when Caspar Whitney tossed it away, once named as an All-American a man who was dead at the time he was selected, and that another man got on an All-American team though he had been graduated from his college a year previous. These items may or may not be true.

For this one, however, I can vouch. A noted selector in the Middle West was accustomed to make annual selections, using three weeks to get his ideas across adequately. The first week he named his All Western Conference team. The next week he widened the field and named the All Western team. The grand finale came in the third week when the All-American Team was revealed. I gave up the year a man appeared on the All-American from a Western Conference university, the odd feature being that this man had *not* been considered good enough to be named on either the All Western Conference or the All Western.

CHAPTER 18

Landis Walks In

I HAVE concerned myself thus far with a variety of characters in many fields of sport. I come now to a consideration of the one I unhesitatingly name as the most interesting person I have ever known, in sport or out of it, Kenesaw M. Landis.

I met him for the first time when he came unannounced to my office in Chicago, under circumstances that then seemed unusual. As my acquaintance with him ripened into a firm friendship and a very close association, nothing that he ever did surprised me. I knew he acted seldom, if at all, upon impulse, and that for all of his theatrical mannerisms, no kindlier soul, no more sincere person ever lived.

I had known Landis by sight, of course, long before I first met him. I saw him coming toward my desk, and rose to greet him.

"My name is Landis," he said, and I asked what I could do for him.

"I was in New York a few days ago," said Landis. "I met up with one of your confraternity who used to work in Chicago. He used to drink in Chicago. Too much. He was fired. He was on the bum. He has pulled himself together. I made inquiries about him. I want to help him. I want to send him some money. I don't want him to know, in my lifetime, that it came from me. I will leave it to your good judgment how best to get it to him."

With that Landis placed on my desk a draft for a considerable sum.

I began to protest that he was placing a great deal of confidence in me, whom he was meeting for the first time.

"I don't want to hear any more about it," he said. "You work out whatever plan seems best. And one thing more . . . if he ever learns where that money came from, I will make it my business to stage the greatest gut-letting this community has known since there were Indians around Fort Dearborn. And they'll be your guts. Good day, sir."

A few steps toward the door, Landis turned, grinned broadly, and waved his cane in a salute.

With the aid of Jim Crusinberry, whom I knew to be a confidant of the Judge, a plan was worked out whereby the indigent journalist in New York got his stake, not all at once (since neither Jim nor I held the confidence in his reformation Landis did), but a little at a time. I would like to be able to report that our man resumed his place in sports writing and was forever after both sober and industrious. But unfortunately this was not so. He used up the last installment from his unknown benefactor to get gloriously drunk, and passed out, not only from whatever chance there was for him to rehabilitate himself, but from this story.

This was the first Landis decision with which I became personally involved. To me, it was far more important than any ban he felt called upon to place on strayers from baseball's straight and narrow path. It impressed me more than that fabulous fine he inflicted, as a federal judge, on the Standard Oil Company.

I spent a great deal of time in the company of Landis in all parts of the country during his lifetime. It was the popular belief that Landis sat up nights worrying about the dread influence of the race track and race-track operators on baseball and the people of baseball. No doubt as commissioner he did frown upon race betting activities involving ball players, but this seems as good a time as any to clear up what seems to be a general misunderstanding. He had no intense feeling, one way or another, about horses, horsemen, or horse players.

One of his best friends in later life was Colonel Matt Winn, of Kentucky Derby fame. I was the medium through which they met for the first time. They visited frequently. Not very long before Landis went to the hospital for his final illness he called upon Colonel Winn, then resident in Chicago. For more than three hours they sat and reminisced. Since their lives covered such a tremendous span of this country's existence, I have always regretted that session had no transcript.

Landis had no persistent opinions for or against horses and horse racing. They were not his business. I have known few men in my lifetime who were so careful about minding their own business as was Landis.

Long before baseball reached forth and adopted him as its commissioner, Landis was a fan. He was a fan after he took charge of baseball, but he schooled himself to restrain all natural impulses that come to every fan in a ball park.

He was baseball's only neutral. He even had to indicate that he liked umpires ... publicly. I suspect that he hated them just as much as any fan ever did. I have suspected that since one day at Wrigley Field, Chicago, when I sat beside him for a while, and there was a not too accurate decision at the home plate that caused a small-sized riot among the players.

Landis sat there, arms on the box rail, chin on arms. He studied every move of the principals. He weighed every word that could be heard, and some of them could be heard a half block away. At last he turned to me and said, "Do you know something? If it were possible, if it were permissible, there ought to be one day set aside each year in each park. On that day, if a bum decision came up, the fans should be permitted to leap out of the stands and take after the umpire. Why, if that ever came to pass, there wouldn't be a park in the country large enough to hold the crowds!"

In his out-of-the-office moments, Landis privately had many

a chuckle over hearings that had taken place before him.

In a world's series between the Chicago Cubs and the Detroit Tigers, the bench jockeys became so violently abusive one with another that Landis had to call a halt, much as he regretted this, for he had been majoring in free-style language for more than three score years and ten.

Another time he had some of the Cubs and an umpire before him as the result of a row in which many naughty words were exchanged. He cross-examined each offender and elicited from him, statement by statement, the complete report of what had been said. Afterward, and off the record, he confessed that all his life he had prided himself on knowledge of and ability to sling violently expressive words around, but from those ball players and the umpire he had learned of new flights of descriptive fancy he had not known were in existence, much less had been explored.

At most of his hearings he had all the principals before him at the same time. He had a disarming technique to open proceedings. Two persons who had been involved with each other would appear before him. Landis would insist on introducing them to each other.

"They would look at me," he once said, "and I could tell they were wondering what kind of simple-minded old so-and-so this was. Didn't he even know that they knew each other before coming in? That's when I'd have them where I wanted them. If they thought, coming in, that I was too smart, they'd be more apt to keep their guards up."

During one spring training trip around major-league camps in Florida, I was basing in St. Petersburg. Landis used to spend part of his winters at a resort hotel near Clearwater. On the docket this particular spring was the hearing of a famous but eccentric player who had been accused of breaking an agreement to take part in an exhibition game promoted by a southern minor-league club operator. The minor-league executive took the case to Landis, and he chose to have the hearing at Lakeland, which was handy for the player involved.

Landis phoned me asking about the proper procedure for getting the findings to the various press associations. I explained that the major press associations undoubtedly had correspondents in Lakeland, or close enough to get them there. Besides, there would be enough journeymen baseball writers on hand to get sufficient coverage for the story when Landis released it.

I decided to go to Lakeland. The hearing of testimony took two days. At the beginning of the second day's session, Landis started reading from the transcript the ball player's testimony at the opening session.

He proceeded a little way when the ball player protested, saying, "I didn't say nothing like that, Judge."

Landis ignored that and proceeded with the reading. He was soon interrupted again, the player insisting that he hadn't said nothing like that yesterday.

Landis read on. When a third interruption took place, Landis halted the reading and looked over his glasses.

"You know this is an exact transcript of what was said here yesterday?" he remarked.

"I don't know nothing about transcripts," said the player. "All I know is that I didn't say nothing yesterday like it says there today I did."

"Were you here yesterday?" asked the Judge.

The player solemnly swore that he was.

"You're sure we're not wrong about that?"

The player was sure.

"That's all," said the Judge, abruptly ending the hearing. In his own good time he proceeded to find for the complaining minor-league club operator.

One of the Landis exploits that I have always treasured in memory took place in the midst of the uprising in the 1934 world's series, after Joe Medwick of the Cardinals and Marvin Owen of the Tigers had their set-to at third base. The umpires failed to expel the fighters from the game, and presently the entire park was in an uproar. The game was held up while Medwick was showered with fruit and vegetables by

Tiger fans. Pepper Martin and Rip Collins began a juggling act with some oranges that had rolled in their direction. The Judge watched this for a time. Then he left his post at the rail and went back to speak to some of his series guests who were seated well behind him.

In the meanwhile the rioting grew in fury and finally somebody thought of consulting with Landis. The umpires had a little difficulty in finding him, but eventually he came down to the rail, held a hearing with Medwick, and banished him from the game.

The game resumed then, but when it was all over I was still curious to know what had taken Landis from his familiar post at the rail at the height of the excitement.

He disclosed that he had been studying Pepper Martin's technique with a chew of tobacco. He had hastened to explain to his guests that all his life he had been trying to master the fine art of spitting tobacco juice through his teeth. And only then, by observation of Martin, had he learned the secret.

In his private moments he was a little discouraged with his umpires for having failed to quell the trouble at its outset by removing the offending player from the game. The umpires' defense was that prior to the series they had been instructed by the Judge that they were not to eject anyone from the game unless it was for very serious offense. This instruction had arisen from an incident in a previous world's series when Heinie Manush, one of Washington's better hitters, had been chased by an umpire for what seemed to many a mild infraction of baseball's law and order.

After the Detroit–St. Louis umpires brought in their minority report, Landis delivered himself of a speech. The umpires didn't hear it, which was just as well, but I did, while having dinner with the Judge the night after the incident.

"Suppose," he said, "Medwick had slid into third base, risen, rushed into the clubhouse, and extracted from the trainer's bag a scalpel or sharp scissors, then returned to the

field, and in the presence of fifty thousand people threw
Owen to the ground, hog-tied him, and proceeded to carve
his name and forwarding address on Owen's bosom . . . do
you suppose the umpires would have considered *that* serious
enough to merit putting a man out of the game? Damned if
I'm sure that they would!"

Most of the time Landis reached his conclusions on baseball matters only after long and most thorough consideration
of all available facts. Rarely did he give out any vocal statements on matters of state in baseball. When his associate
Leslie M. O'Connor had reduced the findings to type,
whether the announcement was of ten or ten thousand words
in length, that was it. It brooked no misquotation. No matter
how close a friend might be to Landis, it was useless to try
to get him to amplify or explain any of the printed findings.
That was it. Happily, there was never much chance for misunderstanding what Landis had decided. Anyone able to read
could get it.

There were times, however, when he went into action
without recourse to the research department. Such an instance took place during the 1922 world's series when umpire
George Hildebrand called a game while the score was tied
at 3 to 3, saying that it was too dark. He was the only person
in the Polo Grounds who thought so, and great was the dis-
order that prevailed immediately.

Many of the fans, thinking that it was Landis who had
halted the game, crowded around his box and did their raving. That didn't disturb the Judge too much. In his time
he had heard all the accomplished ravers in action many
times. What bothered him was the possible kickback against
baseball, since the tie might be the occasion for a series going
into eight games when the rules called for seven.

This could well have started a belief that it was all a plot
to get the magnates the extra money. A tied game did not
count for either side, and fans who had paid their way in to
see a decision were deprived of it because of an impulse of

an umpire. The aftermath could have put baseball's money-changers in a bad light.

Within a matter of hours Landis decreed that the entire revenue of that tied game should be taken out of the world's series pool, and that it be distributed to various New York charities.

As the series turned out, it did not even require seven games. The Giants turned the Yankees back in five, winning all but the one in which umpire Hildebrand rewrote Joshua's famous act with the sun. But the Judge took no chances, just the same.

Umpires were forever getting in his hair, and for all his years there was a lot of Landis hair in which they might get.

CHAPTER 19

Good Morning, Judge

THE public life of Judge Landis was exploited sufficiently to need no complete recapturing here. That is why I have been content to follow through with a side of his character that was not generally known.

For all his glowering appearance, Landis had as fine a sense of humor as anyone I have ever known. He appreciated pranks, and he was not above playing them himself.

He was very fond of Westbrook Pegler. On one occasion while in New York, he tried to communicate with him. Peg lived in Connecticut, or thereabouts.

The Judge tried to get through to him on the long-distance phone, and met with repeated failures.

"That fellow has himself cut off from the world," Landis told me. "It's getting so now, whenever I pick up my hotel phone the girl on the switchboard is liable to say, 'If it's Pegler you want, excuse it, please.' Do you think he has taken the veil?"

Landis persisted in his attempts to get through to Peg, but failed utterly and presently went back to Chicago.

A few weeks later Pegler was in Chicago and phoned the Judge's office. Landis was out at the time, so Peg left his hotel's name and his room number.

Landis did not call back that day. Instead he waited until very early the next morning. Then he went to the hotel and up to Pegler's room. He suspected his friend would be sleeping the sleep of the just, so he did not bother to phone from downstairs. Instead he lifted his cane and began banging on the door. The startled Pegler awoke and demanded to know what the hell was coming off. Landis continued the banging.

"Get away from that door," yelled Pegler. Landis stayed in the batter's box and kept swinging. A neighbor must have phoned for the law, because a house officer soon came on the run. He saw and recognized Landis, and was somewhat taken aback. Landis signaled for no comment and whispered to him what was going on. Being an affable house officer, as are all those in Chicago, he turned to and began helping out with the door beating.

That was too much for Pegler. He rose and opened the door, prepared to start a little swinging of his own. When he saw it was Landis, he demanded, "Why in hell didn't you phone?"

"I have no faith in telephones," said the Judge, "especially when I am trying to get Pegler on the other end. I was just returning your call."

Whenever he was in St. Louis, Landis counted that day lost in which he was unable to visit the zoo. He made a practice of carrying a bag of cinnamon buns with him, and would have a great time tossing them to the Kodiak bears. He invited me to go along one morning.

"There is one fellow I particularly want you to see," he said.

One of the bears, when the bun-tossing began, lumbered into position and stood up on his hind legs, front paws outstretched much as a catcher preparing to take a pitch.

"That's the one," said Landis. "Doesn't he remind you of somebody?"

"Lombardi?" I hazarded.

"I was thinking of Shanty Hogan," said Landis. "Now watch."

He tossed the bun straight at the outstretched paws of the bear. The lazy lout did not make a move until the bun thudded against his chest. Then he slowly bent over and retrieved it.

"For years," said Landis, "I've been trying to train him to make that play properly. I'm afraid it's no use."

It was in that same St. Louis park where the zoo is located that John Kieran, the "Information, Please" expert of experts, led Landis and me on a still hunt for a species of acorn that was supposed to be very rare. It was too rare for us, and eventually Landis and I left Kieran to continue with his search.

Some of the adventures of Landis with the radio reporters who came into existence during his regime were very interesting. He supervised radioratory very carefully, especially in world's series, and all-star game, time. His rules were not very complicated, but they were meant to be obeyed ... or else. He reserved the right to say who might broadcast and who might not, regardless of the sponsor's cravings.

Several times I served as a commentator at world's series games, and thus was enabled to attend the Landis previews. In one series able announcers Red Barber, Red Manning, and Ty Tyson were to do the play-by-play, and I accompanied them into the meeting.

Landis welcomed the three journeymen announcers. Then he greeted me with an inquiry as to what I was doing there. As if he didn't know. I told him, however.

"You will never learn to keep your mouth shut, will you?" he observed. Just to prove I could, I said nothing.

"You men," said Landis, "are skilled broadcasters, otherwise you would not be here. I want to tell you that Mr. Harridge and Mr. Frick have favored us with four men who are assumed to be capable umpires. They are all we will need to call the balls and the strikes, the safes and the outs. They will not need any help or any second guessing from you gentlemen. Is that clear?"

Messrs. Barber, Manning, and Tyson said it was. I kept my mouth shut.

"Fine," said the Judge. "That concludes the meeting. Now we can have a visit."

I encountered another side of Landis in his relations with

broadcasters one day on a train carrying players, league executives, and a goodly portion of the press and radio to the
site of an important skirmish. There were several visitors
in the Landis drawing room, one of them being a broadcaster of whom he was very fond.

That broadcaster fancied himself as a bettor, and talked
frequently of various wagers he had made and of books in
which he had made them. If Landis was interested, he gave
no indication.

Later on he sent for the broadcaster and asked him some
leading questions.

"I will be the last to tell any other man how he should
regulate his conduct," said Landis. "But I want to put this
situation up to you in a way that may never have occurred
to you. You have a vast listening audience. I know that. You
must know it. Those people hear you talk about the ball players and their every action. They must feel that no ball player
has any secrets from you. You are their pal.

"Now, I heard you talking publicly about your betting.
Again I say that's your business, in one way, and not mine.
In another, it's very much mine. As I propose to explain.

"If you talk about your bets elsewhere as openly as you
did in my presence, it is logical to assume that it will be repeated by others. Suppose, now, that there's a ball game
being played on which you have a big bet. Suppose that
game is decided because a player makes an error at a critical
time, and you win your bet. You might not have seen or
talked to that player before the game. But don't you see
that there might be somebody suspicious enough to suppose
that you, the see-all, know-all, was in cahoots with that player,
and knew about it before the game?

"I don't have to tell you what that might lead to, though
I know and you know that the suspicion was entirely un-
founded, and probably never would happen.

"I think it might be a damn good idea if you quit betting
on ball games."

The broadcaster thought it was a damn good idea, too. He hasn't made a baseball bet since.

It was not very often that Landis volunteered advice to his fellow men, though he always stood ready to give it if asked.

At the time Charles H. Strub was putting Santa Anita across as a major racing project, he still retained his interest in the San Francisco baseball club. On one of his early trips through the Middle West and the East to interest leading stable owners in sending their horses to Santa Anita, Strub called on Landis.

"If you think it wise," he offered, "I'll get out of baseball. I understand you don't think it proper to mix baseball and racing."

"Have I asked you to get out of baseball?" Landis countered.

"No," said Strub, "you haven't. But if you do not approve of baseball and racing interests coinciding, I surely don't want to embarrass you."

"Don't you think," replied Landis, "that it will be time enough to worry about that when I request you to get out of baseball?"

The request, of course, was never made.

Landis himself could not have been more severe in his methods of keeping racing and baseball interests apart than Strub. At one time he let it become known that he would be very happy if ball players and umpires did not go to Santa Anita at all to bet upon the Thoroughbreds.

There was a popular belief at one time that Landis had warned a certain umpire to stay away from race tracks. The "inside" of that story is that it was a practical joke that got out of bounds. This umpire prided himself (as all umpires do) on his sharpness of eye. He was a horse player in his off season. He was a very noisy horse player. The relative unimportance of his personal cash contribution to the development of the Thoroughbred by way of the pari-mutuel machines did not prevent him from letting his own corner of the world know at all times whether his horse had won or lost.

He was a steady patron of the racing arts at Santa Anita in its first few meetings. One day he was attracted to the mystery of the camera that photographs close finishes. Sometimes there is a delay while the film is developed before the exact order of finish is made known. Many of Santa Anita's action-cravers hit upon the idea of wagering on their own judgment against that of the camera, while waiting for the picture. The umpire knew that no camera ever made was as accurate as an umpire's eyes. So he joined in the action. When he was right, which was very often, he could be depended upon to make noise about it.

Some Chicago newspapermen, in southern California with the Cubs and White Sox, made note of the umpire's noise-making at Santa Anita and decided to do something about it. Their plan took the nature of a telegram suggesting that he curb his enthusiasm at the track, or else. The telegram was signed "K. M. Landis."

Then the newspapermen began telling friends and acquaintances of the umpire about the warning. The telling was in "strictest confidence," of course, all newspapermen knowing that this was the surest and the most rapid means to get general circulation.

The umpire began to get the least bit irked when person after person began asking him what was this they had heard about his being warned off the track. He could hardly wait to get back to Landis and tell him where he got off. They couldn't do that to him.

Meanwhile, the conscience-stricken practical jokers decided it might be well to advise Landis on the play-by-play to date. Fortunately he thought it was funny, too.

Thus when the umpire eventually called upon him to plead his right to life, liberty, and the pursuit of happiness, Landis heard him out, and at the finish simply said that a man was known by the company he keeps. Landis meant the newspapermen, but the umpire thought he meant race-track habitués.

The umpire was seldom seen on a race track again. Not even after his newspaper pals confessed that the entire incident was a rib. He used to explain his reformation by saying that he would not go to a track again until both he and Landis had a good thing running.

Next to baseball, golf was the sport that Landis liked best. He played the game frequently and most violently. He was not very long off the tee, but he usually managed to keep to the fairways and putted with considerable skill.

All the expressions that his role as the Great Neutral forced him to keep pent up when he was in a ball park were given a complete airing when the Judge took to the golf course.

He was a member of a foursome that played a memorable engagement at Glenview, near Chicago, one midweek day. Host was Michael McKinley, University of Iowa's athletic hero of the good old days, and a noted jurist. The other members of the foursome were Edward J. Hughes, Secretary of State of Illinois, and a Chicago newspaperman who played his golf under protest, but who would not have missed this one.

Jock Hutchinson, famous professional, was in charge at Glenview. He came out to the first tee when the fearsome foursome was taking some practice swings.

To the newspaperman, Landis said, "You and I will play these politicians."

Hutchinson offered to go around and keep score.

"We are reasonably honest," said Landis, "and trust each other to some extent."

Hutchinson stood by and watched the foursome drive off the first tee in four different directions. Then he apologized to one and all.

"It was a natural mistake," he said. "I thought you had come out to play golf. Yours is some new kind of game. I don't think I will like it."

Glenview, one of the most beautiful of the courses in the Chicago district, has its fairways crossed at many points by winding brooks. One of these is so situated that a fairly long wallop will clear it. A conservative will not make the attempt save with fear and trembling.

Landis, in making his shot, delivered himself of a sort of line drive. It went sailing straight down the fairway, landed, and started bouncing toward the brook. As soon as he had finished the swing Landis started forward. He sensed trouble ahead. He began jumping up and down, somewhat in tune with the ball bouncing upward and onward toward the watery hazard.

Then he began yelling, "Sit down, you little white ball. Sit down! Sit down!"

He made his way as rapidly as possible to the other end of the shot, and found the ball hanging on the very bank of the brook.

"It heard me," he said. "I didn't think it would."

"You underestimated your vocal range," said McKinley, the jurist. "They probably heard you in Scotland, where the game of golf originated."

CHAPTER 20

Break for the Player

THE advent of Judge Landis as baseball commissioner rapidly established the fact that the ball player's rights were to be protected, something that was debatable in the previous existence of the game. It did not matter how lowly the player. If he had merit in his case, he was assured of prompt action.

In the early twenties, Bill Cunningham of San Francisco was a National League outfielder. He served with pennant-winning New York Giant teams, and afterward with other clubs. He was a nephew of William H. McCarthy, then president of the Pacific Coast League, which ambitious body did not see eye to eye with the major leagues and with Landis on a variety of subjects, particularly the matter of the selective draft.

The Pacific Coast League, following the practice established by the San Francisco club, thought in terms of $100,000 and $75,000 sales prices for its major-league prospects, rather than the modest draft price. Landis, of course, argued that the draft was the only protective measure by which a ball player had a reasonable chance to advance in his profession. Without it he might have been shunted about in minor leagues for his entire career, subject to a minor-league wage.

Toward the end of his playing career, Cunningham felt that he had been given shabby treatment by a major-league club with which he was associated. It involved salary remuneration and hospitalization costs for an injury sustained in the line of duty.

Cunningham, friend and former opponent of mine in California during his younger days, came to see me in Chicago. He wanted to place his case before Landis, but he was uncertain of the approach.

"He'll probably throw me right out in the alley," said Cunningham, "since he probably knows Billy McCarthy is my uncle. They haven't been getting along too well."

I suggested that Cunningham did not have anything to lose, even if he did land in the alley. The alley near the Landis office was a nice alley, as Chicago alleys go.

Cunningham reported at the Landis office and stated his case. Afterward he related to me some of the circumstances, and said that Landis had promised to investigate the matter.

"But that isn't what got me," said Cunningham. "He didn't mention my uncle, and neither did I, until we were all through with the business that brought me there. Then all of a sudden he wanted to know how my uncle was. I told him he was fine, last time I had seen him. 'He's a fine man, Bill,' he said. 'He likes to stand up on his own two feet and say what he thinks. Wish there were more like him in this game. It's the behind-the-hand talkers we have to watch, Bill.' "

The Landis investigation established that Cunningham had right on his side.

One of the more notable of the Landis baseball decisions was that which involved minor-league or "farm" players belonging to the St. Louis Cardinal and Detroit Tiger "chains." Dozens of players who had been moved around and about among various minor leagues, and thereby had their rights to rapid advance up the baseball scale retarded, were declared free agents by Landis in a sweeping decision.

Many of the players were thus enabled to negotiate for new contracts in the open market, and the sums obtained by them for "selling" their services were considerable. Benny McCoy, freed from the Detroit Tiger farm system, was reported to have obtained $40,000 as a bonus for signing a contract with the Philadelphia Athletics. Others did proportionately well.

It is worthy of report, as a commentary on the genus professional ball player, that not one of the more than ninety declared free agents by Landis ever thought of sending him as much as a postal card expressing thanks for the break he had given them.

In his dealings with the press, Landis was well liked and respected by practically all save those who had aligned themselves under the banner of Ban Johnson, American League president, and a man of czar tendencies when Landis entered baseball.

Landis and Johnson were seldom in agreement about anything, and while the Commissioner was very careful in his public and private conversations, Johnson was not. Nor were his sycophants among the sports writers. They went out of their way to take sly digs at the Commissioner, but their attacks were slowed down greatly in time. About the only weapon they could use was the Landis posturing over the rail of his box at ball games, or his style in hats, most of which looked as if they had to be run over by an hour's Michigan Avenue traffic before they were shapeless enough to suit his taste.

For the most part, Landis worked in conjunction with the presidents of the National and American Leagues. He seldom departed from his theory that the league presidents should look after their respective affairs. It was only when something was out of line that he entered the picture. Then a league president was as certain to be told where to get off as was any club owner, club executive, or player.

It was charged often enough that Landis made his own rules, and that his interpretation of the baseball code was peculiarly his own. Perhaps he did not always act by the book, but in his long tenure in office the game prospered as it never had before, and the public's confidence in it was sure and steady.

The world's series was strictly a Landis concern, as were

the once popular meetings of the Cubs and White Sox in Chicago city series. The league presidents would designate two umpires each, and it has never been known that Landis objected to any of their choices. Before each series began, however, he called the umpires into session and advised them on proper procedure. They were now under his direct control.

He always attended the world's series, but would designate some baseball dignitary as his representative at the city series. Such a person was in charge fully as much as the Judge himself was at the world's series, though none ever did more than a routine figurehead job at it.

Appointment of scorers for the world's and city series was part of the Landis program. In the world's series it is customary to have three scorers. The president of the Baseball Writers Association of America is chief. A baseball writer selected from each of the two contending cities completes the trio. The city series called for but two scorers as a normal quota, but once it was played with no less than four, and Landis was responsible for that.

This was in the early thirties. At the time several newspapers were ceasing publication. Many baseball writers were temporarily out of employment. In conjunction with the Baseball Writers Association, the Judge decided that it would be proper to assign as world's series scorers, wherever possible, a man or men who had no regular employment at the time. A sizable fee is paid each series scorer.

In Chicago it happened that two long distinguished members of the craft had been dismissed, presumably for cause. Landis, mindful of the other ruling, decided to extend it to cover this case. He appointed as his scorers for the city series the two who were out of work.

The Chicago Chapter of Baseball Writers did not care particularly for this ruling. In fact, they were very mad about it. They met in session and decided to appoint scorers of their own, and did so. Thus the city series went on with one set of scorers functioning for no wage, but with the righteous knowledge that the Chicago papers would print their findings. They labored for love. The Landis or phantom set of scorers were just as particular. They kept score, turned in their balanced sheets, which no one save Landis and perhaps his aide, Les O'Connor, ever saw, and were duly paid the $300 or whatever it was that was standard wage for city series scoring.

A good time was had by all.

The Landis procedure for appointing his scorers consisted in wiring—or in the case of Chicagoans, of phoning—asking whether the individual he had selected would oblige him by being scorer. I have never heard of anyone thus invited sending in his regrets, though H. G. Salsinger of the Detroit *News* and I, who served as scorers in a Cub-Tiger world's series, have often thought that we should have replied, "No, thanks," if the honor were ever again bestowed upon us.

In our scoring adventure our chief, the president of the B.W.A.A., was having himself one of those times throughout the series, as sports writers often do when an event of consequence is up for grabs. Maybe it's the strain.

Sal and I did not see much of our colleague throughout the series. We went ahead doing the best we could at deciding routine and knotty problems involving hits and errors, the chief worry of any official scorer. We made some judgments that did not coincide with the opinions of many others.

The final game of the series was to be played in Detroit. At the ball park before the game, Sal suggested that I remain over in Detroit until the next day, and that we compile all the official score sheets. I could then take them back with me to Chicago and turn them in at the Landis office. By so doing, Sal would be able to plunge at once into his worries about football at Michigan. I could catch up with Notre Dame, Northwestern, and whatever other teams were on my calling list that season, and we'd both be very happy.

Our colleague was at the park, for a change. We asked him to remain over. He said it was impossible. He had to hurry to his eastern base. He might even have to leave before the final game was over if it dragged too much, he said.

Sal and I worked the day after the series ended, and made all the box-score sheets come out even. I returned to Chicago to deliver them to Landis and forget about it.

In the course of the games there had been several criticisms over our scoring judgment on a play or two, and in the series rehashing these plays were dissected in many sports columns. However, we were utterly unprepared for a treatise that our colleague, who had cast so many absentee ballots, wrote for publication. He wrote, among other things, that Sal and I would not let him sit near us; that he had not been consulted in any of the questionable scoring plays, and that he refused to take any blame for the scoring.

He did take the fee, no doubt.

Neither Sal nor I worried too much about it. It was not mentioned to Landis until some time later, when it came up as a matter of routine discussion.

"You fellows should not feel badly about written criticism," he said. "You ought to see the kind they write about me once in a while."

Of all those connected with organized baseball, Landis had the calmest viewpoint on the immediate future of the game when World War II broke out. It was obvious that most of the players would be taken into various branches of the service, but what most baseball operators worried about was the reaction of the public to the play of those who remained. A similar situation had arisen in World War I, and the "work or fight" legislation ultimately caused baseball to curtail one season.

Landis adopted a sensible attitude. He was certain that baseball would furnish an emotional outlet for the public caught up in the demands of war. Therefore he proposed to keep the game going "as long as the clubs were able to put nine men on the field." He spent some time in Washington, not pleading for any favors for baseball, but rather in stating its case clearly. He came away from there with the assurance, afterward widely publicized, that President Franklin Delano Roosevelt wanted the game to go on.

Go on it did, and it served a useful purpose. In the major leagues, toward the end of the war, the baseball was far below any previous standard, but the public, whether it saw games in early afternoon, by twilight, by night, or even in remote cases in the morning, established early and often that it was in favor of the game's continuing.

In retrospect, baseball came through World War II with few if any needs for apology. Its own service flags were studded with proportionately as many stars as those of any other business. That it got that way was due in no small measure to Judge Landis. Early in the situation he made it clear that baseball asked and would accept no favors. But he did insist that it had rights to be respected as long as such rights did not interfere with the progress of the war.

One of baseball's toughest wartime problems was that of travel and hotel accommodations, since baseball is essentially a game of movement. It was customary for the major-league clubs to train in the South, the Southwest, and the far West, and play their way back to their own territory after camps had been broken. Landis put a stop to that. He drew up the famous "Landis line" below which no major-league club was permitted to go for spring training. The hundreds of thousands of travel miles thus saved were no small contribution to keeping the war's traffic jam of men and materials from becoming much worse than it was.

The training periods spent in the North did not seem to impair the efficiency of the athletes remaining in baseball action. While there was some grumbling about it by sports writers who craved a sight of Florida's palm trees and the delights of Texas and California, eventually everyone became adjusted to it.

As a further contribution to travel mileage saving, Landis, the major-league presidents, Will Harridge and Ford Frick, and their schedule makers so arranged the war seasons that no more travel than was absolutely necessary was involved.

After sufficient practice, an able traveling secretary could tell without research when it was in order to travel by day coach and when by Pullman.

The ball players were not always happy and comfortable. If any of them were unselfish enough to go in for reflection, they must have remembered that travel conditions were not always ideal through the South Pacific, north from Italy, or east from the coast of France about that time in the world's history.

When the history of baseball is finally written, there will be revealed in it no figure who played a more important part in enabling it to reach its present estate than Judge Landis. On the playing field, Babe Ruth and all his imitators made the baseball world home-run conscious. There is no doubt but that the Babe's mighty wallops came in very handy as a counterirritant for the running sores inflicted upon the game by the unworthy White Sox of the 1919 world's series. So far, no other figure has advanced to the plate and delivered himself of a wallop commensurate with the Babe's normal healthy swing. But when Kenesaw M. Landis was in there swinging, he never failed to get both distance and volume when it helped the most.

He left behind him a game that was much better for his having administered its affairs for so many years. So in order was the baseball house that his successor, the former Senator A. B. "Happy" Chandler, after a few false starts because of inexperience and overeagerness to please, was soon able to say (as he did on the slightest provocation) that his was the ideal job, and he could ask no more.

It was, because Kenesaw M. Landis had made it so, in his own time, and in his own peculiar way.

CHAPTER 21

The Portable A.C.

WHEN I took up residence in Chicago, late in 1923, the questionable sport of prize fighting was being conducted on a scale peculiar to that area. It was not too hard for me to adjust myself to the surroundings. After all, I had served my time years before, keeping up with the oddities of the four-round game as practiced in California before the game became legalized there. Chicago's loosely run game would have to move very dizzily to surpass my beloved four-rounders.

On some of these four-round fights I have reported already. They were served in San Francisco and Oakland on a regular weekly show basis. Real headliners by any boxing standards would participate occasionally, as was the case when Willie Ritchie, the former lightweight champion, essaying a comeback, was cast as an opponent for Benny Leonard, then the champion of all the world, and so skilled there was a constant argument whether he or Joe Gans had been the greatest of all the lightweights in history.

Benny was not geared for the four-round game. Ritchie, having emerged from it, was able to fit his comeback to its requirements. One night in the Civic Auditorium Leonard was somewhat embarrassed when Ritchie hit him a harder punch on the nose than anyone had ever done before. It surprised Benny, but it did not surprise me.

In the four-round game I had learned to expect almost anything. That schooling prepared me for Chicago's boxing, which was of the bootleg variety and presented under something called an injunction, in the days before the solons decided to legalize it.

Nowhere else in the country have I ever witnessed more remarkable exploits of the prize ring than those that Chicagoans patronized when James C. Mullen was promoter and matchmaker, and his club was known to the trade as the Portable A.C.

The reason for that name was valid. Sometimes the shows took place at Aurora. Sometimes they took place at East Chicago. At irregular intervals Mullen would attempt to put over a fast one and come right into a Chicago arena. Usually there were difficulties that only the most resourceful promoter could surmount.

Mullen, for all his promotional eccentricities, was a splendid matchmaker. He might have prospered greatly and found himself ranked with Tex Rickard were it not for one strange turn of his nature. He fancied his ability to find promising fighters and build them into great drawing cards. This he did many times. Then he could hardly wait until he was able to find someone to knock his star crowd-gatherer over. Most promoters other than Mullen have been very careful to protect their drawing cards in and out of all matchmaking clinches.

Mullen was not able to produce any such memorable attractions as Ah Wing, Tanglefoot McGovern, and Cockey O'Brien of my younger days in San Francisco. But with what he had, Mullen did all right. He was a law unto himself. Perhaps that is why he was able to stage some notable events upon which any legalized commission would have frowned quickly.

There were in Chicago's Loop a couple of characters belonging to the set I was pleased to term the Rover Boys of Randolph Street. Each had a leg disability causing him to limp. They became involved in an argument one evening in Henrici's Restaurant, and were about to start swinging when Mullen suggested that they hold their fire. He could use them. He did, too, and after sufficient exploitation the pair appeared in the ring at Aurora as an added attraction to one of Mullen's shows. On that night Randolph Street was as quiet as the main street in Fork-in-the-Road, Utah. Everybody was at Aurora.

Playing baseball (it was alleged) for the White Sox was a character out of Texas, Art Shires, who styled himself "The Great." He thought well of himself as a fighter. First thing he knew he was given a match on one of Mullen's East Chicago cards. When his opponent went out on schedule, Shires became a great attraction.

His major showing in the ring was against George Trafton. Trafton had been a famous Notre Dame center and was later even more famous as a player with the Chicago Bears. The fight between these two created as much excitement among Mullen's clientele as any event he ever staged. It went to East Chicago. It was an awful fight to behold, but it did provoke an incident that indicated the occupational hazards of broadcasting from the ringside.

The broadcaster, Pat Flanagan, a famous figure on Chicago's air lanes, had established his reputation on baseball and football. He was taking this epoch-making fight in stride and showering the air with hysterical words and phrases as Shires and Trafton lumbered about the ring, each wondering what to do next, or whether to skip the whole thing.

Right behind the broadcaster sat one of Trafton's teammates on the Bears. He had come to the show properly fortified with emotional outpourings. In the very thick of the furious battle in the ring, he detected something the broadcaster said that he thought reflected on the fighting character of his pal Trafton. Being a man of action, he reached over and popped the broadcaster right in the nose. This caused a sudden flow of expression that set new heights for airways ring reporting. In the confusion that followed, the fight came to an end, with the sneak-punch victimized broadcaster utterly unable to let his clients know who had won.

Not that this was unusual for radio broadcasting in the twenties. I once sat directly behind Graham McNamee while he was describing the Gene Tunney–Tom Heeney fight. That contest, which marked Tunney's farewell, came to an end under somewhat unusual circumstances.

The champion had steadily cut Heeney down to size, and at the very end of a round deposited the Australian on the floor. Punches were flying from Tunney's fists so fast that McNamee was several wallops behind in his description.

I don't know whether Graham noticed that Heeney was on the floor, or that his seconds had rushed across the ring to carry him to his corner as the bell rang. I know he paid no attention to their frantic efforts to get him up and out for the next round.

For Graham, at the instant the bell sounded, plunged into a dramatic reading of the commercial, which was due then in behalf of the tire company that had sponsored the broadcast.

The commercial was timed for a minute's reading. Graham finished just on the dot as the bell for the next round rang. It rang for everybody but Heeney, who couldn't hear it. The fight was over. That much McNamee gathered from a quick survey, but what had caused the sudden ending seemed as dark a mystery to him as it must have been to his listeners.

Under any other circumstances he might have explained, after a quick brushing up on the facts. But it was customary in those days to get at that windup commercial as soon as the fight ended. That's what Graham did, and presently he was on his way out of the arena. He was content to let his clients find out what they wanted to know by reading the papers. Or perhaps he suspected that they had been just as bored with Heeney as he was.

The listening audience of the broadcast of the Shires-Trafton fight was hardly comparable to that of the Tunney-Heeney, but soon after that Mullen came up with another fight project that promised to be national in its scope.

Shires, the White Sox "fighting" first baseman, had been getting so much attention that friends of the Cubs, hated rivals of the White Sox, began to resent it. They looked around for a Cub who might have ring aspirations. In no time at all they found one. At least, Mullen found one for them. One day he announced that "Hack" Wilson, the home-run hitter of the Cubs, would be the next opponent for Shires. That was all the notice this event needed. From then on Mullen had to worry about finding an arena large enough to seat the crowd that wanted in on this battle.

The papers played it up with might and main. There is no telling what might have happened if the event had ever gone through. Even if it did not revolutionize boxing, as it threatened to do, it offered numerous other possibilities. So many, in fact, that Kenesaw M. Landis summoned Wilson and Shires into his presence. He told them how much he appreciated their willingness to prove their athletic versatility, but that he would be sore as hell if he ever heard another word from either of them about fighting each other in a public prize ring as long as they were identified with baseball.

In my private list of the great fights that never took place the Shires-Wilson affair is near the top. It belongs on the same card with the main event of Jack Dempsey in his prime versus Joe Louis in his.

Right beside them is the one that Mullen arranged at East Chicago, outdoors, involving Mickey Walker and Billy Wells, an English warrior who was being handled in this country by Charley Harvey. Harvey was one of the last of the honorable old-line managers and affected a curling, very black mustache.

Walker was a great drawing card, and Wells was a likely enough opponent, so that the arena was sold out many days in advance of the date of the fight. On the day it was scheduled, rain fell, and Mullen ordered a postponement.

Next day he was called by Harvey, who wanted to know if the promoter had any idea where Wells was. Mullen had not. Nor did anyone else. The English fighter simply disappeared. It was several months afterward before he was heard from again. By that time he had crossed the Atlantic.

But never a word why he had walked out on an engagement that figured to return him more money than any in which he participated before or since.

Walker was a performer in several of Mullen's extravaganzas after boxing had become legalized in Illinois. In one of them he was given the decision by referee Benny Yanger over Tiger Flowers, a verdict that made Mickey world's champion. This distinction he held with honor for a long time thereafter.

In its own quiet way, this bout created as much furor as the "long count" episode in Tunney's fight with Dempsey at Soldier Field. There was so much adverse comment over the decision, Yanger was hailed before the Commission to explain.

He told an interesting story. He quoted the rules under which boxing was conducted in Illinois, particularly that part treating of "flicking or hitting with an open glove," a practice at which Flowers was adept. The rule, Yanger went on to say, stated that it was at the discretion of the referee to disqualify the offender *or* award the decision to his opponent.

"With all those people there, I thought there might be trouble if I disqualified Flowers," Yanger explained. So he took the other alternative, and gave the decision to Walker at the end of the fight.

"Oh," said the august Commission, in effect.

Which was all right, except for the fact that the law did *not* offer any alternative. What it said was that the referee at his discretion could disqualify the offender *and* award the decision to his opponent. In other words, the referee, if he were to call into effect that rule, had to do so as soon as he was convinced there was an offense. He was not justified in waiting until the fight was over. But the Commission didn't read the rules too carefully, either.

Well, we had situations like that when Chicago's boxing was very young.

Yet another of Walker's Chicago appearances under Mul-

len's direction was in a bout with Mike McTigue. The latter
was the light-heavyweight whom the incredible Battling Siki,
the Singular Senegalese, had the temerity to fight in Dublin
on St. Patrick's Day, with the world's championship at stake.

McTigue was something much less than a champion on
the night he met Walker. Perhaps Mullen realized that, for
in his advertising material he announced that every fight on
the card would end in a knockout. It did, too, with Walker
draping the unconscious McTigue across the ropes with a
punch or two. All of Mullen's clients were back to their
normal haunts before ten o'clock from a complete fight show
that did not begin until eight-thirty. There should be more
of those.

The advent of legalized boxing in Illinois found Mullen
putting on the first show, a lightweight contest between
Sammy Mandell and Rocky Kansas. Kansas was the lightweight champion going in, but Mandell, a clever sort, out-
speeded him and emerged with the title. It was a popular
decision.

No other two citizens of Illinois did more to make possible legalized boxing than Ed Hughes, then a member of
the Senate, and Michael Igoe, then of the House. They were
both regular patrons of the fine arts on display at the Portable A.C.

Once boxing was legalized, it was interesting to observe
the demands of the solons for complimentary tickets as their
just due for having fostered the sport. But it isn't as interesting as a notation in the memory book of Sol Katz, who was
Mullen's head box-office man in the Portable A.C. days and
who followed him into the presentation of Illinois' first legalized contest.

His first two purchasers of tickets were Hughes and Igoe,
who had put the bill across. Neither had ever acquired the
habit of mooching complimentary tickets. Neither cared to
start, now that boxing—it was piously hoped—was going on
a scale in Illinois that might one day rival New York.

Save for the Dempsey-Tunney opus at Soldier Field, and a

few other presentations, it never has. But it was a good idea at the time. If Hughes and Igoe in their respective later lifetimes turned to the development of the Thoroughbred as an outlet for their sport enthusiasm, with a generous dash of baseball and football thrown in, I will never question their judgment. Chicago's boxing in the post-Mullen and Rickard days has been strictly of the bush-league variety. Such promoters as there are usually wind up with what the well-dressed operators of New York's arenas throw away.

CHAPTER 22

The Thoroughbred Develops

My interest in racing dates back to the early days of the century, when the Thoroughbreds were being developed at Emeryville, across the Bay from San Francisco and down the peninsula a piece at Tanforan.

It was Bud Fisher, the cartoonist, who made me conscious of the fact that horses ran and people bet upon them. In a San Francisco paper Fisher created his famous character, A. Mutt, who began his pen-and-ink life as a horse player. A daily record of A. Mutt's play and the size of his bank roll, increasing or shrinking, went along with the drawings of his adventures. In the years that A. Mutt has been featured in cartoon strips he has gone in for many other adventures, but there are still many of us abroad in the land who like to remember him as a horse player.

At Emeryville in A. Mutt's horse-playing days the star rider was Walter Miller. In the 1906 racing season Miller rode 388 winners. That record has never been threatened seriously since. It is the more remarkable because there were not as many tracks, summer and winter then, as there are now, on which a jockey might ply his trade for 365 days a year if he so desired.

Miller's riding deeds are all in the book. Since this story tries to concern itself mostly with matters that are not to be found in record books, I intend to take up the subject of Miller the ball player.

Five or six years after he had ridden his 388 winners,

Miller was appearing with the Emeryville semipro team, which used to engage similar organizations from around the Bay section. One of these was the strong Pall Mall Pool Room team, which has figured earlier in these jottings. Its pitcher was Walter "Dutch" Ruether. Miller, a left-handed hitter who played outfield for Emeryville, stood up to the plate and hit Ruether as if he owned him. That is something I could say about few left-handed hitters who ever faced Ruether in collegiate, semipro, or minor- or major-league settings.

Once in a great while, as in the case of Ellsworth Vines and Mary K. Browne, who were tennis champions and became sound golfers, you run across athletes who are or could be proficient in two sports. I have no doubt but that Miller the ball player might have graced any major-league line-up with a little schooling. But then, I doubt if any major-league club, past or present, could have paid him a salary commensurate with what he was accustomed to make booting those horses in.

It could have been, of course, that I caught Miller in an atmosphere in which he felt at home. For the Emeryville ball park used as its outfield barrier the stables in which were kept some of the horses that used to go to the post on the track not far away.

When racing dropped off the legal calendar in California, it remained for James W. Coffroth, the former fight promoter, to revive it at Tijuana, close enough to San Diego, and on a clear day to Los Angeles, to make the venture profitable.

At Tijuana both forms of wagering, books and pari-mutuel machines, were in vogue. It sometimes seemed as if the racing association made up its rules as it went along, but the track, both in its original form and later in its more pretentious Agua Caliente setting, supplied many noteworthy happenings.

This was the track that came up with racing's first $100,000 added event, the Coffroth Handicap. It was the site of the first, last, and only North American appearance of the great

TELEPHONE MESSAGE

7 ___ 19 50   TIME __ 4 30 P M.

M? _Richard Goldman_

ROOM _1008_

'HE FOLLOWING MESSAGE WAS RECEIVED DURING
YOUR ABSENCE, FROM

M_____ TEL. NO._____

Call

Operator 115-

Asbury Park N. J.

ACORN STAT. CO., N.Y.C. STOCK FORM NO. 144

Australian stake horse Phar Lap. It was, and this was where I checked out, the scene of Cotlogomor's gallant but futile bid to win the 1927 Coffroth Handicap. Beset on all sides by three Seagram stablemates of the eventual winner, Sir Harry, it also had to carry the additional burden of trying to win in the future book $9,000 for the $60 investment of three Chicago newspapermen, Andy Griffin, John Carey, and the man who had discovered Cotlogomor racing in Florida soon after its arrival from France.

These three incidents alone would cause me to remember Tijuana, Agua Caliente, and the original $100,000 added handicap.

The big money event was staged for the first time in 1926 and was won by Carlaris. In the following year, several weeks before the running of the Coffroth Handicap, Cotlogomor was glimpsed in the results from Florida, a fast-finishing second. In Chicago a sports editor noticed that and made a note to bet it next time out. Cotlogomor won next time out and paid a fair price.

The sports editor had something to say, naturally, and it was heard by his racing writer, Griffin, and his assistant, Carey. Griffin had on his desk the latest future book quotations on the Coffroth Handicap, and remarked that Cotlogomor was entered and was quoted at 200 to 1 to win, 150 to 1 to place, and 100 to 1 to show.

"Well, why not?" asked the sports editor. A quick frisk of himself and his two associates revealed $60 that could be spared. It was dispatched to Coffroth's future book operator at Tijuana without delay.

In due time the ticket came back, but as is the practice of future book operators the world over, the price had been cut following Cotlogomor's victory. The Chicago syndicate held a ticket at 150 to 1, or $9,000 against their $60. The place and show prices, with which they were not interested, had dropped to 100 to 1 and 50 to 1.

Cotlogomor raced again in Florida and won. It was shipped to New Orleans, raced in the New Orleans Handicap on a muddy track, and won that, paying more than 20 to 1, because no one had any line on whether the imported horse could go on an off track. All the while Cotlogomor's price was dropping in the Tijuana future book. Once the horse actually arrived on the track, it was moving toward even money. When it won its breather over the Tijuana track a week before the running of the Coffroth Handicap, it became a certain posttime favorite, in spite of the fact that the powerful Seagram stable was sending an entry of four horses into the race.

One of these was Sir Harry, and the other three seemed cast in the role of blocking backs. It was a roughly run race. Cotlogomor was almost knocked to his knees at the barrier. Once he got running and moved into contention, he was sloughed into the rail on the way around and an ugly slash was torn in his side.

With a quarter of a mile to go, Cotlogomor was nineteenth in the field. He finished third, beaten a couple of heads for it all.

I guess Man o' War was a great horse, all right, but in the book of three Chicago newspapermen, Big Red has nothing on Cotlogomor.

Phar Lap, winner in 36 out of 50 races in Australia, came to these shores for extensive campaigning and chose the Agua Caliente Handicap, nee the Coffroth, for its debut in 1932.

The Australian was trained as no American Thoroughbred ever was. Brisk walks and mild trotting, no time trials, no possible chance for the early morning railbirds to get an accurate line on the visitor. But once the racing began, the mighty Phar Lap made a joke out of the mile-and-a-quarter race, winning as he pleased in the very creditable time of 2:02⅖.

It was after this smashing inaugural victory that Phar Lap contracted an ailment while resting in California. Death came speedily, and it was said that it was due to poison. Many were the wild stories that followed. As late as World War II when American soldiers were based in Australia, many of them never having heard of Phar Lap, they were in a constant turmoil when some of the old settlers insisted on bringing up the foul plot that brought about the untimely death of the greatest horse Australia ever sent overseas for racing purposes. That there was any plot at all, or that the poison was administered by anything but sheer accident, was never proved.

Save for an occasional visit to tracks in the New York area and a vacation visit now and then to New Orleans and Agua Caliente, I did not encounter much turf action until the twenties.

There was some racing then in the Chicago area. It was not legalized, but by a process similar to that by which James C. Mullen was able to stage prize fights in a state that had not yet legalized them, racing, such as it was, was held.

My first adventure with the Kentucky Derby and the beginning of a long friendship with Colonel Matt J. Winn began in 1924, the year Black Gold won and just about ruined all the future book operators throughout the country. A couple in Chicago were particularly hard hit. The long-distance wagering had begun when Black Gold won the Louisiana Derby during the winter season.

It was the 1925 Derby, won by Flying Ebony, the first and only "field" horse ever to score in the event, that satisfied me that though races might come and races might go elsewhere in the country, the Kentucky Derby was the top event for story purposes. I have never changed that opinion.

Until the night before the Derby, I had not heard the name of Flying Ebony mentioned much at all. Everyone was discussing the chances of Quatrain, probable posttime favorite.

Into the midst of a select group of newspapermen strode Damon Runyon, a horse player of long standing. He announced that he had the winner, and that it was Flying Ebony. Very promptly he was asked how he got that way, and just as promptly, he told.

He had been talking, he said, to G. A. Cochran, owner of Flying Ebony.

"The man says he's too lucky to lose," said Runyon.

"A few hours ago he didn't even have a jockey for his horse. Now I have just learned that he has secured the services of Earl Sande. The man's lucky."

Sande's original Derby mount had disappeared from view, leaving that great rider on the outside looking in, until Cochran made a deal with him.

One of Runyon's audience, who prided himself on his knowledge of the ways of horseflesh, objected to Flying Ebony.

"He can't stand up unless it's an off track," he said.

"All right," Runyon conceded. "Then it will come up mud before Derby time. The man's lucky. Told me so himself."

The man *was* lucky, too.

One of the most drenching rains in all Kentucky Derby history turned up before the race. The track was called sloppy. That was an understatement. By a little stretch of the imagination it could have doubled as the transplanted bed of the Ohio River.

Flying Ebony had been held at 40 to 1 in the future book, but the presence of Sande in the saddle, coupled with the fact that six others of the seventeen-horse field ran with it as the "field," i.e., bet on one and you bet on them all, shoved the posttime price down to less than 4 to 1. Even so, Quatrain left the barrier as favorite, not quite 2 to 1.

Sande, greatest rider of his time, got Flying Ebony away smartly, reserved him for a mile just off the pace being set by Captain Hal, and then set him down. The Cochran colt went under the wire to win by a length and a half. The favorite, Quatrain, was a bang-up twelfth.

The following year I was present at the Derby victory of Bubbling Over, second of Colonel E. R. Bradley's series of four winners of this event. I had missed the Bradley victory debut in 1921, when his entries, Behave Yourself and

Black Servant, finished first and second. This caused great glee to everyone save Bradley, who had backed Black Servant heavily in the future book. The jockey aboard Behave Yourself didn't behave himself, and in a furious stretch battle with the stablemate his owner favored, was up to win by a head.

If I missed that one, I was to see many years later a similar and happier event when Charles S. Howard's great campaigner Seabiscuit went to the post for the last time, running as an entry with Kayak II in the $100,000 Santa Anita Handicap.

Howard wanted Seabiscuit to win, since it meant he would take top ranking among the money winners of all time up till then. Kayak II had won the event the year previously. There are many who think he could have won this one. However, no mistakes were made. Kayak II was far back until the stretch was reached. Though an amazing finish carried him almost abreast of Seabiscuit in the stretch, the more famous old Thoroughbred put on one last, blistering surge and won by a length, setting a new track record of 2:01⅕ for the mile and a quarter.

In the 1926 Kentucky Derby, Bradley held all the cards. He had ready three three-year-olds, Bubbling Over, Boot to Boot, and Bagenbaggage. It is a matter of record that Bubbling Over could beat either of the other two, that Boot to Boot could beat Bagenbaggage, and that Bagenbaggage could beat any three-year-old not owned by Bradley.

Not being a selfish man, Bradley decided to start but two in the Derby. He kept Boot to Boot out, which is the sole reason he isn't the only owner whose entry has ever run one-two-three in the event.

After the Bubbling Over victory, the next Derby that was productive of peculiar interest for me was the 1928 event. In it the favorite was Reigh Count, belonging to Mrs. John D. Hertz. It was also productive of a field of twenty-two, largest number of starters ever to go to the post in the Derby.

The newspaper that employed me was affiliated with a radio station, which elected to go in for broadcasting the Derby Day's events in a big way. As luck would have it, the sun was decidedly not shining bright on the old Kentucky home that day. It rained and the visibility was very poor. The radio announcer calling the early races was having a terrible time trying to keep up with the parade. I could foresee that when it came time for him to unscramble a twenty-two-horse field in the Derby, chaos would be a mild term for the conditions.

I left the rooftop where the microphone was and went down to the ground level to look for help. There I encountered E. Phocian Howard, the well-dressed owner of a weekly sports paper. With him was Clem McCarthy. Around McCarthy's neck hung a pair of field glasses that looked potent enough to bring into focus the houseboats on the canals of Mars, even with visibility as bad as it was at Churchill Downs that day.

I knew that McCarthy was an experienced caller of races, and that he was one of the real racing experts of his time. I explained our problem up on the roof, and asked if he would like to help out and call the Derby for us over the radio.

"For an old pal," he said, "what can I lose?"

Thus was thrust into radio for the first time the man who has been, from scratch, its foremost caller of races.

In that murky setting at Churchill Downs, working with little or no preparation, and with his only script the racing program, Clem McCarthy reeled off information about each of the twenty-two starters as they paraded to the post. He gave their records and bits about their jockeys and trainers, their odds, and all the interesting essentials. Once the race began he turned in a magnificent description of it, for all the wild scramble out of which Reigh Count and Chick Lang emerged in the stretch to go on and win.

That broadcast established McCarthy. What he had done for an old friend, for the hell of it, that afternoon at

Churchill Downs, was to bring him regular bookings on national radio chains as often thereafter as he chose to accept them.

On that count alone might rest my case that the Kentucky Derby, more than any other racing event in the year—any year—is where you must go to find the human interest story without which the development of the Thoroughbred would be dull indeed.

CHAPTER 23

Derby Delights

*F*OR a comparatively long stretch I have been looking at renewals of the Kentucky Derby—long if you don't recall that Colonel Matt J. Winn has seen 'em all since Aristides won the first one in 1875.

It has been my luck to see the Derbies resulting in new track records. First Twenty Grand in 1931 lowered the mark for the mile and a quarter to 2:01⅘. Ten years later Whirlaway made it in 2:01⅖. It was worthy of note that each of these two record-makers reached their objective by the same method, both going into the lead when the stretch turn was reached and drawing away to lengthy leads.

However, I have seen several Derbies won by famous three-year-olds that led most of the way, some of them, as in the case of Bubbling Over, Clyde Van Dusen (1929), War Admiral (1937), Johnstown (1939), Count Fleet (1943), Hoop Jr. (1945), and Jet Pilot (1947), practically from the rise of the barrier to the finish.

Since 1924, when I saw my first Derby, there has been but one whose issue left a reasonable doubt. That was the 1933 race, when Bradley's Broker's Tip got up to win by a nose over Head Play. This was the race that was featured by a stretch wrestling match on horseback between jockey Fisher on Head Play and jockey Meade on Broker's Tip. Both violated most of the code of riding sportsmanship, but the order of finish stood.

Bold Venture, winning in 1936 from the heavily backed

Brevity, did so by a head, but it did not seem to me then or now that this was close enough to worry about. Perhaps that was because Bold Venture was trained by Max Hirsch, who sprang Assault on the Derby in 1946 and took him on from there to be the horse of the year—and then some.

Merely by way of proving that in horse racing as well as in baseball you must never take anything for granted, I saw Assault run sixth in a six-horse race, the Arlington Classic, in that same 1946. Prior to that Assault had cleaned up on the Derby, the Preakness, and the Belmont, thereby becoming another one of those known as "triple crown" winners. Sir Barton, Derby winner of 1919, was the first of these, and he was joined eventually by Gallant Fox (1930), one of his sons, Omaha (1935), War Admiral (1937), Whirlaway (1941), and Count Fleet (1943).

In my Derby doings I was privileged to see Earl Sande ride the last two of his three Derby winners, Flying Ebony and Gallant Fox, and see Eddie Arcaro move into that select jockey circle with his three, Lawrin (1938), Whirlaway, and Hoop Jr.

All these past performances of horses, riders, and trainers who saw that both were ready form a component part of the Derby history. But the main story is not that of a horse, an owner, a trainer, or a jockey. It is of Colonel Winn. He *is* the Derby, and has been since he took charge at Churchill Downs, which would be nigh on to fifty years ago.

There is a legend that Winn as a very young man saw his first Derby from a spot in the infield. Sometimes, the tale goes, he saw it from the limb of a tree. Sometimes it is related that he saw it from the tail gate of a grocery wagon. All that matters is that he saw it, as he has seen every Derby ever run at Churchill Downs, and since he took charge in 1902 he has further seen to it that each successive renewal finds the ever increasing crowds marveling at his remodeling of the country's most picturesque racing plant.

Many years before the current growth and expansion of legalized racing in this country, Colonel Winn foresaw and openly stated that crowds of 100,000 or more were not only possible but quite probable. He was to live to see the Derby Day on which he could have staged his Derby before many more than 100,000, were he able to find a place to put them. Year by year he has been trying, and year by year, no matter how Churchill Downs has expanded, the demand invariably exceeds the supply.

During World War II, when transportation troubles beset all sports catering to the public, there was some doubt that the Derby would be held. Colonel Winn, proud of its unbroken record since 1875, said that the Derby would be held if he and the necessary staff of officials were all that saw it. He compromised by going the limit with the Office of Defense Transportation, and refused to sell his precious accommodations to anyone who came from outside the corporate limits of Louisville, wherein Churchill Downs is located.

To be sure, there were some cheaters, those of the "it doesn't mean me" type. But on the whole, when Colonel Winn ruled that it would be a streetcar Derby, he came very close to making the event strictly for home consumption. That the number of "residents" in Louisville seemed to increase greatly by Derby Day was commented upon, of course, but in the main the general idea was carried out, and thousands of Colonel Winn's steady Derby patrons who came from afar sat the war presentations out.

Perhaps the most remarkable circumstance of the Derby as held during the war was the unwillingness of Colonel Winn's annual box-seat patrons to give up their priorities. Scores of them, accepting the ruling that it was for "residents only," sent in their checks just the same and instructed Colonel Winn to distribute the valuable seats to members of the service, many thousands of whom were in training in the vicinity of Louisville. It is doubtful if Colonel Winn would have scratched any of these from his regular annual reservation list, but none cared to take the chance. Some of them had waited a long time to get a regular location at Churchill Downs on Derby Day, and they did not want to lose it.

The setting at Churchill Downs, almost as old as racing itself in this country, has never been geared to the high-pressure salesmanship of the more modern tracks. Until a few years ago, such a thing as an electric totalizator was not used, though it was in vogue at most other tracks. Churchill Downs patrons were accustomed to take it easy, and if the mechanical speed-ups were not there, no one worried much, unless it was some big operator from Broadway or Hollywood or even from Chicago's Loop.

While racing is on at Churchill Downs, Colonel Winn lives at the track. He watches many of the daily races, but can't tell you when he last made a bet upon one. Neither is he given to discussing chances of any of the Derby candidates except in a general way. He is given to one statement, however, that turns up sometime between the close of one year's racing and the running of the next year's Derby.

Invariably he foresees a "very open race," and he hopes for "a pretty day."

That his public invariably hits upon a favorite and makes it a one-horse race doesn't enter into the conditions of the statement-making. Colonel Winn can be depended upon to say the same thing every year, just as surely as Ford Frick, president of the National League, and Will Harridge, president of the American League, can be depended upon at the start of each baseball season to say that they look for a close race right down to the finish.

That such statements have been made prior to races in which a pennant winner clinches the championship by Labor Day never seems to deter these presidents from saying it all over again the following spring.

An annual guest of Colonel Winn at the Derby, and an associate of his in racing, is Edward J. Fleming, a business-man of Chicago. Fleming is a horse player who will never die broke. He has too many systems, and most of them have proven successful . . . it says here. One of them I am anxious to record, since it portrays as well as anything else the camaraderie that exists at Churchill Downs in Derby Week.

At one stage of his horse-playing career Fleming had his own clocker, and a rather famous one. Shortly before the running of the first race Fleming's constant companion, Pete O'Neil, would obtain the clocker's markings. He would then go to the clubhouse, where Fleming was invariably entertaining a gathering of friends from all parts of the country.

On the day before one particular Derby, Fleming was host to Maury Burnett of Cleveland, Steve Hannagan of New York, Judge Michael Igoe of Chicago, Bill McCormick of New York, John O'Neil of San Antonio and Los Angeles, and Joe E. Brown of stage, screen, radio, and the old Minneapolis American Association infield.

The markings were duly distributed. Burnett did not care for the choice in the first race. The price was too short. He bet against it. The choice won.

"It's a cinch the guy will not have two in a row," said Burnett. So he bet against the clocker's choice in the second race. The choice won.

"Nobody ever had three winners in a row at this track," concluded Burnett, and again the choice won.

That was the way it went throughout the long afternoon. That clocker's markings indicated eight straight winners, and Burnett, who started even with all Fleming's other guests, went right through the day without betting on one of them.

He was out bright and early the next day, however, resolved not to make that kind of mistake again.

Again the markings arrived and were duly distributed.

Burnett went into the pari-mutuel mart with greater confidence than he ever had before in a battle with the "iron men."

He wasn't going to weaken this time. He didn't, either. He kept on playing those choices from the first race through the seventh, and in the seventh race he was rewarded at last with the clocker's lone winner of the day, which happened to be Johnstown, sixty-fifth Derby winner. Its price was $3.20.

To me much of the fascination of racing comes from the

patrons of the pari-mutuels. Theirs is a never ending tale, which does not seem to differ greatly whether you hear it at Churchill Downs, Santa Anita, Belmont, River Downs, Fair Grounds, Pimlico, Rockingham, or at the lowliest of the half-milers, many of which have been on my calling list from time to time.

In the case of Gallahadion, longest priced winner of modern renewals of the Derby, a $72.40 number, or Bay View, Santa Anita Handicap $118.40 winner, the most astonishing thing to me is not that they won, since anything can happen in a horse race, but that the prices were as high as recorded.

By actual count, I have heard from enough people afterward who "had" the winner to have made either of these no more than odds on favorites, instead of long shots. Perhaps that is because I am a good listener.

There was one time when I was a good teller of the tale, however. That was when Sun Beau came out to Hawthorne for the first time to compete in the Gold Cup race.

Most of us around Chicago were Misstep-minded, and had been for some time. Just to make sure that nothing promising got away, I gave the *Racing Form* a particularly fine going over the night before, and decided that Sun Beau's record indicated it might be worth worrying about.

At the track a little while before the running of the Gold Cup race, I was in company with Ed Hughes, Secretary of State, Fred Stirling, Lieutenant Governor of Illinois, and Richard Barr, a veteran legislator. All were horse players. All were Misstep men. I took up the subject of Sun Beau, and spoke with such conviction that all three decided that Sun Beau, which was a much longer price, was good enough for them.

We all started for the mutuel windows, and I was last in line of the four. One by one I could hear my friends call out the number of Sun Beau and see them accept their tickets.

Then it was my turn. I did not hesitate. I gave my number. It was Misstep's.

That particular Gold Cup race was as spirited a mile-and-a-quarter competition as I have ever seen. It was strictly a two-horse race, and the two were Sun Beau and Misstep. From flag-fall to finish, never more than a head separated them. But always it was Sun Beau's head.

Three leading lights of the Illinois political world came rushing up to hail me as the greatest handicapper of my time. Maybe I was, but darned if I could get anything from the mutuel cashiers for my own private choice, Misstep.

The race that gave me the biggest thrill in all the thousands I have watched was the 1940 Santa Anita Handicap, won by Seabiscuit.

I had seen this persistent old equine hero beaten by a head in his first try in 1937 by the Duponts' Rosemont. Seabiscuit, a grandson of Man o' War, had raced into the front rank of Thoroughbreds after a discouraging two- and three-year-old existence. It moved on Santa Anita after having demonstrated speed and endurance at San Francisco.

Gene Normile, an associate of James W. Coffroth and Jack Dempsey, whom he managed for the first fight with Gene Tunney, had told me about the threat to Rosemont, the probable posttime favorite and my original choice to win the Santa Anita. Normile was a friend of Charles S. Howard, the owner, and his wife.

"I am worried about this race," Normile said. "I don't like to think about the Howards. If Seabiscuit doesn't win, one of them will be so disappointed she'll drop over, and if Seabiscuit does win, the other one will be so excited he'll drop over."

It was a race exciting enough to cause even a Dupont to drop over, but they paid off on Rosemont, and Seabiscuit had to wait another year.

For the 1938 running of the Santa Anita, Seabiscuit's place in the racing world was so well established that most of the patrons were content to wager upon him, and he went to the post a 9-to-5 favorite. His chief competition was expected from a three-year-old, Maxwell Howard's Stagehand, which trainer Earl Sande had sent to the post to win the Santa Anita Derby a short while before. Stagehand, eligible for the Handicap, drew the light weight allowance of one hundred pounds, and there were those who claimed when the race was run that the thirty-pound pull in the weights was what got Stagehand home a head in front of Seabiscuit. However, the race was run in 2:01⅗, which was a new track record, so for all his weight and advancing age, Seabiscuit was not exactly loitering.

This second disappointing defeat by a head caused Charles S. Howard to retire Seabiscuit, and the following year he was represented by an imported starter, Kayak II, which clipped another fifth of a second off the track record.

A life of ease did not suit Seabiscuit, and he was back to the races in time to start in the 1940 Santa Anita, coupled with Kayak II. It took no handicapping skill to realize that either of these could win the race, and the 7-to-10 price was the result. But it was equally obvious that all of Santa Anita's patrons were hoping that the old-timer, now seven, would be the half of the entry to get home first.

I have always prided myself on ability to refrain while occupying a working seat in a press coop from giving out with any vocal demonstrations. But this was one time that I was willing to stand up and root Seabiscuit home.

The race served as a complete vindication for the old-timer, as well as for his jockey, "Red" Pollard, who had been criticized three years before when Seabiscuit blew the lead to Rosemont just before the wire was reached.

It was a race always to be remembered fully as much for what happened then as for what did not happen in the other renewals of the Santa Anita. For it is a historical fact that two heads, Rosemont's and Stagehand's, and Bay View's neck, which was his 1941 victory margin over Howard's Mioland, were all that kept one owner from winning a $100,000 race five consecutive times.

I doubt if the entire history of racing will record another set of circumstances similar to these.

CHAPTER 24

For Ways That Are Dark

*I*N all the people of sports who have come to my attention, none have been more consistently curious than the professional wrestlers. I know that Bret Harte once decided that for ways that are dark and tricks that are vain, the heathen Chinee is peculiar. But that was simply because Harte had not seen professional wrestlers at their diversions.

I became an observer of them in San Francisco early in my sports-writing career. Frank Schuler was promoting wrestling and had a show every week. Sometimes the vaudeville bill at the Orpheum wasn't up to standard and I became accustomed to patronizing the antics of the "beeg, strong fellers."

Once in a while Schuler would call at my office with a wrestler in tow. He arrived one day with John Pesek, who was billed to meet somebody within a day or two. Pesek was a fine conversationalist, as are most of the wrestlers. In the course of his visit he made mention of the fact that he had once lain down on a street and permitted an auto to pass over his body.

"That I would like to see," I told him.

Pesek offered to oblige, and before he had a chance to change his mind the demonstration was arranged. Schuler was to provide the auto, and I rounded up my paper's cameraman and also notified Otto Stolberg, International newsreel cameraman in that area.

We chose a vacant sand lot near the post office but Pesek asked that we abandon that site. He was fearful that the wheels of the auto would be unable to get traction. He did not object to a car using him for a highway, but he positively refused to become a parking area.

We picked another spot in the street. Pesek, who was in wrestling togs, placed his bathrobe on the street and prepared to recline on it, only to be halted by Stolberg.

"If you don't jump up right away," he said, "everybody will think it was a fake."

Pesek promised to jump up. Schuler, his five-passenger car laden with witnesses, started his car, and presently the wheels on the left side ran across Pesek's midsection.

He did not get up, and the cursing of Stolberg could be heard downtown. Pesek was very obliging. He was anxious to please. He reclined again, and after the car passed over him once more, he leaped up and did a handspring.

The still pictures of that made the front page of my paper, and Stolberg's newsreel shots went all around the country's movie houses. From then on I had a steady clientele of wrestlers. Each one that came to San Francisco to wrestle for Schuler seemed to know that I was a soft touch for the unusual.

"Toots" Mondt, who came to be something of an organizer later on, was featured in two of our productions. He had a long, narrow iron bar placed in his teeth, and while several kids pulled down from each end of it, Mondt thrust upward. It was a tough struggle. Blood oozed out of his teeth and the veins appeared like cords on his forehead. It was a complicated way to make a huge hairpin, but we made it.

At about this time there was considerable agitation on the subject of boxer versus wrestler. Strangler Ed Lewis, the wrestler, and Jack Dempsey, the heavyweight champion, were getting a great deal of publicity mileage debating this issue. With the co-operation of Schuler and Mondt, a test was made in Dreamland Rink, San Francisco.

Selected as Mondt's opponent was a four-round heavyweight who could punch, and little else. He came into the ring wearing regulation gloves. Mondt wore wrestling togs, but I noticed that he had shoved down the top of his trunks a length of stout cord.

It was agreed that the boxer could swing punches whether he was on his feet or on the floor, and the match began. Mondt came out of his corner hunched over, arms wrapped around his head. The boxer came toward him and let go a punch. As he did so, Mondt dove forward and tripped him, and as they went to the floor the wrestler was on top.

He spun the boxer around quickly and clamped his hands. Then he reached into his trunks, produced a cord, and proceeded to tie the boxer's wrists. This done, he swung around and applied the toe hold, which presently had the boxer writhing in pain. The meeting was stopped before Mondt had time to twist off the leg and throw it into the face of the nearest believer that a boxer could ever defeat a wrestler.

Joe Stecher, one of the more famous of the wrestlers, came to San Francisco for an engagement about the time the Pacific Coast League baseball season was coming to a close. Stecher said he was a baseball player and had worked at first base for his own team in Nebraska.

In San Francisco that week was the Salt Lake club, which was going nowhere in the league. Nor was its manager, who happened to be a friend of mine. It was not too difficult a task to get him to play Stecher at first base in a regular game. The wrestler seemed very muscle-bound in a baseball suit, though he was sheer grace on the mat. However, he managed to keep from getting killed with batted or thrown balls, and actually did deliver a single that scored a run.

To San Francisco came a veteran wrestler called John Olin. The best extracurricular offering he had to make Stolberg and his newsreel camera happy was a promise to permit an anvil to be suspended from his teeth while he defied blacksmiths with sledges to dislodge it.

Our main problem was to find blacksmiths, but a search was rewarded. Accordingly a heavy rope was bound around an anvil. Olin had a leather mouthpiece with hook attached, and to this hook was fastened the anvil. There was some difficulty in getting the blacksmiths to understand the rules, but after a time they learned that the object of the experiment was to knock the anvil loose from Olin and not vice versa. Either way seemed to suit them. They swung their sledges with might and main as Stolberg's camera whirred, but the anvil did not drop until Olin got ready to spit it out.

Jack Kearns tried to break in as a wrestling promoter in San Francisco running opposition to Schuler, whose current "house" man was Ad Santel.

Kearns aligned with Jack Curley, and the proposed match involved Wladek Zbyszko and someone known as Jirza. All we were able to learn of Jirza was that he spoke several languages and wrestled in all of them. Much of his training was to be done in secret.

It so happened that Santel didn't like the idea of these interlopers moving into "his" town. So one day he dropped into Jirza's training quarters, where he was not recognized, and offered to work out with him. The offer was accepted. Santel threw Jirza so many times the workout grew a bit boresome to a sports writer who was on the scene by the merest coincidence, so he went back to his office and wrote about it. When the story appeared there was no further need of a Zbyszko-Jirza match.

As far as I know this was the beginning and the end of Jack Kearns' career with the wrestlers.

Perhaps the strangest of all the wrestling adventures that came to my attention was a series of incidents involving one Gobar, who was in San Francisco to meet Stecher, the body-scissors exponent. Stecher was strictly in our league to prove that wrestlers could do other things more interesting than grunt and groan and make faces. His first appearance had been preceded by stories of the crushing effect of his scissors. When Joe wound those long legs around an object, it was supposed to be just too bad for that object. Tales were told of his bursting open huge sacks of grain, and of how he had once forgotten himself while horseback riding and applied too much pressure, killing the horse.

My long-time associate Edgar T. "Scoop" Gleeson thought it would be a wonderful idea if Stecher would agree to crush a calf to death at the corner of Third and Market Streets. So did Schuler, who was sure that Stecher would oblige. The experiment was never made because the S.P.C.A. threatened to get out injunctions and all that sort of thing.

This was the object, then, of Gobar's attentions when he first came to San Francisco. He was said to be a native of India and a graduate of the University of Calcutta. I did not have any proof of that, but I did have means to find out.

When Schuler brought him to my office, Gobar proved to be an intelligent conversationalist ... up to a point.

He spoke of his training, and I asked where he trained. He said he trained in his room, taking various exercises.

For instance? He showed me. As an encore he let me in on one of his own secrets. That consisted of putting a finger over one nostril and inhaling through the other. The breath would be held while the finger moved to the opposite nostril. Then the exhaling took place.

"I do that a thousand times a day," said Gobar.

"What in hell for?" I asked.

"It lessens the carnal appetites," he said. I should think it would.

Gobar said he ate gold leaf and silver leaf daily. One gave him strength and the other acted as a sort of purgative. I don't know whether he ever ate gold leaf and silver leaf before or since, but one day in my office in the presence of witnesses he ate two sheets of each ... and liked it.

At the University of California at that time was a professor who was a close friend of my editor, Fremont Older. The professor, I knew, was a native of India. I arranged to have him meet Gobar in my office.

The professor was a tiny man. Gobar must have weighed 250 pounds. When I introduced them they began verbal sparring, but did not seem to get anywhere. I found out afterward they were trying out dialects to find one that suited the occasion. I left them to their workout.

I was not gone long before I heard their voices getting louder and louder. It sounded as if it were leading up to a fight. Presently I was sure of that, and as I started for my office to see what it was all about, the door burst open and the little professor dashed out. He was very mad indeed. He grew no quieter when I stopped him and asked if Gobar were really a native of India. He kept right on going.

Gobar was still in the office, and seemed calm enough. I asked him what it was all about. He said that when he came to our country he had to promise that he would not discuss Gandhi and the political situation.

"Your friend," he said, "wanted to discuss nothing else, and we lost our tempers."

When I reached Chicago to start working there, the wrestlers were quite the rage. In those days it was customary to have the matches go on for quite a while before a fall was scored. The modern speed-up system I prefer. It is both louder and funnier.

Chicago went through the long-drawn-out wrestling matches perhaps because there was no one with the lively interest that actuated Scoop Gleeson in the old days in San Francisco.

The Civic Auditorium in San Francisco, which was rented from the city for major sports spectacles, was often used by the wrestlers. There one night a match between Strangler Lewis and Wladek Zbyszko was so long delayed in getting started, and then endured for such a length of time, it was well after midnight before it reached its conclusion. Gleeson decided to take steps. He sought out the city father in charge of renting the auditorium and asked him if it were possible to rent the place for two days for the price of one.

"Of course not," said the city father.

"Then why do you keep on doing it?" demanded Gleeson. He pointed out that one day ended when midnight was reached and another day began.

"These wrestlers," argued Gleeson, "should be charged two days' rent instead of one, since they are in the building past midnight."

"You have something there," agreed the city father. "I shall so notify the promoter."

He probably did, for never again in San Francisco was there a wrestling match that lasted until midnight, much less beyond it.

I don't suggest, you understand, that there was any pre-arrangement. The wrestlers were just being careful, that's all.

My study of the wrestlers began when the sport (?) did not savor as much of the burlesque as it has in recent years. Nowadays, in such communities as tolerate the antics of the wrestlers—many state commissions refuse to hail their meetings as contests but as exhibitions—it is no novelty to find a man who wrestles in the main event on one card appearing in a twenty-minute preliminary on the next. The next is usually the next night, either in the same city or one that can be reached handily.

In the days of Frank Gotch, Hackenschmidt, the Zbyszkos, Joe Stecher, Earl Caddock, Strangler Lewis, and Jim Londos (in his earlier stages) there was probably just as much hokum, but it was not as barefaced hokum. There was a Masked Marvel who came on the scene many years ago, but through the grunting and groaning wrestling forties the country was overrun with men of mystery. They would appear in masks, in hoods, and in all sorts of disguises.

One spring in Los Angeles such a mysterious character was all the rage. The papers were filled with yarns about the attempts to find his identity. He packed 'em in every time he appeared. He spoke to no one. No one spoke to him. There was such a terrific drive on to find out who he was, Charlie Grimm, the Cubs' manager, Bob Lewis, and a pair of Chicago newspapermen decided to go see the man of mystery.

It was the custom then to call attention to celebrities at

the ringside, and Grimm and Lewis were duly presented just before the main event began. The man of mystery was sitting in his corner at the time, peering out through the eyeholes in his hood.

As he was summoned to the center of the ring for instructions, the man of mystery paused for a moment and leaned over the ropes, speaking in a low voice that was heard only by Grimm.

"Is Clyde McCullough here with you?" he asked. McCullough was then a rookie catcher seeking a place with the Cubs.

Somehow that seemed to spoil the illusion for me, but when ringsiders pressed around Grimm to ask what the man of mystery had said, Grimm straight-facedly explained that he didn't know, it was in some language he could not understand.

Lewis was more explicit. "He wanted to know where the men's room was," he said.

Gobar, of whom I have written, was the only wrestler from India I ever saw, but I always enjoyed hearing international wrestling figures tell of one Gama who was supposed to be the greatest of them all. Or was until I heard tell of yet another wrestling native of India who used to toughen his stomach muscles by lying flat on his back with a board over his tummy, across which a herd of elephants would walk.

These days Londos is the only wrestler I visit with very much. I like him and he likes me, probably because I don't talk wrestling with him. We discuss Greek politics, the difference between classical and modern Greek, and whether it is proper to attempt to drink real Greek coffee with a spoon or eat it with a fork.

But then, Londos and I are old friends. He was an ambitious young amateur wrestler at the Olympic Club in San Francisco when I was a member of its baseball club.

It is an admitted fact that years do not seem to hang

heavily upon a professional wrestler. I suspect that Londos must be about my age, and I went into athletic retirement in 1914. Londos is still going. He is ageless. He is one of the most remarkable athletes I have ever known.

CHAPTER 25

The Customer's All Right

*I*N the preamble reference was made to the people who have the news thrust upon them. I have not forgotten them in this leisurely trip through a half century of sports. I come now to the customers, the fans, the alumni, those who voice their opinions from ringside, from galleries, from box seats or bleachers. Nor do I intend to slight those who take pen in hand and write letters to the sports departments. No, indeed. Constant Reader will have his turn, too.

I even intend to give an inning to those members of the public who love to call up on the phone, if not very late at night when the boys are gathered in the back room, then surely just when the phone-answerer is right on a deadline at his office. They shall bat first . . . and go out quickly. For after due deliberation, I must classify them as pests. Not so much of a nuisance, perhaps, as the writers of letters who are fearful of signing their own names to a document panning a sports writer who was willing enough to affix his name to what he had to say. But nuisance enough.

Especially the sort that gets in an argument, let's say over the age-old subject: Did Jack Johnson win the world's heavyweight title when he knocked out Jim Jeffries, or did he win it when he knocked out Tommy Burns? Or: Was Joe Louis champion when Max Schmeling knocked him out?

One man calls up. He gets his answer. But that is not enough.

"Tell it to this fellow, will you?"

So you tell it to the other fellow, wondering all the while why he should believe you, when he will not believe his friend the first time around.

After many years of trying to fashion a defense for these "Tell it to him, will you?" plays from the boys in the back room, I hit upon one that has proved adequate in San Francisco, New York, and Chicago. I imagine it will work elsewhere as well.

When the first fellow calls up and wants to know if Louis was champion when he was knocked out by Schmeling, you tell him no, which is correct.

When he says, "Tell it to this other fellow, will you?" you ask the second man what the question is. It's the same question, of course: Was Louis champion when he was knocked out by Schmeling? You tell him yes, and hang up quickly.

The battles that have ensued after this sort of treatment must have eliminated an awful lot of those phone callers from the back room. At least I don't seem to get many of them any more.

My first experience with a sports crowd took place at Dreamland Rink in San Francisco. I was covering a fight show and the decision given in the main event displeased a galleryite, who hurled a beer bottle at the referee. His aim was bad. The bottle hit the top rope of the ring directly opposite me. The neck of the bottle broke off and the jagged butt sailed across the ring and caused quite a divot in my right hand. If you care to drop around someday I'll show you the triangular scar.

The only time I was ever involved in a barrage by an aroused baseball crowd took place at St. Louis during the 1930 world's series between the Cardinals and the Athletics. This series was being broadcast by my old pal Graham McNamee. In those days the wise powers of baseball did not segregate the broadcasters from the baseball writers, and McNamee worked from a spot in the press coop with baseball writers in front of him, behind him, and beside him. In back of the press rows, cash customers filled the upper stand to its roof.

This series had begun in Philadelphia, and the partisan St. Louis crowd had gained the impression that McNamee's account was biased in favor of the Athletics. The Cardinal fans were very mad about this. Long before McNamee arrived, these fans were milling around the press stand, where baseball writers were trying to work. The fans were asking that McNamee be pointed out to them. They had so many different McNamees pointed out that it's a wonder they didn't give up and forget it. But just before the game began, when Graham took his place at the microphone and started describing the climate and the St. Louis sky line, the fans began to get the range.

Throughout the game they pelted him with rolled newspapers and rubbish generally, with peanuts and anything else that was throwable. As usual, their aim was bad, and I'm quite sure that if the hunting laws set a limit on baseball writers that year, each one of those enraged St. Louis fans must have bagged his quota, but not one of them caused McNamee to skip a single beat in his flow of language.

The most childish display given by spectators at any sport anywhere is that offered by the patrons of the Black Hawks' hockey games at the Chicago Stadium. For a long stretch before each game the galleryites amuse themselves by making gliders out of paper, which they sail down onto the ice. After the games begin, when anything irks them, and sometimes when anything pleases them, these galleryites toss out packs of playing cards, rolls of ticker tape, and all sorts of missiles, representative of animal, vegetable, and mineral kingdoms. No matter what attempts have been made by the management to curb this senseless practice, it is as much a part of professional ice hockey in Chicago as are the Black Hawks.

It is from the crowds at baseball games and boxing matches that you are most likely to hear individual attempts at witticism. College and professional football games are more organized in their cheering or booing, as the case may be.

It is a question whether the comments are more savage from spectators at baseball or at boxing. I have heard representatives from each class put forth efforts that merit consideration if there is ever to be an award for free-style criticism. And each city I have visited has had its own challengers for this award.

The only concerted display of ill-mannered crowd comment I have ever observed at a college football game happened in the Pittsburgh stadium in 1930 when Notre Dame met Pittsburgh. The Panthers were a formidable team, and their violently partisan crowd expected them to turn back Rockne's team quite handily.

When Notre Dame first got possession of the ball it was on their own thirty-yard line. Pitt's goal was seventy yards away. Quarterback Frank Carideo called signals. The Notre Dame backs shifted, not with their usual snap and precision, but awkwardly. Carideo checked signals quickly.

As Notre Dame prepared to line up again, from the crowd on one side of the field burst forth a series of derisive comments. The great Notre Dames didn't know what they were doing. Is that the fancy Rockne stuff we've been hearing about? And so on.

Carideo's signal-calling done anew, the backs shifted and the ball was snapped. It came back to Marchy Schwartz. He started off tackle. No one stopped him. He was through the line ten yards without a hand being placed upon him. In a leisurely fashion he made his way the rest of the route for his touchdown. It was leisurely because there wasn't a single Pittsburgh player left standing to challenge him or pursue him once the Notre Dame blocking had been completed.

The largest crowds I have ever seen at any competition are those that attend the annual 500-mile race at Indianapolis. This event was given big-time publicizing by Steve Hannagan and his associates for a long term of years, and as a result the crowds were so large that almost any figure in excess of 150,000 would be credible. These Indianapolis crowds occupy stands spotted at intervals around the two-and-a-half-mile course, mill around on foot in the tremendous infield, or sit in or on top of thousands of parked automobiles.

Thousands of them have been in line for days before the gates are thrown open. Thousands of them pay no attention to the race save for an occasional glance, and picnic the rest of the time in the infield or wander about surveying each other.

They are not the most mobile crowd at sports. That distinction will have to go, I believe, to a race-track crowd. Not very many people go to a race track for the purpose of watching a race. They go for the purpose of betting and watching. They are forced to walk around to a mutuel window to buy tickets, and if they're lucky, to another window to cash them. They visit the horses in the paddock. They gad about, always on the alert for last-minute information. They are the most restless of sports crowds.

They are also the longest suffering. At Churchill Downs, where the country's largest race crowd gathers annually for the Kentucky Derby, it is impossible for many of the thousands present to get as much as a fleeting glance at the horses going by. They know that before they ever start for the Downs, but start they do, and when they get back home they have just as much to say about it as the man who sat in a box on the finish line and watched the horses all the way around with powerful field glasses.

The patrons of any sports event of importance fall into two general classes, those who want to see and those who want to be seen. The latter class are numerous enough to have made possible the $100 ringside plaster Mike Jacobs attached to his ringside seats for the Joe Louis–Billy Conn championship fight, to which Conn, the challenger, supplied about thirty cents' worth of actual fighting. The $100 ringsides were sold out so quickly Jacobs had to get a new batch ready. The fans who wanted to see had a better view on the merits of that championship fight, and remained away in large numbers.

I have noticed one crowd reaction that is not peculiar to any sport. That is the utter inability to remain in a seat when the action starts.

Baseball fans come closer to keeping their poise than any others, but even they will leap rapidly to their feet when a ball is driven down along the foul line, causing the broadcaster to go into his routine: "It may be fair, it may be foul, it looks ..." etc., etc., etc. If they had remained seated the crowd would have discovered in ample time what it was they wanted to know.

Football crowds jump up at the kickoff, and spend the rest of their time getting up and sitting down as the play goes on. There isn't a thing that could possibly happen on a football field that they couldn't see if they remained seated, but up and down they go, just the same.

At a track meet, in stands parallel to the straightaways, the sound of the starter's pistol brings everyone erect. It also keeps about two thirds of the crowd from seeing anything, whereas visibility would not be bad at all if everyone had kept his seat. But up and at 'em is the rule.

Most unmanageable crowds of all are those that follow golf matches. All kinds of methods have been used to keep them out of the line of flight of the ball, or from encroaching upon the greens, but no satisfactory system has yet been devised. Galleryites, striving to get a point of vantage, are liable to cross the fairway without warning. Sometimes they line the fairways so densely they furnish stories that were not in the original prospectus.

I was following Bobby Jones one round in a National Amateur at a course near Boston. The spectators were closely packed all along the fairway, which made its way through a wooded area.

Jones hooked badly off the tee and his ball, traveling far down the course, landed in the crowd. Instead of continuing on into the woods, it was seen to rebound and land out on the fairway. By the time Jones and his retinue reached the vicinity the neighbors were giving first aid to a galleryite off whose head the ball had bounced. It saved Bobby some extra strokes, but it did not increase the victim's appreciation of golf as a spectator game.

The most active of all baseball spectators I have ever encountered are those who attend games at Brooklyn. There is no end to their antics to keep themselves amused. They are not especially unruly, and mad as some of their pranks are, I prefer them at their vociferous worst to any congregation of the fair sex or of the kiddies gathered for a free day at a ball park.

I have witnessed crowd disturbances at ball games in Detroit, Cleveland, St. Louis, Chicago, Pittsburgh, and Brooklyn in which everything from a pop bottle to a patron was thrown, so I assume fans are much the same emotionally wherever they are encountered.

It is the practice of most operators of sports projects to make a few rules of conduct for their patrons and then forget about enforcing them. I have been in attendance at collegiate football games in stadiums well placarded with signs telling what will happen to anyone who brings intoxicating liquors into the place. And in those same stadiums I have seen about as large a collection of drunks as can be encountered at any sport event.

However, I do insist that crowds can be educated. Charles H. Strub, directing force of Santa Anita, proved that when he drew up his own code of rules and regulations.

One of these was that there were to be no passes distributed. He followed the sensible theory that anyone who was unable to pay his way into a race track had no business on it. This no-pass rule was supposed to strike at the very foundations of racing, since one of the chief purposes of the sport is to get as many people in the vicinity of those pari-mutuel machines as possible.

Strub went through with his plan. He was helped, of course, by the fact that legalized racing was new in southern

California when he started. There was some grumbling by those who had known how freely passes were distributed at other tracks throughout the country, but before long Strub's public was adjusted, and Santa Anita's paid gate receipts are not the least of the tremendous revenue that the track gets year after year.

If Los Angeles can take its racing pass or let it alone, not so Chicago. That is a very pass-conscious community, especially for races. Some of the tracks distribute passes even to people who do not ask for them, which is the height of something.

In recent years there has been a great deal of comment about the presence of gamblers in sports crowds. Almost any observer can spot them, since they are on the go constantly, as the tide of battle shifts. They are to be seen at Madison Square Garden and at the Chicago Stadium and in any other major arena in the land. They are at fights and ball games, football games, particularly among the professionals, at hockey and basketball games. They are a nuisance to other spectators who are able to get a kick out of a given competition "without having something on it." But very little is ever done about it. In all the time I have been looking over the sports field, the ejection of gamblers from the San Francisco ball park by Strub, and their being kept out, is the only definite move against these obnoxious creatures I have ever noticed.

My last category of people who have the news thrust upon them takes in the ticket seekers, those who want to buy and those who want to mooch.

I have known many men well able to pay their way into any event who would rather boast about having made it on a pass. I have known others who might have been given a pass on one occasion who have been off me for life because I was unable so to outfit them for subsequent events. I confess freely that I hate ticket moochers. I hate them as much as I do the friends of the big boss who do not hear about a world's series, a championship fight, or a big football game until the very day it begins, and then put pressure to bear on some luckless sports writer, who must produce two, four, six, eight, or ten tickets inside the first five rows ringside, between home plate and first or third base, or on the fifty-yard line . . . or else.

May I add that these are the only members of the public, my public, whom I do not love dearly, and never will.

CHAPTER 26

Meet My Gang

MEET now the gentlemen of the press and radio, as I have been meeting them daily for many and many a year. Some of them, as much the actors as the reviewers, have been touched upon already in these pages, but I have reserved the general roundup until now.

From a very early age I have been in association with newspapermen. I have worked with them. I have associated with them. I have written of them and at times they have written of me. I have met them at exhibitions of practically every form of sport on the calendar. I have been with them at national conventions, at famous trials, at opening nights in the theater. I have been with them on regular beats and in their offices. I have played with them, cultivated them, and fought with them. I have had experience with newspapermen in all the major cities of this country, and many of the smaller.

Before going into my all-out recital of what experiences of theirs I deem part of this story, I have one statement to make regarding the members of my craft. Wherever I have met them, or under whatever circumstances, whether famous or inexperienced, they were my kind of people. In my whole life I have met but three members of my profession, oddly enough all in Chicago, whom I would classify as Grade A jerks.

Those three, contrasted with the hundreds or perhaps thousands of others I have known and liked from coast to coast, can be forgotten. The others, individually and collectively, make up a cross section of America with which I am everlastingly grateful for being identified.

When I broke into the newspaper business, the way of the cub was as rough as it was for a rookie trying to make his way in baseball. There were few encouraging hands lent him. He had to prove his worth first, and the hard way. Woe unto him if he attempted to crash into batting practice while the regulars were so occupied. A dozen harsh "Get out there and shag, you busher!" would resound in his ears. He took what was left and did what he could with it, and was grateful.

I wouldn't have missed that rigorous system, but I can see where it is much happier now for cub reporter or for rookie ball player. Right from taw they can sit with the mighty, in their card games or at their table. They can get into their arguments. They can bat for them or with them, and nothing is said about it.

I took up the sports-writing chore about the same time an associate of mine in semipro baseball also made a bid for his by-line. His name was Tom Laird. In the San Francisco sports-writing fraternity we were the two "bushers." The stars on the baseball beat, at least, were Al Joy and Harry Smith. They gave Tom and me the back of their hands at every opportunity. We bushers were in veritable quarantine in the press box at Recreation Park. Not exactly pariahs, but we would do until a couple came along.

One day Laird and I came up with our first big story. We were both on afternoon papers, and therefore had it in print hours before the Joy and Smith follow-ups hit the street.

We went to the ball game next day prepared to take bows on our feat. The first person I saw was one of the principal characters in the story. He greeted me with the statement that that was certainly a swell story Joy had in the *Examiner* that morning, wasn't it? The guy didn't even know I'd had the story and that Laird had had it the afternoon before.

From then on I haven't bothered my head too much about "scoops." They're nice to have, but I have long since reached the conclusion that the reading public doesn't always know or care which paper or which reporter got there first with the news.

In this instance, however, Joy and Smith knew that the bushers had beaten them, and Laird and I were frowned upon more than ever.

After exhausting the possibilities of our scoop as a press-box topic, Joy polished us off with this:

"Well, anyhow, I'm the highest paid sports writer in town and I don't care who knows it."

That certainly put in his place young Brown, who was getting the interesting amount of $25 a week ... and had been wondering how long this had been going on.

I don't mean to rush ahead too fast in this, but there was an incident in Fresno, California, many years later. Joy had long since left the newspaper business and occupied an important and lucrative post with the Raisin Growers Association.

I had changed my base of operations to Chicago, and had come out to Fresno to interview "Dutch" Leonard, a former famous American League left-hander. It was in the interest of checking up on a story involving several of baseball's super stars, and Commissioner Kenesaw M. Landis had been trying to get Leonard to come to Chicago and tell his story. Leonard refused.

I arrived in Fresno a few hours after the story broke in Chicago and went at once to Leonard's home. When I arrived the phone was ringing. Mrs. Leonard answered it and shooed away the caller, who wanted to talk to Dutch. The phone kept ringing. Mrs. Leonard kept shooing 'em away. I found out whatever it was Leonard wanted me to find out, and still the phone rang.

I suggested that Mrs. Leonard take a breather and let me answer a few calls and tell them I didn't know where Dutch was, either.

The first caller was most businesslike.

"This is Al Joy," he said. "I want to speak to Dutch Leonard."

"He isn't here," I said.

"But I have to reach him somehow," Joy insisted. "Cobby of the San Francisco *Examiner* has asked me to do a story for him and he's in a hurry."

"Tell Cobby he'll get his story in a hurry," I said. "That's why I'm here."

"Who is this?" demanded Joy.

"This is the highest priced baseball writer in Fresno, Al, and I don't give a damn who knows it," I told him.

"Well, you elephant-memoried son of a bitch!" said Al Joy. An hour later we held a joyous (no pun intended) reunion in his office, and it was on his typewriter that I composed the story for which Cobby was waiting.

My first experience with a writer from the big time was with Charley Dryden, generally considered the master baseball reporter of them all, and certainly entitled to rank with Ring Lardner, Damon Runyon, Grantland Rice, Bill Mc-Geehan, Charley Van Loan, and Hugh Fullerton, all in the starting line-up of my own all-star team.

Dryden came to San Francisco with the Cubs at a time when Laird and I were still in quarantine in the Recreation Park press box. When all the Chicago writers were assembled, and were hobnobbing with Joy, Smith, and "Spike" Slattery, another of the San Francisco veterans, it was Dryden who noticed that we two bushers were being ignored. For the Cubs' entire stay in our midst, Dryden sat with Laird and me and discussed baseball and baseball writing and affairs of state with us as if we had been leading lights of the country's greatest newspapers. For that I never forgot Charley Dryden, and if, in my time, I have resisted the urge now and then to brush off some upstart who has let his newly acquired by-line throw him, it is entirely because of that memory.

If there is such a thing as a godfather for a youngster trying to make his way in the newspaper profession, mine was T. A. Dorgan, better known at Tad, one of the best of all the cartoonists, and an accomplished turner of the sports-page phrase. It is a matter of debate whether it was Tad or Runyon who contributed the more to the slang expressions that swept the country from time to time.

Tad had made his start in San Francisco under Hy Baggerly, the sports editor who gave me my first chance. Perhaps Baggerly had written him about me. At all events, on one of Tad's infrequent visits to his old home town he sent for me to have lunch with him.

When I arrived he had a copy of our paper in which I had a story of which I was inordinately proud. I really had turned on the best of the English I had learned in my senior year at dear old St. Ignatius.

"Bag wanted me to talk to you," he said. "What's your ambition in this business?"

"To get to New York," I told him.

"Why?" said Tad.

"That's the big league, isn't it?"

Tad did not reply to that. Instead he took up a new form of questioning.

"Do you read papers a lot?"

I said that I did.

"What writers do you like best?"

"Arthur Brisbane on general subjects, and Runyon in sports," I decided.

"Why?"

I gave that some thought, and finally explained somewhat haltingly that I guessed it was because they were easy to read and because I could always understand what they were getting at, whether or not I agreed with them.

Whereupon Tad put his finger squarely upon the story of which I had been so proud. "Then why in hell don't you get wise to yourself?" he said.

Since that moment, even though Paddy Harmon, a promoter of Chicago, once said that I wrote with an ax, I have left the flowery expressions in the English class at St. Ignatius, and if they were moved into the University of San Francisco, that's all right by me. Only once since then have I ever had any doubt that my followers knew what I was trying to say. That once came after I had written a story about one of the annual knockdown-and-drag-'em-out football games between Northwestern and Notre Dame.

Among the letters that came in from Constant Reader was one saying that while everybody knew I was a Northwestern rooter at heart, I should try to be fair in my reporting. He cited one passage from the story to prove how biased I was. In the same mail came a letter saying that I ought to be ashamed of myself for letting my love for Notre Dame influence me every time I covered a game in which they played. He cited the same passage to prove his point. I never have been able to figure that one out.

My first general assembly with all the famous newspapermen of the nation took place in San Francisco on the occasion of the Democratic Convention in 1920. The members of the press of San Francisco took charge of the entertainment of the visiting members of the craft. In all history there has never been another national convention covered as that one was. If you think so, may I mention in passing that part of our service to our guests consisted of delivering at the hotel-room door, morning and evening during the entire stay of every visiting newspaperman, a quart of the best. And I don't mean milk.

It could have been coincidence, but I doubt it, that the Democratic candidate nominated that year was James Cox of Ohio, who was a newspaperman. He might have won, except for the fact that his opponent, Warren Harding, had newspaper experience too.

It was at this convention I had the chance to observe the great writers at work and at play. It seemed to me that the more famous they were, the finer company they were. I cultivated Runyon, the number one man in my field.

I was to meet him again at Benton Harbor, when Jack Dempsey met Billy Miske. A few days later, when I was visiting New York and stopping at the Hotel Belmont, where

Kearns and Dempsey resided, Runyon came into the lobby
while I was talking with Kearns and Dick Scollin, a former
San Franciscan, who managed the hotel.

Runyon greeted Kearns and Scollin but paid no attention
to me.

"You know Warren, don't you, Damon?" said Kearns.

"Oh, yes," said Runyon. "You're that fellow from the
Coast, aren't you?"

I said I was from the Coast, and continued, "What did you
say your name was?"

"Nice going, young man," said the greatest of all reporters,
and from that day until his death Runyon and I got along.

It is telling no tales out of the editorial room to say that
frequently the gentlemen of the press, and especially sports
writers, look too freely upon the flowing bowl and become
so dizzy they are unable to carry on their work. Others work
for them, and in the long run it all comes out even.

There is a fraternity among newspapermen the like of
which I suspect exists in no other profession. Only in such a
field could happen a series of events such as befell Hype Igoe.

Igoe was allergic to such things as the six-day bicycle race
in Madison Square Garden and the world's series. In the
early twenties the series was exclusive property of the New
York clubs, Giants and Yankees.

Hype's little woman was fearful about what might happen
if her helpmeet were exposed to one of these series. So she
barred him. She not only barred him, but locked him in the
apartment and took away his outer garments.

Being a newspaperman first, last, and always, Hype was
resourceful. He searched the joint and located a dressing
gown. With that wrapped about his pudgy frame he went out
a window and down the fire escape. He hailed a cab, and
luckily found one driven by a fellow who let nothing that
happened in Manhattan surprise him.

"Drive me to the Commodore," ordered Hype. "I'll sit
in the cab while you go upstairs to the baseball headquarters

and tell them Hype Igoe's in the cab and wants to be bailed out."

The driver did as ordered. Hype was bailed out and smuggled into headquarters, where a lot of jolly good fellows proceeded to raffle him off. The winner was to have custody of him for the duration of the series.

The first problem was to get Hype some clothes. Unfortunately his appearance coincided with Columbus Day, a Jewish holiday, and a Sunday. Search as they might, no clothing store could be found open. Finally far down on the Bowery a foraging party was able to get control of a sailor's suit, several sizes too large. However, Hype donned it, rolled up the floppy pants, and announced that he was ready to see Colonel Huston's Yankees kick hell out of John McGraw's Giants.

"Where's your press ticket?" asked a fussbudget.

"It's home with my clothes," said Hype. "But I'll get by."

Get by he did. From the most accessible bathroom Hype snatched from an essential part of the plumbing a button on which was printed "Press." Even Commissioner Landis would not have dared question the authority of that badge.

CHAPTER 27

Gentlemen of the Press

*F*OR reasons that will appear obvious in detailing the adventures of some of my associates, I shall have to pretend that they had no names.

There was that episode at a national golf championship when a writer from the deep South, fired with enthusiasm over the prospects of Atlanta's Bobby Jones, pulled up very lame. Bob Harlow, former newspaperman who was managing Walter Hagen's affairs, heard of this and proceeded to cover for the stricken southerner, signing the latter's name. Bob neglected to advise others of his friendly deed, and presently two others rushed into action, each filing a complete story, and signing the fallen hero's name. When the third story duly reached Atlanta, a mystified managing editor wired: "Please send no more stories. The last one was best."

A famous New York racing writer came out to the bluegrass region to prepare himself for the story of his life on the Kentucky Derby of that year. He was on the job for weeks in advance, filing beautiful stories. He went right down the line to Derby Eve, when he became embroiled in an argument with the law, refused to tell his name, and was duly locked up. He was in the Louisville brig when the Derby was run and won, and never did see the race for which he had prepared so thoroughly. However, there were no complaints about his story. One of the master craftsmen in Colonel Matt Winn's press box turned to and batted for him, as fellow newspapermen always have and always will.

I have been alter ego from time to time myself for members of my profession. At Benton Harbor, Bill McGeehan had particularly rough going the night before the Dempsey-Miske fight and throughout the day of it. He made his way by forced march to the press headquarters to finish up his story. When he got there the only typewriter available was one of those old-fashioned Olivers, on which the type faces rose from left and right on slender ovals.

As McGeehan thrust his fingers on the keyboard, coils of these type faces rose from both sides and met in the center in an appalling knot. Bill shuddered as he surveyed the scene, rose unsteadily, and made his way out of the place.

He was next heard from when he arrived at the press box in the Cleveland ball park two days later. His clothes and personal belongings were forwarded to him. His story on the fight reached his paper on time. It wasn't pure McGeehan, but it got by.

My most interesting series of adventures in the helping-hand department were caused by the derelictions of a Chicago associate. One football season I had gone to Ann Arbor to cover the Michigan-Illinois football game. Next to me was the wire set up for my friend's paper. I did not know who was assigned to it, but when no one was on hand at kickoff I began sending in the play-by-play and continued to do so for the half.

At half time my friend arrived. He was in a great rage. He was cursing Fielding Yost and all Michigan. He said he had been delayed for an entire half because no press ticket had been made out for him and he couldn't get in without one.

Since he was in now, I didn't bother to ask how he had made it, but assured him that he was all up to date and could go right on with his second half.

"Who covered me?" he asked. I told him.

"They'll know it isn't my style," he said. "They'll think I'm drunk again. I'll send it in again in my own way." Which is exactly what he did.

The following Monday I encountered his boss on the street near our office.

"How was So-and-So Saturday?" he asked.

I said he seemed all right to me. Why?

"He must have been all right," said his boss. "He was supposed to cover the Purdue-Chicago game right here in Chicago and he showed up instead at Ann Arbor."

This same hero went to Columbus one week end for an Ohio State game. The Buckeyes' stadium has two press boxes, one on each side of the field. In one the newspapermen and the telegraphers function. The other is used for scouts and other essential characters. Our hero lost his sense of direction once he got inside the stadium. He climbed the heights to the wrong press box and spent the entire afternoon cursing Western Union for having failed to assign an operator for his paper. The operator, across the field where he was supposed to be, handled the story that I wrote and signed with our hero's name.

The legend of a former sports writer of Chicago contains many passages that are related whenever members of the craft get together for a bull session. He affected a Mexican complex. He went in for sombreros, boots, and a sprinkling of the Spanish tongue. He made frequent sorties across the border and claimed intimacy with all the Mexican notables of his time. He liked to refer to himself as the good *señor*.

Once while making his way back with one of the Chicago baseball teams from the Coast, he paused in a hotel in El Paso. A radio in the lobby was blaring away with the program undeniably in Spanish. He listened attentively and from time to time shook with laughter, saying that the broadcaster was one of the most comical persons he had ever heard.

A native of Texas standing near by also listened and watched the señor with a puzzled expression. Finally he turned to Ed Burns, another Chicagoan, and said, "Is that guy nuts?"

"Not especially," said Burns. "Why?"

"Well," said the Texan, "that program he's listening to

is a weather report from a Mexican station. It may sound funny to him, but I'm damned if it does to me."

According to himself, the señor was also an accomplished engineer, and many was the time while traveling in or out of Chicago he told how he went to the aid of the New York Central, entered the cab of the Century, and brought it in on time.

His imagination was perhaps greater than that of any of his contemporaries, but he seldom overmatched himself. Accomplished as he said he was in the Spanish tongue, he was careful to avoid Moe Berg and Carl Reynolds, two major-league ball players, who could and did read, write, and speak Spanish.

On one of the spring exhibition tours he came again to El Paso, and Burns was with him. They decided upon a trip across the bridge to Juárez, which was then in the hands of insurgents, a revolution being in progress. The señor carefully hid what he said was his commission as an honorary general in the Mexican army.

The insurgents were a motley lot but they were all over Juárez, and the señor led Burns very stealthily through the streets. On their way out of a bar they spotted a pair of heavy hobnailed brogans pacing up and down beyond the swinging door. They were pointed out to Burns, who was cautioned to be careful as it was now obvious they were spied upon.

"The hell with that," said Burns, and went on about his business, which was to purchase and mail a few postal cards. The señor disappeared. Burns took his time savoring the delights of Juárez and returned to El Paso in time to get to the ball park where the Cubs and Detroit Tigers were to play an exhibition game. He arrived to get a welcome that astonished him greatly at first. Later he understood when it was explained that his companion had arrived earlier and spread the word that the last time he had seen Colonel Burns, the latter was being marched to a firing squad, with a bayonet prodding his rear expanse.

The life and times of contemporary baseball writers became much less interesting when the señor retired to become the sedate owner, editor, and publisher of a paper of his very own.

Earlier in the story I mentioned the pre-Lincoln car and engine that Jack Kearns employed to shuttle between Great Falls and Shelby when Dempsey and Gibbons were getting ready for that fight. The newspapermen were continuous passengers.

One of them went to Great Falls, and went into both a decline and a fall. It was decided to return him to Shelby after he had passed out. His companions laid him out on the couch that was part of the car's fixings. His hands were folded across his bosom and candles placed at the head and feet of the bier. Word was sent on to Shelby that we were bringing back the body.

There was quite a crowd at the station when the train pulled in, and the ceremony might have been most impressive save for the fact that just as the mourners began to file in, the body sat up and demanded another drink.

One sports writer operating out of Chicago was assigned to the fight at Shelby to do a series of stories on the participants, leading up to his selection of the winner. On his way out to Montana he locked himself in his room, wrote the exact number of stories, and dated them consecutively. Upon arrival at Great Falls he turned them over to the Western Union with explicit instructions to file one a day, ending with the one that picked Dempsey by a decision.

That accomplished, he proceeded to look for trouble, of which there was all kinds in Montana. He arrived at the Park Hotel in time to participate in a rollicking party Jack Kearns was staging. One drink led to another and he finally passed out in his chair. He resisted all efforts to revive him, so all the other celebrators but one decided to let him stay there. The odd man applied some burnt cork to the fallen writer's face, attached a "For Sale" card around his neck, and with some help took him down into the lobby and parked him there.

At Atlantic City yet another Chicagoan, a two-fisted drinker, arrived to cover Dempsey's camp and was assigned to room with Sid Mercer. The Chicagoan was very faithful in his visits to the camp, but in all the time he was at Atlantic City never once did he touch the keys of a typewriter.

Our man worked on a twenty-four-hour schedule. He would rise from his stupor about noon and go to Dempsey's camp. He would work out there so that he would collapse upon return. About the middle of the night he would recover, join the merry throng at the Beaux Arts, and work himself into another collapse, whereupon he would be aided home by kind friends, of whom he had many.

One night he was late getting started to the Beaux Arts. He was accustomed to rest in the raw. He dressed hastily but limited his garments to shoes, socks, trousers, soft shirt, and coat. Across his broad middle was a belt featuring a gold buckle, diamond studded, a gift from one of the loveliest characters who ever ran beer in Chicago.

Because our hero was late, he worked more rapidly than usual at his hoisting within the Beaux Arts, and very quickly he was being counted out in his chair. There were rumors that the prohibition agents were abroad, and the Beaux Arts proprietor ordered the body removed. A delegation composed of Charles Wilberforce Dunkley and Hype Igoe took the body to the front door and placed it in a boardwalk chair, returning to the table and the party. When the Beaux Arts proprietor discovered the body right at his front door, he demanded that it be taken far, far away. Dunkley and Igoe wheeled the chair and body a block down the boardwalk to the hotel, lifted the body, and started walking it across the well-peopled lobby.

Then only was it discovered that some passer-by had appropriated the fancy belt buckle. In the midst of that crowded lobby the body's trousers dropped, creating a veritable sensation, since there was no draping beneath the trousers. Igoe and Dunkley let go to reach for the trousers. Down went the body. They reached for the body and down went the trousers.

"The hell with it," said Dunkley, and taking out his handkerchief he held it in front of the body while he and Igoe carried it up a few steps to the nearest corridor. There they dropped and left it, returning to the party at the Beaux Arts with all the aplomb of two boy scouts who had done their good deed for both the day and the night.

Cincinnati had a worthy representative in Bill Phelon, who used to collect reptiles of various kinds and carry them about with him for inspiration during many a dull ball game. Phelon had one adventure with the veteran Bill Hanna, a very able baseball and football expert of New York. Hanna's peculiarity (all sports writers have 'em, you know) was that he enjoyed bad health. It was said that while Charlie Dryden would pack up as soon as the baseball season ended and retire to Ocean Springs to fish until another baseball season began, Hanna, as soon as the football season was over, would retire to a hospital for an operation, whether he needed one or not.

He carried with him at all times a bag with a complete assortment of pills and other nostrums. The surest way to earn his undying hate was to meet him and say politely that he was looking well. Phelon, as all of Hanna's contemporaries, knew about this. One day while the Cincinnati Reds were in New York, Phelon was walking down lower Broadway when he espied Hanna coming toward him.

"Hello, Bill," said Phelon, and brushed right on by. Coming up the street was one of those old-fashioned open streetcars. Phelon dashed at it, climbed aboard, and rode about a block. Then he jumped off and started back in the direction whence he had come. Again he passed Hanna, as if for the first time, and went through the same quick greeting and away. Hanna stood looking after him for a while, puzzled, but finally resumed his walk.

There was no streetcar coming now, but that did not stop Phelon. He commandeered a cab and began to trail Hanna. Several blocks from the original meeting scene he dismounted and for the third time approached Hanna, giving him the "Hello, Bill" greeting, and striding right by.

This time Hanna was more active. He rushed after Phelon and caught him by the arm.

"Didn't you just pass me down the street?" he demanded. Phelon gave him a blank stare and asked whether he were drunk. "This is the first time I've seen you in weeks," he said.

Hanna almost collapsed on the sidewalk. "For months I have been fearful my mind was going," he said. "This must be it. I'd better have myself examined by a specialist at once."

These quaint characters of the newspaper profession have always been an active lot, doing good for themselves and for others.

Mark Kelly, a former Chicagoan who operated in Los Angeles for a long time, attended a Pacific Coast League meeting one year. The chief business was the installation of a new president, who happened to be a former newspaperman. How Kelly, who was feeling no pain, ever got into the closed meeting no one will ever know. But there he was, in and seated in the back of the room while all the argument was going on up front.

The Coast League delegates were a willing lot, but what they wanted most was a driving force. They messed around with the subject of the president's salary for a while until Kelly began to get annoyed. In a loud voice he moved that the president be given an annual wage of so much. It was more than any previous Coast League president ever got. No one asked who made the motion. But it was voted.

"And expenses," amended Kelly.

Expenses it was, and when the investigation disclosed who had made the motion, the Coast League fathers very wisely decided to let well enough alone.

CHAPTER 28

Work or Play?

*I*N studying the reactions of my contemporaries as well as of myself when confronted with sports news in the making, I have reached several definite conclusions.

Over the long or seasonal haul, noisiest of all sports reporters are those who inhabit press coops at race tracks generally, and Santa Anita and Churchill Downs in particular. They are louder by far in rooting their choices home than were the Boston baseball writers in the days of Paul Shannon, when "Earache Alley" was just that.

In actual work for their daily bread, the football writers are busiest of all, especially if on play-by-play detail. I say that without bowing in the direction of either ice hockey or basketball proponents, who are in continuous debate as to which is the fastest sport there is. To me, basketball is *just* the game that is probably witnessed by more spectators in the aggregate than any other, and ice hockey is the game in which there is more motion to less purpose than any other I have ever seen.

The most disagreement as to what *did* happen is apt to take place in the working press section at a fight more often than anywhere else on beats I have patrolled. Fight writers who are ever ready to take picks on the referee and the judges seldom agree with each other, either, on the important items of punches and punching power. Many a warrior has gone down from a left hook to the jaw. One man sees it that way.

His neighbor makes just as definite a notation that the end came from a terrific right to the midsection.

It took much study of motion pictures to find out just how many knockdowns there were in the first round of the Dempsey-Firpo fight and who scored them. To this day, as I have pointed out already, there are multiple identities for the man on whose typewriter Dempsey landed when Firpo bull-rushed him out of the ring.

The form of competition that is physically impossible for any one man to report in its entirety as an eyewitness is golf, in early stages of match play rounds or any stage of open play, unless the men who are to finish one-two in the open happen to be engaged in the same twosome.

There is one well-known golf expert for a New York paper who seldom strays from the press tent. He copies scores from the board and interviews reporters coming in from their roadwork around the course. Once in a while he strays into the locker room to talk with players who have finished a round. He winds up outexperting everybody, of course.

Baseball writing is somewhat standardized. It is freer—or was until recent years—from "handouts" of paid press agents than most other sports.

Most baseball writers become rooters. They are in the heights when their team is going well, and low indeed when it blows a tough one. Ken Smith of the New York *Mirror* worries more about the Giants than does Mel Ott. Charley Doyle of Pittsburgh cries aloud when ill fortune hits the Pirates. Jimmy Cannon of the New York *Post* is a hero guy and wraps his choices of the moment in some of the sports pages' most diverting prose. And so it goes.

One of the outstanding examples of the bleeding-heart style of baseball writing took place in the press box at Comiskey Park in Chicago. The White Sox were going nowhere. Cleveland had some kind of chance for the pennant. (It was blown a while later to Detroit when an "unknown" pitcher, Floyd Giebel, won from the great Bob Feller.)

The Chicago authors were in midseason form with their

noisemaking, even if the ball club was not up to American League contender standards. The uproar in the press coop was deafening.

Ed McAuley, a Cleveland writer, stood it as long as he could. At last he turned and pleaded, "Don't you fellows realize that *we* are fighting for a pennant?"

The baseball writers hobnob with players. There is very little of the life and habits of a star or a rookie that does not find its way into print in some fashion. Perhaps there seems to be more to say about baseball people than about other sport participants because baseball is productive of more characters, on the field, among the umpires, in the business offices, and right on up to the league presidents and the commissioner himself.

All of these who go to make baseball the national pastime get to know all the baseball writers. In the main, they have confidence in anyone who owns a membership card in the Baseball Writers Association of America. Few members of that order have ever violated any trust placed in them, and many have carried career-shaking secrets for a long time because such matters came to them as privileged communications. Many such as Joe Williams, Grantland Rice, Dan Parker, Bill Corum, Ed Bang, Tom Swope, Lou Smith, John Carmichael, Bill Cunningham, Harry Salsinger, Roy Stockton, Sid Keener, Ed Wray, Dan Daniel, Frank Graham, Jimmy Powers, J. G. Taylor Spink, Stanley Woodward, Ed Burns, Red Smith, and Arthur Daley have played a more important role in the development of baseball and sports generally than perhaps they realize. They have never pulled punches. They have been ever ready with criticism or sound advice. And their all-time average is very, very high.

In spring training and on the road during the regular season baseball writers travel with the team and are routed along with the party. Their papers are usually billed by the clubs for traveling expenses, monthly, though at one time there was a practice of having the representatives of some papers "cuff" their way around as the club's guest.

Traveling with a major-league ball club is really a soft touch for anyone who wants to see America in comfort. From the time he joins up in the spring until the world's series is over, if his team gets into it, the baseball writer has no travel cares at all. His baggage is handled for him. His rooms are ready for him at any hotel upon arrival. His railroad tickets are bought for him and all he has to know is the time of departure. The traveling secretary tells him that, as well as his Pullman space. If he has to make a quick trip from ball park to station, cabs are reserved for him, as they are upon his arrival in a city.

Traveling secretaries, who look after all this, are bound to be regarded as wonderful by baseball writers, and most of them are, anyhow. If they were not, they would go daffy first time around the circuit.

The only other personages in sport I have found who are comparable with traveling secretaries are the collegiate student managers, who have to look after large parties en route to games that involve travel. The student manager technique, such as is in vogue at Notre Dame or Northwestern, with whose teams I have traveled most, is somewhat different from that of a baseball traveling secretary, but both come out even in the long run.

Normally a traveling secretary looks after only the writers covering for his own city's papers. If the team is in the race, going through the last few critical weeks, he begins to hear from writers from various other cities in both major leagues. To the best of his ability he adds them to his list of charges.

Once a team gets into the world's series, there are always many writers who want to travel with it. It is standard practice to have at least one press special train, but as many writers as can do so like to crowd on the train with one team or another.

To the journeyman sports writer there is no great mystery to his work, though the public always seems to find it so. It seems a never ending source of amazement that a man in a press box with a telegraph operator at his side is actually depositing in his newspaper office, hundreds or thousands of miles away, a reasonable facsimile of that material which is rolling out of his portable typewriter.

In my own case, when I am in a press row at ball parks, football games, or prize fights, the copy is much more legible when the telegraph man in the office listens to his sounder and transcribes what he hears in excellent typewriting. Many years ago I found that press rows were too congested to use a portable typewriter, however small, without interfering with a seatmate on either side or having him interfere with me. So I generally write longhand, or, when a familiar operator is assigned, dictate into his shell-like ear.

Overnight stories—that is to say, those that are not from the field of play—I bat out on a typewriter, as I do my column. I make no claims to inventive genius, but I have succeeded in making converts to my longhand spot news reporting system. One of them is Ed Burns of the Chicago *Tribune*. He has a distinct advantage over me. He writes legibly in longhand, and usually with a fountain pen. I'd no more think of that than I would of trying to work a diagramless crossword puzzle in ink first time around.

I said at the outset of this consideration of the members of my profession that they measure up as my kind of people, generally. Perhaps I should take an exception or two at this time.

I have a distinct dislike for the sports writer, often a Johnny-come-lately, who is forever worrying about the "fix." He believes that a race is seldom run on the track that has not been decided in the owners', trainers', or jockeys' rooms the night before. He is forever looking for "angles" on every prize fight, and writes or talks knowingly about "tankers," "dives," and so on.

He belongs in the same category, in my private rating, with the sports writer who puts the blast on a one-sided match, generally in boxing, but who has gone right along helping build it up for days or weeks, when his better judgment, if he has any, must have told him that what *did* happen was inevitable from the day the match was made.

As an outstanding example of this, I believe the Joe Louis–Billy Conn fight, first of the postwar heavyweight championships, will always stand as a record for "experts" reversing their own field.

The most ridiculous incident I have ever encountered at a race track took place just before the running of the 1936 Santa Anita Handicap. This race was for $100,000 added. It attracted many of the most famous Thoroughbreds in training, among them A. G. Vanderbilt's Discovery. Discovery was the posttime favorite, held at about 8 to 5 on the board.

A Los Angeles sports writer who had been suspicious since his childhood of the circumstances of Grant's victory over Lee was trying to get himself in the frame of mind to make a bet on the race, and he was inclined toward the favorite, Discovery.

He approached Ed Burns, who was covering the race for his paper. "Do you know Vanderbilt personally?" he asked.

"Sure," said Burns. "*All* the Vanderbilts and Whitneys, two Rockefellers, and one Ford. Why?"

"I'm serious," said the Los Angeles man. "I'm thinking of making a bet on his horse. I'd like to know if he's shooting, with the price as low as eight to five."

One hundred thousand dollars at stake in the purse, and the skeptic was wondering if an owner—any owner—wasn't shooting!

One of the best known of the "my boy" school of sports writing was Tom Laird, who operated out of San Francisco, whence came many famous major-league players.

For years Frank O'Doul was Laird's "boy." O'Doul, whether in National, American, or Pacific Coast League, could do no wrong. In later years Joe Di Maggio became Laird's "boy," but since Tom was noted for his violent temper, none ever attempted to extract from him an opinion on who was the greater, O'Doul or Di Maggio. Since Laird's

retirement, Jimmy Cannon of the New York *Post* has succeeded to the "my boy" school title.

Once in a while in the progress of their daily chores,
sports writers carry on a seemingly endless drive against an
individual or events over which an individual has control.

In bygone years Bill McGeehan took the New York State
Boxing Commission for a ride day after day. He entitled
them the Dumb Dukes. There was nothing vicious about Mc-
Geehan's attack, but there must have been times when the
Dumb Dukes wished there were. It was the lampooning rather
than harpooning that got 'em in the long run.

Dan Parker, of those now actively engaged in sports col-
umning, is more apt to belt around the body politic than any
other writer since Westbrook Pegler set his sights on other
targets. Parker's pen is mightier than any sword. Dan has
carried on feuds with many characters in the years he has
been writing. Sometimes he has made converts out of a few
of his objects of scorn or derision. Not often, but enough to
keep him on edge for anything else that comes along.

In Chicago Gene Kessler, a sports columnist, at one time
dedicated a great deal of his prose to the proposition that
the Chicago Cubs' James T. Gallagher was someone he didn't
like. From time to time Kessler blamed on Gallagher everything that happened to the club except the occasional tur-
bulence of the channel the Cubs must cross each spring on
their way to training camp at Catalina. At first Gallagher, a
former newspaperman, was inclined to fire as soon as he saw
the whites of Kessler's eyes. Presently he realized that the
best way to annoy any writer is to pretend that you do not
read him at all.

If Gallagher chose to ignore criticisms directed at him,
there have been other major-league club executives who
relish brushes with the gentlemen of the press, and sometimes go out of their way to invite them. Perhaps the leader
of this sect is Larry MacPhail of the Yankees. Scarcely a
season goes by that does not find MacPhail the object of some
writer's unaffectionate prose. He has been one of Dan

Parker's favorite subjects, and others have argued with him or against him as long as he has been in baseball.

My own experience with MacPhail dates back to the time he was a football official in the Western Conference. This was before he became a minor- and later major-league executive. Even though it be treason in the eyes of several of my colleagues, I must say that MacPhail has never yet told me anything for the record that he was unwilling to stand for later on, whatever its repercussions. Nor has he ever given me a bum steer on any story in which I was interested. More, I have not yet asked of anybody.

CHAPTER 29

"Please Use and Oblige . . ."

As sports, professional and amateur, assumed big-business rating, every form of it has gone in for public relations men or press agents.

No college of any importance is without one. By degrees most of the major-league and minor-league baseball clubs have them in one form or another. Fight promoters and many individual fighters have their personal "please use and oblige" men. And so it goes through professional football, basketball in all its phases, golf and golf clubs, racing, bowling, billiards—everything in sport, from archery to yachting.

Many of these press agents are former sports or general assignment reporters. Some prepare copy and make work easy for the journeymen who are apt to be on the lazy side or who are in need of a relief driver. Some are best as idea men, planting stories or tips and letting the reporter's nature take its course.

One of the more notable in this last group is Joseph Chesterfield Farrell, who is the Chicago Black Hawks' tub-thumper. He seldom commits his ideas on the Hawks to type, but no public relations specialist ever gets any more attention to his game than Farrell does for his ice hockey. This is the more remarkable since Farrell in his earlier days was an avowed baseball fan and a disciple of Charles A. Comiskey, original owner of the White Sox.

Farrell once toured the world with the White Sox–Giants party, and one of his favorite reminiscences has to do with his explanation of the American game of baseball to the royal family of England. Now he explains the Canadian game of hockey to Chicagoans.

The best free-style, all-around exponent of public relations is Steve Hannagan, an Indiana boy who made good in the Big City. He does not trouble himself about sports promotions now, save in the role of spectator. But there was a time when he and his associates Larry Smits and Joe Kopps did more to get those crowds of upwards of 150,000 moving to Indianapolis each Memorial Day than did any driver from Barney Oldfield's time on. When Miami Beach was in the process of being discovered, Hannagan and his two aides made the world acutely aware that swimming suits were far more useful pictorially than for the execution of crawl strokes, back strokes, or high and low springboard diving. Hannagan was once public relations counsel for Gene Tunney, and thereby learned a lot of new words.

Hannagan once essayed the promotional publicity work for the Arlington Park race track, which is one half of Chicago's big-time racing, Washington Park being the other. He lifted that form of press agentry to a new level, but abandoned it before the stretch turn was reached. Chicago was not quite ready for all that high-powered activity.

Of the currently functioning press relations men around race tracks, heading the list is Fred Purner, who presides at Santa Anita. He has been there since Charles H. Strub first left San Francisco with the idea and began drumming up investors within the state.

Santa Anita's press arrangements could well be a model for all other tracks. Some have attempted to copy its format but none has quite succeeded.

Purner and his staff have the situation so well under control that the only thing they do not attend to is furnishing the wherewithal for investments in the pari-mutuel machines. However, a season or two ago Purner did cause to be placed adjacent to the press box a battery of $2 machines, sellers, and cashier. The cashier, since sports writers are notoriously bad pickers when it comes to putting their own money through the machines, is usually forced to play solitaire while the races are run, just to pass the time away.

The Santa Anita press box is furnished with a complete café. It has all modern appliances for getting information from any part of the course most quickly. It has a private elevator and entrance, and obviously, a clear view of the course for all save the most important race on the Santa Anita calendar, the $100,000 guaranteed handicap.

For eight races a day every other day of the meeting and for seven races the day of the Handicap, the writers, however many there may be, remain in their allotted seats and see all that is going on. But let the Handicap starters begin their slow pace to the post and there is a general exodus through the windows. The writers sit on the sills. So generally do they get in each other's way, very few have a clear vision of what is going on.

In this the writers prove that they are emotionally no different from the rest of the public they serve. Earlier in this story I remarked the tendency of the customer to jump up in his seat when action is about to begin, thus making it tough for himself and all around him to see clearly. More might be made of that were it not for the fact that everybody around him is doing the same thing at the same time. It may be mass hysteria. I must look that up sometime. For the present I prefer to call it just a nuisance.

The college press agent, of whom many are most capable as writers and as cover-up men, is busiest in football and basketball time. Football is a game in which every coach, for publication, looks on the side least bright. Consequently, these college publicists are all masters of the sob story. Heading toward a big game, they can make a shaving cut seem like a capital operation, if that's what the coach wants.

The college publicist whose team is a winner has other troubles besides getting his copy across. He is plagued by late-arriving experts who need someone to square them with an innkeeper that they may have shelter overnight. He has to diagram and assign seats in a press box for writers with telegraph operators and without, for scouts and friends of the management, of whom there always seems to be an adequate supply. He has to look out for the broadcasters' needs, which are many and complicated. He has to know which photographers want on the roof, and which want somewhere else.

In such spare time as he has, the average college publicist may serve as correspondent for several newspapers, furnishing a hundred words or so on daily workouts. Sometimes he covers games when their importance is not such as to warrant a staff man being sent to the scene by the paper or papers he represents and press association reports are not adequate.

In football season most colleges stage a press party on the night before the game. Here the publicist has to double as host and master of ceremonies, though the latter function is invariably taken off his hands and tossed up for grabs as the visiting authors become imbued with the spirits of the occasion.

Press agents abound in a championship fight promotion. One of the heavyweight extravaganzas staged by Mike Jacobs in recent years usually calls for at least three. There is the club's own man, who functions the year round. Each fighter's camp is manned by a director of public relations, who issues a daily release and looks after all the requirements of writers who pour or are poured in from all parts of the country.

One of the most versatile of the press agents in the ground and lofty division is Harry Mendel, long associated with the quaint art of the six-day bicycle race. For many years it was believed that Mendel was one of the very few people who ever knew what a six-day bicycle race was all about. As a consequence, he found it necessary to appear in the press section periodically to explain that in the last jam the team of Broccoli and Asparagus lapped the field.

No one at six-day races, not even the public address man, ever seemed to know for sure when a lap was stolen or how, but if Mendel said one had been, then that made it official.

Mendel has served time at many a fight camp, and has dabbled in other enterprises.

Most prolific of all the fight camp publicitors is Francis Albertanti of New York. He has prepared more warriors for the opening bell than anyone else I know. It has always been a source of regret to me, if I may borrow a phrase from the turf, that the starters from the Francis "stable" could not always run back to the rating his intense ballyhooing touch gave them.

When he isn't running someone's camp, Francis is certain to be a daily visitor at some important ring affair. He appeared frequently at Billy Conn's camp when the latter was getting ready for whatever it was he had in mind against Joe Louis. Francis listened to and read the ballyhoo pronouncements, which were setting a new high. One day he subjected himself to an interview, saying, "Conn looks great. He is faster than ever. He is punching better than I ever saw him. He is boxing more cleverly than anyone since Gene Tunney or perhaps Jim Corbett himself. He is game. He is determined. He has the will to win." Francis then paused and wound up with a lethal wallop at ballyhoo's body: "I pick Louis to knock him out any time he wants to."

It is said that Conn was very mad at Francis for this. Too bad someone didn't say something to get him mad at Louis.

The most unusual as well as one of the most successful fight press agents I have ever known in sports was Ike Dorgan, brother of Tad, the cartoonist. Ike was in charge of Tex Rickard's boxing enterprises from the time Tex came into the New York area.

I can testify that in all the time I knew him when he was functioning as front man for the Rickard shows, I never saw Ike write a line about any of them. Nor was he a very talkative man. Yet in his time Rickard's shows, great and small, seemed to get more than their share of attention in the public prints. Everyone liked Ike and was ready to rally to his cause.

By the very nature of their association, many sports writers have become accused wrongfully of doubling as press agents for individuals.

In the twenties Bobby Jones did not make a golf shot without the redoubtable O. B. Keeler of Atlanta being as close at hand as his press credentials, the gallery marshals, and the surging crowds would permit. Nor was Bobby very far away from Keeler in his off-course activities. There is no question but that other Atlanta writers were equally fond of Bobby, but O. B. made a profession of it.

During the reign of Jimmy Dykes as manager of the Chicago White Sox, he was adopted by John Carmichael. Once in a while one of the other Chicago writers might take exception to some of the Dykes acts. Invariably Carmichael would rush into print with a column extolling the man whom he believed had advanced managing a major-league ball club from the farthest point ever reached by a McCarthy, a McGraw, or a McGillicuddy.

It was alleged that in the lifetime of Charles A. Comiskey, the Old Roman of the Chicago White Sox, he would go further and do more for sports writers than he would for his ball players. I have no direct evidence of that on either count. I doubt if Commy's lavish entertainments for his friends of the press were any more complete in details than those that Colonels Jake Ruppert and Til Huston used to whip up for New York Yankee followers among the writers or Horace Stoneham now concocts for those who travel with the Giants. Nor have I heard too many complaints around either major-league circuit for the manner in which the average present-day club owner sees to it that the sports writers go first cabin all the way.

Commy could have been years ahead of his time, as far as the sports writers were concerned. As far as his ball players' wage scale went, it is on the record that there are some very successful major-league clubs of the present era whose guardians of the purse strings are never going to scatter about salaries with reckless abandon.

To be sure, the free-wheeling owners are the ones whose

clubs usually get the most attention, but I have yet to hear of any money-making magnate abandoning the game because he didn't always have a favorable press, or because his ball players wished fate had placed them with another club that had ideas of salary grandeur. Nor have I ever heard of any ball players, save Comiskey's shoddy-souled group of 1919, who put forth niggardliness of the owner as an incentive for not giving the best they had all the time they had it.

In the public relations field in these modern times the gift of public speaking is extremely valuable. More demands are placed upon the talents of football coaches than upon anyone else in sports, though every field has found it either necessary or advisable to furnish spellbinders for all sorts of occasions, from dugout interviews to full-scale banquets.

In the coaching profession, the two most sought-after speakers now seem to be Jimmy Conzelman of the professional Chicago Cardinals and Bo McMillin of the University of Indiana. Conzelman, a gifted writer, musician (even to the affectation of long hair), and actor, has the professional touch. His routine is as well organized as any big-time vaudeville monologist's ever was. When he has to, Jimmy can speak extemporaneously, but so far his act, instead of growing familiar with usage, still wows 'em from coast to coast. So he sticks to the script. McMillin is a storyteller who fairly drips with the southern accent when he has to . . . which is nearly always. If either of these two accepted all the speaking bids that come their way, neither would have time to diagram as much as a kickoff formation, much less a long-gainer.

In a former field of always entertaining storytellers, Knute Rockne and Bob Zuppke ranked at the top. Every coach has to go in for a great deal of this personal appearance work. Most of them have ready a yarn or two that might be calculated to cause the audience to take a liking to them, and perhaps think of steering that local high-school football prodigy their way.

Baseball's entertainers, on and off the field, have been many and varied in their talents. Of those now active in the major leagues, Charlie Grimm of the Cubs is in a class by himself. Grimm is a great storyteller, with or without gestures. In this respect he differs from Casey Stengel, formerly on the major-league circuit. Stengel needs plenty of room when he starts spinning yarns, because if the routine calls for a slide, Casey may decide to execute one. He believes in acting out all parts.

Grimm is an accomplished instrumentalist and also sings. He will never chase Bing Crosby out of business, but neither will he chase out any audience he happens to face. He has worked single, but he is at his best in a duo with Bob Lewis, the Cubs' traveling secretary. Lewis is the finest nonprofessional pantomime I have ever seen, and should have been in the movies years ago.

As a rule the major-league managers have their public address innings at baseball writers' annual dinners. Thus they are facing receptive audiences. Football coaches may light anywhere from an alumni luncheon to a meeting of the Chamber of Commerce. They are the better prepared to take on all comers.

I have known of but one instance in which an attempt was made to get some public speaking done by a manager and a coach on the same program. It had interesting enough results to warrant mention here. The incident took place at baseball headquarters in New York during world's series time shortly after John McGraw had replaced himself with Bill Terry as Giants' manager. There had arrived upon the New York scene one Jimmy Crowley, not long out of Notre Dame, who was taking charge of Fordham's football prospects. Christy Walsh, who operated a sports syndicate specializing in ghost writing, thought the baseball headquarters, where sports writers from all over the country were gathered, would be a fine place to have Crowley introduced. He also thought it would be nice if McGraw introduced him.

In the midst of the jollity McGraw was persuaded to rise and rap for attention. He had some difficulty in getting it, what with the clink of glasses and one thing and another, but eventually a semblance of calm prevailed.

Calmest of all was a sports writer from out in the Middle West, whose last slug had brought him down, head on arms, arms on table, near where McGraw was about to go into his speech.

"This young man," said McGraw, "is Jimmy Crowley, the new Fordham coach. . . ."

The man whose head was on his arms now lifted it and said aloud, "We know that's Crowley, but who the hell are you?" Then the head dropped back and the voice was heard no more.

A long time afterward I related that incident to Bill Terry, whom I had known since he broke in with the Giants, and whom I have always liked, most of my New York baseball writing friends to the contrary notwithstanding.

Terry did not think it was as funny as I did.

"I guess that's what is meant when they say fame is fleeting," he said.

Well, if that wasn't, Bill Terry, great ball player and great manager, lived long enough to find out what was . . . and in that same New York.

CHAPTER 30

It's a Promotion

WHEN I broke into sports writing, the covering of events was considered the chief duty of the staff men, whereas the sports editor busied himself with writing, budgets, expense accounts, make-up of pages, art display, frantic pleas for more space, and fewer demands from ticket moochers. Now all that has changed. A sports editor and all his staff are required to have a working knowledge of promotion and make practical application of it.

My own promotional ventures have been few and far between. I'll get rid of them quickly and proceed to a discussion of some of the real champions in the class.

My masterpiece was one that was calculated to end all newspaper sports promotions, and very nearly did. It was beyond a doubt the noisiest event ever put on. It struck at the very foundations of promotion in the sense that no tickets were sold. Our show was, as Dr. Andy Lotshaw put it, "free of gratis." I regret to say that it was a success, and became copied elsewhere.

It was an outboard motor regatta. It was staged originally in one of the lagoons of what was afterward to be the grounds for the world's fair in Chicago in 1933.

My venture into the promotional field was at the behest of Victor Watson, who was my boss pro tem. He became very enthusiastic about it. When the original event was held and a gratifying number of people showed up to see it, it was decided to repeat it the following year. Again it was a success. This time it had been incorporated into the world's fair program. When the world's fair came to a conclusion, took an encore, and bowed off after that, the outboard racers were ready for yet another presentation. They were moved northward in Chicago and cut loose with their deafening racket in the waters near Lincoln Park.

While the regatta was in its ballyhoo stages, Watson had taken a trip to California. He returned to Chicago late in the evening before the big day and retired to his apartment, which was within earshot of the outboard racers' course.

Very early next morning scores of the competitors were on the course tuning their motors. The outboard motor din makes the noise of autos speeding around the Indianapolis brick track seem like a lullaby by comparison. The noise woke Watson, as it must have awakened everyone else for miles around. But Watson was the only one who did anything about it.

He called our newspaper office and aroused the lobster shift man, saying that he thought it was an outrage that all this target practice should be held so close to the residential district. He wanted the cops called, but quick.

The lobster shift man began, "But, Mr. Watson . . ." and was shouted down. Victor wanted action. He raved and ranted and complained that the noise was so great he couldn't even hear himself speak . . . which must have been the most crushing blow of all.

"Who are these people?" he finally yelled into the phone. "Have them arrested and see that they are prosecuted if we have to run page editorials every day. Will you call the cops, or must I do it myself? Who are these people?"

"They are your paper's outboard motor regatta, Mr. Watson," the lobster shift man finally got across.

The cops were not called. Neither have I ever been called again to be a sports promoter.

It is certain that my absence from the field will never be

missed, because all over the country scores of other sports writers are at it. They promote fights. They promote football games. They promote basketball games. They promote baseball games. They have even promoted wrestling matches, which are an all-time low. They have gone in for golf, tennis, swimming, track and field, bowling and ice skating. They have sponsored racing to the extent of cutting in on revenue.

No sport is safe. No sports writer is invulnerable when the promotional bee with his stinger aimed at circulation and/or profits starts buzzing.

Top man in this field, with none close to him for all-around effort, is Arch Ward, the scholarly-appearing sports editor of the Chicago *Tribune*. He has brought into existence the All-Star baseball game between the two major leagues. He thought up the All-Star football game, which annually matches the National Football League's champion of the previous season with the pick of the graduating collegiate crop. There is a question whether Ward or Paul Gallico invented the Golden Gloves, but there is no question but that Ward has done more swinging with them.

He came up with a complete new professional football organization, the All-America Conference. He has promoted skating meets, bowling meets, and frequently has been persuasive enough to talk Chicago race-track promoters out of part of their dates for charity purposes, with his paper sponsoring the show. There is no other sports editor in the country who classes with him for consistent success as an all-around promoter.

Ralph Cannon, of the Chicago *Herald American*, gained a newspaper decision over him in 1946 by staging a game between the Chicago Bears and the New York Giants. It was held in Wrigley Field, which has a capacity of approximately forty thousand.

This game was not considered as a rival to the All-Star contest, which drew double the crowd in Soldier Field, but victory rested on Cannon's banner when it was revealed that his promotion was able to realize more for the charity to which it was dedicated than did the extravaganza between the Cleveland (now Los Angeles) Rams and the All Stars. The practice of employing the services of professional football teams for preseason exhibitions to raise funds for charity is now carried on by several other papers in various parts of the country.

Boxing shows have long been a standard production, with newspapers sponsoring them. Most famous of all were the series in New York that had as their object the raising of money for the Milk Fund. The New York *American* and the New York *Journal* stood squarely behind these projects. They began in Tex Rickard's time and continued into the regime of Mike Jacobs. Ed Bang of Cleveland has a long record of annual Christmas boxing shows for a charity fund, and all have been successful. Joe Williams of New York has explored with interesting results the probabilities a golfer has for making a hole in one. His annual tests for this are one of sport's most unusual newspaper promotional stunts.

One of the interesting features of these sport promotions by individual newspapers is the manner in which their rivals have contributed much of their own space to the cause. That was true of the Milk Fund boxing shows from the start.

Most of the time newspapers that have sponsored a show of any sort from its beginning have clung to future renewals of the event. The exception was the All-Star baseball game.

When it was designed by Ward, the process of selecting the teams was by poll of readers, and he had to do a masterful job of salesmanship to get the two major leagues to go along with his idea.

The game was a tremendous success from its inaugural in Comiskey Park, Chicago, in 1933. It was such a success that the major leagues promptly reached out and took it for their very own. Various schemes of arriving at the identity of the proper All Stars have been tried since that first game. The managers of the world's series contenders of the previous season are usually accorded the honor of leading the two teams, National and American League.

At one time these managers were asked to pick their own squads. Later all the managers of each league were asked to submit selections and a consensus team was chosen. There was criticism right along. Some fair-haired baseball boy was always being ignored. For the 1947 renewal, which went back to Chicago but this time at Wrigley Field, the original policy of permitting newspaper readers and radio listeners, in other words the fans themselves, to make selections was restored.

From the point of view of the manager stuck with an All-Star team, the best he can get is the worst of it. He is wrong if he does, and wrong if he doesn't.

Managers of teams have been accused of using star pitchers just ahead of the All-Star game, thus limiting to some extent their capabilities. Other managers have been accused of not using their star pitchers because of the impending All-Star game, and thus have gummed up a series in the regular league race, which is supposed to be their chief worry.

The ball players themselves have not always gone cheerfully into the All-Star fray. It is customary in arranging major-league schedules to allow a few days in midsummer to permit assembling of the All Stars, and getting them back to wherever their respective clubs happen to be resuming play.

The ball players not engaged in All-Star play usually get what amounts to a few days off with pay, though some clubs are not above scheduling exhibition games to take in the slack. More than one player of prospective All-Star quality would just as soon have the days off to go fishing or visit the race track, and let somebody else do or die for his league.

Nevertheless, the public goes for the game in a big way. After a doubtful competitive start, the two leagues are now able to get as worked up over this one game as they do over an entire world's series.

Some of the most remarkable feats of the track and field athletes have been performed under sponsorship of newspapers. The Chicago Stadium rafter-brushing vault of Cornelius Warmerdam, who soared to the existing world's record height, was made at the Chicago Relays, an annual presentation of the Chicago *Daily News*.

Of all the sports that depend for their existence to a great extent upon the attention the press gives them, ice hockey seems to be the one that has lent itself least to the direction of any sports department's promotional ideas, at least in the United States.

So far, since I abandoned my career as an outboard motor regatta promoter, no newspaperman has gone in for watersports promotion in a big way, though routine sponsorship of swimming meets is common. I can understand that. Great care must be exercised, lest one day a promoter find himself confronted with an event such as the Catalina Channel swim of 1927, which was devised by William Wrigley, Jr. It offered a prize of $25,000 for the first man to swim from the island to the mainland.

I covered that event, and did everything but rub grease on the winner, George Young, a Canadian, the only one of a starting field of 101 to complete the course. Much of the time I was on the press boat, filing short takes by radio-telegraph to the mainland, where it was relayed by the telegraph to which I was more accustomed.

In that race "my boy" was Norman Ross, whom I had watched develop as one of the world's greatest swimmers at the Olympic Club in San Francisco and later at the Illinois Athletic Club in Chicago. Ross was beyond a doubt the most talented swimmer in the field, and the fastest, but he was carried off his course and had to give up, as did all the others save Young.

Since I entered the newspaper profession I have covered practically every sort of sport there is in all parts of the country. I have never covered an event quite as daffy as that Channel swim.

The oddities began when the competitors assembled many days in advance of the race. Each one had his (or her) ideas of what kind of axle grease or oil was best calculated to nullify the chill waters of the Channel. "My boy" Ross argued against grease of any kind. He maintained that most of it would soon wash off, and therefore its cold protection was not lasting enough. Furthermore, it was his opinion that the heavier greases might develop into lumps and ridges that would retard smooth stroking. He made no converts at nightly discussions among the swimmers.

Two of the contestants had original ideas of using some substance similar to novacaine, which would deaden the person to a slight depth below the skin's surface.

"If you take a club and bat each other over the head you will get the same effect," Ross advised.

One of the starters who wanted to keep warm donned two woolen union suits and smeared them with a thick coating of grease. It was almost necessary to use a crane to get him out of the water. Another brave competitor strode boldly off the sands of the isthmus from which the start was made, waded into the water until it was about belt deep, and then was hit in the face with an oncoming roller. He gave up then and there. The race had a legless swimmer. It had one who wore a two-part rubber suit, form fitting, which had tiny openings for eyes, nose, and mouth. He didn't swim very far, and he was quite put out when some of the gentlemen in the press boat kept shouting encouragement to him—encouragement, that is, if insistence that he give himself up and claim the reward can be called that.

By long odds that Channel swim was the most complicated event in which I was ever involved. If I needed any lasting proof, it came about six months afterward when I was trailed to my office in Chicago by a bill for the radio-telegraph tolls from boat to shore, which, it seemed, everybody else had disavowed.

I have never been able to swim a stroke. For that I have never been as grateful as the day and night I spent in 1927 trying to keep up with Mr. Wrigley's 101 characters, who were all wet, from scratch . . . or for it.

CHAPTER 31

Behind the Box Score

I HAVE a peculiar viewpoint on supposedly funny stories of sports-page characters. Most of the time I am fearful of relating any of these, lest the reader has read them elsewhere or heard them before. I appreciate the fact that any story, however ancient its origin, is still new to anyone who hasn't heard it. Yet I remain timid about making such an attempt.

As a case in point there was the episode of Casey Stengel's home run inside the park for the Giants, which beat the Yankees a game in the 1923 world's series. Casey was a veteran at the time and as he touched first base his steps seemed to falter. He was laboring fearfully in his stride as he went around the bases. Practically every writer present had something to say about Stengel's famous run, and attributed its weaving and bobbing to Father Time, who was pacing him.

In those days there were not as many clubhouse reporters as now swarm around world's series games. Such as there were apparently failed to discuss the run Stengel made with its chief character. Which could account for the fact that after reading all the references to his struggle to finish out that mighty dash, Casey himself finally had to offer the true explanation. No sob story was his.

As he tagged first base his shoelace broke. What he fought against all the rest of the way around was not advancing age, shortness of breath, or anything else. He was hoping and praying that his shoe would not fall off. In his heart of hearts he knew that John McGraw would have clubbed him to death with a baseball bat if he blew the game's deciding run because of carelessness in not looking to his shoelaces before setting foot on the field.

When Casey told me that story I hesitated about printing it, assuming that it must have been common knowledge by that time. Apparently it was not, for when I did get around to it, I was accused of having spoiled many a tear-jerking report from the scene.

McGraw and his players were always good for stories, since the Giants in his time invariably had a great case of characters, on and off the field. One such was Irish Meusel, who specialized in driving in tough runs. Irish had been with McGraw long enough to know about his rigid enforcement of training rules, but he also knew that the one thing McGraw detested was any attempt of a player to lie out of trouble once he had been suspected.

Irish went off the reservation on one trip to Chicago, and was hailed before McGraw. No defense was offered. Irish pleaded guilty and Irish was fined $100. Another member of the club lied out of it, and escaped without a reprimand. This caused Meusel to sulk, and he refused to play for a few days, though he did not tell anyone why. It was accepted that the fine was the cause. No one save Meusel and his companion ever did know that there had been anyone else on the AWOL junket but the man who drew the fine. The Giants were very much in the race at the time, but Meusel would not budge. He wanted his $100 back. McGraw was just as stubborn. So Irish hugged the bench.

There came a game at Boston that would decide the pennant in the Giants' favor if they won. They had the proper runners on base late in the game and Meusel was asked to go up and pinch hit. He forgot all about his fine, grabbed a bat, and drove in the precious runs.

McGraw was so elated at the pennant clinching he invited Meusel to accompany him to New York after the game, and before the team had finished its series, since the remaining games were now meaningless.

In the dining car all was merry and Meusel decided this might be a good time to ask for the $100 back. It was, but the fine stood just the same, McGraw said. With him it was a matter of principle. Rules were rules, and all that sort of thing.

Meusel played famously in the world's series, which the Giants won, and again he suggested that he would like that $100 back. McGraw still insisted that the fine stood.

Following the series McGraw and a party of ball players, Meusel among them, sailed for Europe. At the bar one evening ten persons were having a good time, and Meusel made his final bid for the remittance of that $100 fine.

"All right, Irish," said McGraw. "You've been pestering me long enough. I'll give you back the hundred on one condition. You must buy a drink for the crowd."

Meusel accepted hastily.

"Bartender," ordered McGraw, "champagne for all Mr. Meusel's friends."

Champagne it was. The tab came to an even $100.

Meusel had long since retired from the major leagues when he told me that story. Doubtless he had told it many times before, but it was new to me, and apparently it was new to print when I finally got it there. So one never knows.

There have been so many stories of the antics and escapades of Dizzy Dean I have hesitated to make any selection for inclusion here. At spring training camp with the Cubs in 1947 Milt Stock, one of the club's coaches, related a yarn I had never heard before. It took place when Dizzy was in the Texas League, toiling for Houston. The Cardinal aggregation I was to nickname the "Gas House Gang" had not yet been favored with his engaging presence.

Dean was warming up on the side lines, getting ready to pitch for Houston on the afternoon the story broke that he had been sold to St. Louis. Headlines shouted the news. Newsboys raced through the stands yelling, "Dean sold to Cardinals for twenty-five thousand dollars and a player."

"Who's the player—Lefty Grove?" remarked Diz, without missing a beat in his warming up.

Grove of the Philadelphia Athletics was then the top-ranking left-hander in either major league. Even before Diz became the common property of all baseball writers he was not inclined to underrate himself.

One of the earliest of the baseball characters I ever encountered was umpire Bill Guthrie, who came from back of the yards in Chicago. He toiled in the Pacific Coast League before being summoned to the American League.

It is related that Guthrie blew his big-league job because of a jam with Miller Huggins, the famous New York Yankee manager, who introduced the "four straight" world's series design the Yankees favored much of the time thereafter, both for Huggins and for Joe McCarthy.

Huggins, a diminutive person, came raging out of the dugout when some of his players were embroiled in a row with Guthrie. He arrived just as Bill was about to shoo a Yankee player from the game. Having delivered this verdict, he turned to start dusting off the plate. As an afterthought he called over his shoulder, "And take de bat boy wit' you," indicating Huggins.

I have always been partial to umpire Bill Klem's statement that in his long and famous career he never called a wrong decision. I knew—though many reviewers have chosen to ignore the fact—that Klem invariably accompanied the statement with a gesture indicating his heart. At heart I am firmly convinced neither Klem nor any other umpire of consequence ever has called one wrong.

However, I like Guthrie's philosophy equally well. I heard it expounded for the first time in San Francisco at old Recreation Park, where the press and the patrons were very close to the participants.

Guthrie was umpiring at the plate one day and there came a play that precipitated a furious argument. It got nowhere with Guthrie. As the squawkers began their retreat, one turned and let go a parting shot: "You'll have to admit it was close."

"In dis game," replied Guthrie, "dere ain't no close ones. It's either dis or dat!"

Of the same pattern as Guthrie was "Biff" Schaller, an outfielder the Chicago White Sox sent to the Coast League. When Schaller visited Salt Lake for the first time, he had heard much of the rarefied atmosphere that caused a baseball to take long flights. As he stepped from the train Schaller began to take deep breathing exercises. Asked what was the idea, he said he was "getting a load of dis high multitude."

At one hotel on the Pacific Coast League circuit Schaller expressed himself as more than pleased with the surroundings. "Finest joint I ever stopped at," said Schaller. "Why, de rugs is so t'ick, when you spits a chaw of tabacco on 'em, it soaks right in."

Fat Willie Meehan, the Dempsey nemesis, was encountered one day on Powell Street in San Francisco carefully studying the rear end of a new Pierce Arrow automobile. Asked why he was casing the car, Willie said, "I'm trying to figure out how them shock observers work."

In latter-day baseball, the only consistent .400 hitter in the malaprop league I have met is Andy Lotshaw, the Cubs' trainer. For all I know, he may be the all-time champion. I have known him for more than a quarter of a century, and he can take as many falls out of the King's English now as when I first encountered him.

In charge of the first landing party of Cubs going to training camp in the spring of 1947, Lotshaw gave them strict orders not to wander away. "I want all you fellows to congratulate in one place so's I'll know where to find you," he said.

No ramble through sports' lanes would be complete without something about the most unique setup in all ball parks, major or minor, the Booze Cage of old Recreation Park in San Francisco. My contemporaries all have their favorite stories of happenings in Baker Bowl, Philadelphia, once the home of the Phillies, and I have mine, some of which were told in my book *The Chicago Cubs*. But for every ludicrous happening in Baker Bowl, I have one to match from the Booze Cage in San Francisco.

This was a section paralleling first and third base. It was at ground level, protected by a heavy wire screen. It was not more than ten or fifteen yards removed from either base line. Access to it was by way of general admission plus a carrying charge, part of which was redeemable in trade. It was after the redemption had started that the carrying became a problem. As games wore on and many refills were taken, no baseball park ever held so many violently vociferous fans congregated in one sector as did the Booze Cage. Woe to any ball player who attempted to bandy words with the denizens of the Cage!

One tried, and his story must be told. His name was Smith. He was a rookie brought out to Paso Robles, California, one spring to train with the White Sox. He would have served as a working model for Ring Lardner's "Al."

When the Sox played their first exhibition string in San Francisco, Smith and the Booze Cage engaged in exchanges of repartee, much of which was unprintable.

The White Sox closed out their exhibition stay in California with a Sunday afternoon game in San Francisco. That night the team was to start playing its way back to major-league territory. The following Tuesday the Coast League season was to open. Just before the Sunday game started, Smith decided to pay his final respects to the Booze Cage. He walked slowly from one end of it to the other—on his side of the wire screen, of course. As he walked, he kept doffing his cap, repeating over and over, "Good-by, you native sons of bitches. I'm going back to the United States tonight!"

That's what he thought. When the Sox started homeward that night, Smith was left with the Vernon club, which was to open the Coast League season in that same park the Tuesday following.

Smith was on his way back to the "United States" without too much delay, at that. The Booze Cage drove him.

He was not the first player who made the fatal mistake of talking back to the fans, nor was he the last. He was just the one who was overmatched from the start. His career might have been successful, or more successful than it turned out to be, but for his failure to realize that there are times when it is much better to be seen and not heard.

Rightfully or wrongly, many fans, particularly those who pay their way into baseball games and prize fights, seem to accept it as part of their contract to abuse the principals shamefully. There are instances on record of players going into the stands after particularly vituperative insulters, but the average ball player, if he cares to endure, learns early to pay no more attention to the billingsgate of the fans than he does to the jockeying that emanates from rival dugouts.

For my purpose, I prefer to go into the always diverting sport of professional wrestling for my best example of fan conduct and participants' reaction. One of the "beeg, strong fellers" had just lost a match in Los Angeles amid excruciating circumstances. He finished on the mat, utterly unconscious. No effort to revive him was successful. At last a squad of huskies entered the ring and performed the major operation of lifting all 270 pounds of the stricken wrestler over the ropes, and started carrying him to the dressing room, presumably for rapid medical attention.

As the sad journey was being made, a fan who was a bit of a skeptic decided to pursue a restorative measure of his own. He was smoking a cigarette. As the funereal procession went up the aisle beside him the fan reached over and applied the lighted end of his cigarette to the nearest exposed portion of the wrestler's broad expanse.

That did it. The unconscious wrestler shook himself loose from his handlers, gained his feet, and offered to break the neck of the so-and-so who had branded him.

It was the most remarkable recovery I have ever witnessed on the field of combat. It must have been lasting, for the wrestler who was thought on his way to the nearest pulmotor when the cigarette was applied was able to fill an engagement the very next night at a neighboring city.

I could detail many other strange recoveries of wrestlers, but do not intend to do so. Many years ago I attempted to interest medical science in this field and failed to get any encouragement. So what's the use? There are none so deaf as those who will not hear . . . but in sports, there are none so dumb as those who *will* hear, as many a competitor found out when he tried to talk back to the fans in the stands or at the ringside.

CHAPTER 32

My Team — All Mine

S OMEWHERE along the line I promised to express some personal choices in the matter of teams and individuals who have appealed to me as they have applied themselves to their respective trades. Here and now, I make these selections.

In baseball, the best team I have ever observed was the 1919 Chicago White Sox, some of whose members turned sour. This team had everything. It had so much of everything that in the 1920 season, while its eight larceny-minded players were still active, it nearly won a pennant despite the fact that some of its principals were probably trying to lose it. I have seen all of the great Yankee teams and the various Cardinal and Athletic stand-out combinations, but I'll still take those White Sox as baseball's most efficient team ... when it found time to be efficient. I was able to see it on its good days, and will always treasure that memory.

It is silly to attempt to select nine or even twenty-five ball players and say they are the greatest I have ever seen. It is largely a matter of opinion whether Cy Young, as a pitcher, outranked Walter Johnson, whether Johnson outranked Christy Mathewson, whether Mathewson outranked Grover Alexander, whether Alexander outranked Rube Waddell, whether Waddell outranked Bob Grove, whether Grove outranked Bob Feller, and so on.

The same is true of catchers, infielders, and outfielders. If my life depended on it, I would be unable to split out

Hal Chase, Lou Gehrig, and Bill Terry among the first base-
men of note. Nor would I care to have to decide whether I
wanted Ray Schalk, Mickey Cochrane, Gabby Hartnett, or
Bill Dickey to catch for me, if I could have but one.

I've had many a look at Eddie Collins, Rogers Hornsby,
Charley Gehringer, Billy Herman, and Frank Frisch at second base. I would not care to have to point the finger and
say, "That's the one for me."

Perhaps Hans Wagner would satisfy me as a shortstop, as
he seemed to satisfy everyone else. Yet I have very fond
memories of Davy Bancroft, Roger Peckinpaugh, Charley
Hollocher, Martin Marion, Lou Boudreau, and a host of
others who have legitimate claim to greatness at that position.

At third base Buck Weaver is my man. Nobody else. Buck
Weaver. I'm stubborn that way.

In the outfield the standard all-time grouping, Ty Cobb,
Tris Speaker, and Babe Ruth, is good enough for me. Yet
there might come a time when I'd want Joe Jackson's bat.
I know I'd be confronted with old San Franciscans wanting
to know what about Bill Lange, and moderns demanding
recognition of Joe Di Maggio.

By comparison to baseball, boxing's choices are somewhat
limited. I'd endure hardships (and have) to see Jack Dempsey and Joe Louis demonstrate their wares. Along with Bill
McGeehan, I liked Gene Tunney from the start.

These are the only three heavyweights I would care to list
if I had to make a selection of those who came after John L.
Sullivan and Jim Corbett. Jack Johnson was probably as great
as any, when he found the time, but that was so rare I'd
cheerfully pass him up.

Louis, the present champion, is truly great. No boxer who
has ever appeared among the heavyweights has carried the
variety of damaging punches with either hand that Louis
owns. No champion has defended his title so many times in
so many places against so many different kinds of opponents.
Louis has been a satisfying champion. In all his engagements,

from the time he came up through the Golden Gloves amateur ranks, the issue was never in doubt at the conclusion
of any of his fights. In all save his first bout with Max Schmeling, Louis has been the winner, and no argument afterward.
Schmeling's right hand in that first fight clipped Joe early,
but the champion-to-be absorbed fearful punishment for almost twelve rounds before he was battered to the floor and
made to stay there.

He had a return engagement with the German heavyweight, but this came after Louis had knocked out Jimmy
Braddock in eight rounds in Chicago to become champion.
In the second Schmeling fight Louis made no mistakes.
Schmeling was overwhelmed in the first round, but not before he had provided the prize ring with the spectacle of a
beaten warrior screaming aloud from the punishment given
him. In the brief time this fight lasted, Louis more than
made up for any setback he had taken in the first engagement.

As a champion, Louis has been exemplary in and out of
the ring. No matter whom he has been billed to fight, he has
trained faithfully, and when the bell rang his patrons knew
that he was as fit as it was possible for him to be.

Because Louis is a Negro, it was customary for a while to
refer to him invariably as a "credit to his race." One day an
inspired writer came along and said that Louis was indeed a
credit to his race—the *human* race.

He is, indeed, a worthy champion, in or out of the ring.

Of all the lightweights I have ever seen, Benny Leonard
was my favorite. Harry Greb, who fought everything in sight
from middleweights to heavyweights, and who scorned training rules, belongs on my list. So does Mickey Walker, who
ranged up from welterweights to heavyweights, and also had
some peculiar ideas of deportment when he was younger.

Among the tinier fighters, I have fond recollections of
Pancho Villa, the Manila prodigy, of Tony Canzoneri, and
of Bud Taylor. Their appeal was much the same. They were
master craftsmen. They were story makers. Their fights were

characterized by a willingness to give it all they had in boxing skill and punching power. Win, lose, or draw, they were my boys.

I have paid my respects already to football's great coaches and teams as I have observed them. To attempt to nominate individual performers would be as futile as trying to name the Rose Bowl game I liked best. I liked 'em all, else I would not have kept going back for more since seeing the first one in 1916.

In the professional field George Halas and the Chicago Bears, year in and year out, will do for me. I am not too hard to please, as long as I have the best, doing anything.

In tennis Little Bill Johnston of San Francisco has been my ideal. Besides being an international champion, he is the only amateur tennis player I have ever known who gave up the game because he found that it interfered with his chances of making a livelihood. Practically all other amateur tennis players, I regret to say, cheerfully abandon work when it interferes with tennis.

In amateur golf Chick Evans, Bobby Jones, and Francis Ouimet were the beginning and end of my interest. Others I have fancied for short takes, but Chick, Bobby and Francis I'll have to take over the long route. In the professional field Walter Hagen will do for my purposes. Hagen was Hagen and the game will never produce his story-inspiring equal, on or off the course.

In racing I have to consider various phases. In the administration field, over a long stretch, none matches Colonel Matt J. Winn of Kentucky Derby fame. Moving into contention, however, is Doc Strub of Santa Anita. In recent years it has seemed to me that everybody is trying to get into the racing act, but I doubt if any of them will leave behind the record of accomplishment of these two.

Some of these modern adventurers in racing administration, such as the Vanderbilts, the Butlers, and Ben Lindheimer, are big-business men who took up racing as but part of their many endeavors. Winn and Strub are essentially of racing. Any other pursuit they might take up would be strictly an avocation.

I shall not bother to rate basketball or ice-hockey teams or individuals. To me, both of these games, while bewilderingly fast and tremendous crowd pullers, are too much involved with whistle-blowing officials. I am of the old school that maintains that a crowd comes to see the competitors and not the officials. In all sports I have ever watched, it has seemed to me the successful officials, be they referees or umpires, are those who have learned how to efface themselves. Basketball and hockey officials invariably regard themselves as the center of attraction—poor, misguided souls!

Lest there might be a suspicion that I am one of those antiquarians sighing for the "good old days," I must insist that such is not the case. Nor do I care to get involved in arguments as to whether Jack Dempsey in his prime could have licked Joe Louis in his. I'd first have to know under what rules we'd hold this fight. For Dempsey, except in his second fight with Tunney, was not required to retire to a neutral corner after a knockdown. Louis came along when this rule was rigidly enforced.

I once held a session with Gene Tunney, who fought the one and has had many opportunities to observe the other. I might have put the question to him, but did not. He talked interestingly of the two. He characterized Louis as the possessor of as complete a variety of punishing punches as anyone in ring history. Then he posed a question of his own: "Who would you say had the cruelest punch of all fighters?" I guessed that it might have been Ad Wolgast or Harry Greb, who were not particular where or how they hit an opponent, but Tunney shook his head.

"Vote for Dempsey's left hook," he said, "any time you are asked to cast a ballot on that proposition. The ring has never known a more devastating wallop."

Perhaps Tunney would have said Dempsey would beat

Louis. After all, Gene beat Dempsey twice—so why under-rate his own accomplishments? But being a wise man, Gene will probably let the rest of the world argue Dempsey or Louis—and keep a dignified silence himself.

Each decade of sports, it has seemed to me, has been productive of outstanding athletes. In the bodily contact events and in the games of skill and endurance there is no medium by which contestants of one decade and another can be fairly compared. Rule changes, advancement of equipment standards, better playing conditions, all could be determining factors in an individual's or a team's record. Your boys in the back room will never cease arguing about past heroes and present. But they will never reach any accurate conclusion, no matter how many or what expert opinions are sought and obtained.

I do not sit up nights worrying about these things. I take what unfolds before my eyes. I am willing to enjoy what I have in sports, and let the dear past as well as the future take care of itself. Maybe Man o' War, operating under 1947 racing conditions, would have made Assault or Armed stay in his stall. Maybe not. My thought on the matter is that all these greats, humans or horses, were just that when they had it. Whether one was greater than the other is something that makes plenty of conversation but not too much sense.

I do believe that any sports writer can list his preferred stock, and I have done so, by sports and by the persons involved in them. I like baseball and baseball writing more than any other field of endeavor, but even in this always new and always different game, I have some personal choices. Before I trot off this wordy field, then, may I set down my ideal of the baseball organization I'd like to follow and write about, taking its membership from many I've known intimately and some concerning whose exploits I have heard.

My club owners would be Larry MacPhail, of Cincinnati (where he introduced night baseball to the major leagues), of Brooklyn, and of New York, and young Bill Veeck, of

Chicago, Milwaukee, and Cleveland. If their numerous activities would be too much for them to handle the office of general manager, I'd call in James T. Gallagher of the Cubs.

The team manager would be Joe McCarthy of Chicago Cubs and New York Yankee fame. I'd flank him with a coaching advisory board made up of John McGraw of the Giants, Connie Mack of the Athletics, and Hughey Jennings of the Tigers.

When the team went on the field, and I didn't need Charlie Grimm of the Cubs for first base and Casey Stengel of the Giants for outfield, they'd be on the lines coaching, and I know a good time would be had by all.

My pitchers would include Rube Waddell of the Athletics, Grover Cleveland Alexander of the Phillies, Cubs, and Cardinals, Vernon Gomez of the Yankees, Dizzy Dean of the Cardinals and Cubs (and he could broadcast the games when he wasn't pitching), Nick Altrock of the White Sox and his teammate Ed Walsh, greatest exponent of the spitball, Dutch Ruether of all clubs from the Pall Mall Pool Room nine to the world's champion Reds, Yankees, Cubs, Pirates, Dodgers, and Senators, Van Lingle Mungo of the Dodgers, Burleigh Grimes of the Dodgers, and Dazzy Vance, also of Brooklyn.

Gabby Hartnett of the Cubs, Mickey Cochrane of the Athletics and Tigers, and Ray Schalk of the White Sox would be my catchers.

The infield would include Grimm, Hal Chase of the Yankees (or Highlanders), Frank Frisch of the Giants and Cardinals, Rogers Hornsby of the Cardinals and Cubs, Leo Durocher of the Cardinals, Rabbit Maranville of the Pirates and Braves, Pepper Martin of the Cardinals, and Buck Weaver of the White Sox.

In the outfield would range Babe Herman of the Dodgers, Paul Waner of the Pirates, Bill Lange of Anson's Colts, Babe Ruth of the Yankees, Harry Heilmann of the Tigers, Hack Wilson of the Cubs, Ty Cobb of the Tigers, Ted Williams of the Red Sox, and Tris Speaker of the Red Sox and Indians.

Two traveling secretaries would be needed, so I'd have Bob Lewis of the Cubs and Eddie Brannick of the Giants.

Some will argue that not all of these were the greatest players of all time, or that some of them might not have been the greatest of their own era. I am not concerned with that. Every last one of them has contributed and is still contributing to the folklore of baseball. They are the real storied characters of the game whom I have encountered, or whose traces I have run across. Their actual baseball play, while outstanding enough, was the least of the qualities that have endeared them to me and to anyone else who enjoys writing about the makers of sport news.

These men I have named were no nine-inning, three-to-five guys. These were twenty-four-hour men, seven days a week, fifty-two weeks a year. They were not restricted in their activities to the confines of any ball park. They made as much copy away from the diamond as on it. In season or out. Sometimes more. There was never a dull moment when they were around. There could not be. That's why I unhesitatingly list them as my all-time baseball organization.

As long as baseball is played and people talk of it, the exploits of these characters will be recalled by someone. They are the type that has lifted baseball out of the routine compilation of hits and runs and averages. They have made joyous the life and times of baseball writers who have preceded me and most of those who have been my contemporaries.

Let someone else delve into the statistics and come up with the orthodox selections for baseball's hall of fame. I make no protest over that. It is a fine idea and it should be encouraged. All I maintain now, and will continue to do so as long as a typewriter appears before me, is that these are the characters who belong in the baseball writers' hall of fame, and I am sure that if it were ever put to a vote of our organization all whom I have named would go in by acclamation.

Perhaps there will be some who will brush this off with an: "After all, that's just one man's opinion."

Well, did I ever give you any reason to suspect from paragraph one, page one, that all this was ever intended to be anything else?